ETHICS IN TECHNICAL
COMMUNICATION

Recent Titles in
ATTW Contemporary Studies in Technical Communication
M. Jimmie Killingsworth, Series Editor
Published in cooperation with the Association of Teachers of Technical Writing

Writing at Good Hope: A Study of Negotiated Composition in a Community of
Nurses
Jennie Dautermann

Computers and Technical Communication: Pedagogical and Programmatic
Perspectives
Stuart A. Selber, editor

The Practice of Technical and Scientific Communication: Writing in Professional
Contexts
Jean A. Lutz and C. Gilbert Storms, editors

The Dynamics of Writing Review: Opportunities for Growth and Change in the
Workplace
Susan M. Katz

Essays in the Study of Scientific Discourse: Methods, Practice, and Pedagogy
John T. Battalio, editor

Three Keys to the Past: The History of Technical Communication
Teresa C. Kynell and Michael G. Moran, editors

The Rhetoric of Science in the Evolution of American Ornithological Discourse
John T. Battalio

Outlining Goes Electronic
Jonathan Price

Narrative and Professional Communication
Jane Perkins and Nancy Blyler

Technical Communication, Deliberative Rhetoric, and Environmental Discourse:
Connections and Directions
Nancy W. Coppola and Bill Karis, editors

Writing in a Milieu of Utility: The Move to Technical Communication in
American Engineering Programs, 1850–1950, Second Edition
Teresa C. Kynell

Rhetorical Scope and Performance: The Example of Technical Communication
Merrill D. Whitburn

ETHICS IN TECHNICAL COMMUNICATION

A Critique and Synthesis

Mike Markel

ATTW Contemporary Studies in Technical Communication,
Volume 14
M. Jimmie Killingsworth, Series Editor

ABLEX PUBLISHING
Westport, Connecticut • London

Library of Congress Cataloging-in-Publication Data

Markel, Michael H.
  Ethics in technical communication : a critique and synthesis / by Mike Markel.
    p. cm.—(ATTW contemporary studies in technical communication ; v. 14)
  Includes bibliographical references and index.
  ISBN 1–56750–528–7—ISBN 1–56750–529–5 (pbk.)
    1. Communication of technical information—Moral and ethical aspects.   I. Title. II.
Series.
  T10.5.M34   2001
  174'.96—dc21   00–027629

British Library Cataloguing in Publication Data is available.

Library of Congress Catalog Card Number: 00–027629
ISBN: 1–56750–528–7
      1–56750–529–5 (pbk.)

First published in 2001

Ablex Publishing, 88 Post Road West, Westport, CT 06881
An imprint of Greenwood Publishing Group, Inc.
www.ablexbooks.com

Printed in the United States of America

The paper used in this book complies with the
Permanent Paper Standard issued by the National
Information Standards Organization (Z39.48–1984).

10 9 8 7 6 5 4 3 2 1

Contents

Preface

This book examines the relationship between ethics and the professional life of technical communicators. In it, I critique and synthesize the current research linking technical communication and ethics, summarize the main currents of Western ethical thought, and present an approach to ethical decision-making that I believe draws on the best traditional and modern theories. In addition, I apply this approach in examining five topics of particular concern to technical communicators: truthtelling, liability, multicultural communication, intellectual property, and codes of conduct.

My goals are to provide students and practitioners with a clear introduction to historical and contemporary accounts of basic ethics and to suggest how these accounts can help technical communicators think through the kinds of ethical dilemmas that inevitably arise in their working lives.

The book is divided into two parts. The first part, Ethical Decision-Making, contains the bulk of the synthesis and critique of ethical theory, culminating in my own approach. The second part, Issues and Cases, consists of five chapters that apply the ideas from Part I to particular ethical problems faced by technical communicators.

Part I begins with an introductory chapter that defines key terms, justifies the examination of ethics and technical communication, and surveys the scholarly literature on the subject. In addition, this chapter provides an overview of the argument of the book. I would recommend that all readers look at this chapter.

Chapter 2 describes some of the basic assumptions underlying a serious study of ethics. I make several basic points about the study of ethics, such as that it is a rational rather than divine or intuitive enterprise. In addition, I try to counter some common arguments against studying ethics, such as that ethics is a subjective matter and therefore unworthy of study. For readers who have not studied ethics in college, this chapter might be of some interest.

The next four chapters constitute my survey of ethical thought, concentrating on Kantian rights, utilitarianism, the transitional ethical theories of the early 20th century, and several strands of contemporary ethical theory. Although in these four chapters I occasionally refer to technical communication, my focus is not on the sorts of ethical problems faced routinely by technical communicators. Rather, I am trying to explain and critique general ethical theory. Because this material is often challenging, I follow the practice of most ethics commentators in using simple hypothetical examples to communicate the ideas. For instance, to make a point about duty, I am much more likely to refer to the ethical obligations deriving from one person's owing another $5 than to draw on a more complex and realistic example from the professional lives of technical communicators. Simple examples are more effective than complex ones because they highlight the essential ideas under discussion much more effectively.

Although these chapters in Part I do not examine technical communication in any detail, I think they are important because they enable readers to get beneath the surface of the various theories, to see not only the strengths and limitations of each theory but also the ways in which each one addresses a fundamental shortcoming of another. A critical understanding of the ethical theories examined in Part I of this book is necessary for an informed, balanced analysis of the issues presented in Part II. Readers who can see beyond the catch phrases of Kantian ethics or utilitarianism will be in the best position to propose satisfactory approaches to dilemmas related to complex issues such as intellectual property. Just as a practical approach to the problem of automobile emissions relies on chemical and physical theory, a practical approach to an intellectual-property issue such as deep linking in Web pages relies on ethical theory.

Part I ends with Chapter 7, in which I explain my approach, which calls for a fluid, nonhierarchical analysis that draws on the traditional values of rights, justice, and utility, plus the more contemporary value of care. This analysis should be conducted in an open, noncoercive environment, as described in contemporary accounts of discourse ethics. This environment increases the chance that all stakeholders will be heard. In this chapter, I acknowledge the debt I owe to commentators in the field of business ethics. Because they have for decades applied ethical theory to the study of contemporary ethical problems in organizational contexts, business ethicists offer the most insightful and compelling analyses for technical communicators. Part II of this book makes clear, I think, the considerable overlap between our concerns and those of business ethicists.

Part II consists of five chapters, focusing on truthtelling, liability, multiculturalism, intellectual property, and codes of conduct. My method in these chapters is to define the problem, summarize and critique the scholarly literature, and present an approach to thinking about the problem sensitively and realistically, an approach that derives from the ethics theory from Part I. Each chapter concludes with a case about technical communication that draws on the information in the chapter. After each case, I present my analysis of it.

My students at Boise State University and Drexel University will recognize many of the themes and ideas that we worked out together. I owe my students a great deal of credit for the good things in this book. I have enjoyed and profited considerably from the conversations we have had.

I want to acknowledge, too, three colleagues. M. Jimmie Killingsworth and Jacqueline S. Palmer, both of Texas A & M University, provided extremely useful commentary on the manuscript of this book. They have helped me make the manuscript more clear and accessible in numerous ways. I want to thank, too, Scott P. Sanders, of the University of New Mexico, who, as the editor of two articles I published in IEEE *Transactions on Professional Communication*, helped me clarify my thinking significantly. Over the years, Scott and I have had many highly productive discussions of ethics and technical communication. He is a thoughtful and generous colleague, and I have benefited from our relationship.

Brief passages in this book are revised versions of material included in two articles on ethics that I have published: "Technical Communication and Ethics: A Case for Foundational Approaches," *IEEE Transactions on Professional Communication*, 40, 284–299 (© 1997 IEEE); and "An Ethical Imperative for Technical Communicators," *IEEE Transactions on Professional Communication*, 36, 81–86 (© 1993 IEEE). I wish to thank the Institute for Electrical and Electronics Engineers, Inc. for permission to use copyrighted material from these articles.

Kant quotations are from *Foundation of the Metaphysics of Moral*, Second Edition (trans. L. W. Beck), ©1990, and are reprinted by permission of Prentice-Hall, Inc., Upper Saddle River, N.J. Ross quotations are from *The Right and the Good* (Oxford: Clarendon Press, 1930). The case at the end of Chapter 10 first appeared in *Technical Communication*, Sixth Edition, by Mike Markel, copyright ©2001 by Bedford/St. Martin's, and is reprinted with permission of Bedford/St. Martin's.

Finally, I wish to thank the Idaho State Board of Education, which awarded me a grant that helped me research this book.

1

Ethical Decision-Making

1

Introduction

Within the technical-communication community, interest in ethics began a quarter century ago, and it intensifies each year. In his introductory address to the Society for Technical Communication (STC) in 1977, H. Lee Shimberg stated that although most technical communicators are rarely asked to tell deliberate lies, "shading the truth or reporting mostly favorable results or attributes happens often enough to be of concern to all of us who are aware of it" (p. 31). For years, the STC magazine, *Intercom*, has published ethics cases based on workplace practices, then printed responses from readers. In 1998, the Society published "Ethical Guidelines for Technical Communicators," an updated version of its 1980 "Code for Communicators." The Society's annual international conference always includes at least a handful of papers on ethics and technical communication.

TECHWR-L, a discussion list with over 4,000 subscribers, often includes threads discussing ethical issues in the workplace, including topics covering ethical dilemmas related to hiring practices, intellectual-property issues, liability, and truthtelling in product information.

All the major textbooks in technical communication include chapter-length discussions of ethics, explaining how to write honestly and clearly. Often, these texts also include guidelines for avoiding misrepresentation in creating graphics. In 1997, Allen and Voss published *Ethics in Technical Communication: Shades of Gray*, the first full-length treatment of ethics and technical communication. The book was written "to help professional technical communicators and students preparing for the profession to deal with complex ethical issues, both on the job and in the classroom" (p. xix).

Researchers in technical communication have written a number of articles on the *Challenger*, analyzing how the rhetorical dynamics of the exchange between the engineers and the managers led to the fateful decision to launch the shuttle. Recently, graphics scholar Edward Tufte (1997) presented a detailed analysis of the graphics sketched that night, showing how the engineers failed to create clear and compelling data displays that might have persuaded the managers to postpone the launch.

Other scholars have written about the Exxon Valdez case and the company's subsequent handling of the ecological disaster. One scholar (Herrington, 1995) has analyzed the ethics of the design of the "Report of the Department of the Treasury on the Bureau of Alcohol, Tobacco, and Firearms Investigation of Vernon Wayne Howell Also Known as David Koresh." Another scholar (Katz, 1992) has analyzed the ethic of expediency displayed in technical memos written by Nazis about the construction of gas chambers.

Numerous commentators have focused on the relationship between rhetoric and ethics in technical communication, analyzing writers from Plato and Aristotle through Foucault and Lyotard. Topics include the differing views of the classical Greek and Roman theorists on whether a communicator should be an ethical person or merely a persuasive one, whether it is possible to eliminate sexism from technical communication, and whether the use of the impersonal style in technical communication—characterized by the use of the passive voice and the avoidance of "I"—is a ruse.

The scholarship and discussion threads mentioned here suggest that the technical-communication community sees ethics as an important topic in the working lives of technical communicators and technical-communication students. This book is intended to be another contribution to the continuing discussion of the relationship between ethics and technical communication.

In this chapter, I provide a brief overview of the research on technical communication and ethics, discuss the premises on which the argument of the book is based, and provide a brief summary of the argument.

TECHNICAL COMMUNICATORS, CONTEMPLATION, AND ACTION

In his study of the ethic of expediency in Nazi memos, Stephen Katz (1992) makes an important point that constitutes one of the themes of this book. Ethics, which he defines as "human character manifested in behavior," is inextricably linked to rhetoric.

All deliberative rhetoric is concerned with decision and action. Technical writing, perhaps even more than other kinds of rhetorical discourse, always leads to action, and thus always impacts on human life; in technical writing, epistemology necessarily leads to ethics. The problem in technical communication and deliberative rhetoric generally, then, is not only one of epistemology, the relationship of argument, organization, and style to thought, but also one of ethics, of how that relationship affects and reveals itself in human behavior. (p. 259)

Technical communicators must act, both in their professional capacities as communicators and as citizens.

In the workplace, technical communicators create, shape, and transmit technical information so that people can use it safely, effectively, and efficiently. Everything that they do, everything they create in their jobs, entails choices, many of which have an ethical dimension: describing the company's facilities and resources in a proposal, explaining how to perform a task in a manual, constructing a Web site—these and other activities call for an active, questioning, and skeptical attitude toward accepted notions of what constitutes honest information and appropriate professional behavior.

If it is true that technical communicators as employees must take action in an imperfect world, it follows that educators are obliged to help their students expand their understanding of ethics and improve their skills in making ethically informed decisions. James L. Kinneavy (1986) writes eloquently of the need to integrate ethical concerns in the technical-communication course, to make it truly humanistic. A cursory glance at new textbooks shows that this approach is now orthodox; ethical concerns are interwoven throughout the course.

As citizens, technical communicators also must act. Recent essays about the technical communicator's role in society are a healthy outgrowth of similar essays about the role of composition courses in teaching citizenship skills. Against this background, communication skills are seen not merely as job skills but as essential attributes of active, responsible citizenship. Technical-communication education should not be about the mere processing of technical information but rather, as Thomas P. Miller (1991) argues, about educating citizens who "can say the right thing at the right time to solve a public problem because they know how to put the shared beliefs and values of the community into practice" (p. 57). Russell Rutter (1991) writes that technical-communication education should be a "liberal education grounded in oratorical traditions that emphasize the mastery of rhetoric for use in the active life" (p. 149).

The need to act, to make decisions in an imperfect world, is of course the basis of democracy. James A. Berlin (1993) makes this point in describing an approach to teaching writing in which language use is central in defining the writer, the reader, and the message, an approach he calls social-epistemic rhetoric. "The purpose of social-epistemic rhetoric is finally political, an effort to prepare students for critical citizenship in a democracy" (p. 152). In "The 'Q' Question," Richard A. Lanham (1988) describes rhetoric as "an education in politics and management" (p. 692). For Lanham, the institution that epitomizes the decision-making imperative in modern societies is the courtroom, where we "stage a public drama, empanel an audience whom we call a jury, and offer contending versions of reality. . . . The magic moment of transmutation, what drives the system, is the need to *reach a decision*" (original emphasis, p. 692).

My starting point, then, is I think a commonsense idea: Technical communicators, as workers and as citizens, must act in the real world. Presented with inaccurate and incomplete information, assessing unclear and inadequate options, torn between competing claims and goals, they must make decisions.

What kinds of ethical dilemmas do technical communicators face in their jobs? Here are a few excerpts from recent posts to the TECHWR-L discussion list. (I have chosen not to cite these excerpts, because at this point I want merely to suggest the range of topics covered, not to discuss the excerpts.)

The writer quoted in Figure 1.1 is responding to a question about how to document a product that does not yet do all that its manufacturer intends. The writer's frustration, expressed in the last paragraph, suggests that his solution doesn't always work. Truthtelling is discussed in chapter 8.

Figure 1.1
A Post about Truthtelling

What do you do when asked to write about how a system WILL EVENTUALLY behave while ignoring what it actually does. Remember, the person asking you (an engineer or manager) has their job, and possibly an entire team's or group's, on the line.

The obvious strategy is to write about what the product WILL do, not what it IS doing. The reason has nothing to do with ethics, and everything to do with describing the product the customer will see. Some of us call this process 'shooting at a moving target' but it's an activity most of us have done at one time or another.

That said, however, it's important for you to get serious commitment from the developers as to what will and won't appear. If you're going to write what amounts to fiction and put your department's reputation on it, they're going to have to sign up for creating the features that support that fiction. In fact, if things are really political, you might have the development manager sign a statement to that effect, so that if they change the deliverable your department can always point to what they signed up to do.

Unfortunately, this sort of thing happens all the time, despite all sorts of efforts to get products nailed down before the final testing/review cycle. It's one of the frustrations of this business.

Figure 1.2 is an excerpt from a post by two technical communicators who carried out a survey on TECHWR-L about intellectual property law as it relates to information on the Web. This post suggests that technical communicators do not necessarily have a solid foundation in ethics or a thorough understanding of intellectual-property law. As discussed in Chapter 11, the law is not keeping up with intellectual-property issues related to digital communication, especially on the Internet.

Figure 1.2
A Post about Intellectual Property

For those of you who just want a quick summary, here are our two main findings:

1. There was a close correlation between "legal" and "ethical" in people's perceptions. In other words, if a behavior is perceived as legal, it was also perceived as ethical, and vice versa: behaviors that are perceived as illegal are also perceived as unethical. This was somewhat surprising to us, because there is a lot of controversy about the fairness of copyright law, and plenty of people (outside of the population we studied) do not feel the laws line up with ethics very well at all.

2. There seems to be a widespread feeling that giving credit to the creator(s) of the material you are using makes a legal difference—in other words, if there is some doubt about whether or not it's legal (and ethical) to use a given piece of material, the feeling was that if you cite your source, that makes it more likely to be legal. (In point of fact, attribution makes not a bit of difference. If it's illegal to use something, it's still illegal even if you credit the source.)

Figure 1.3 is an excerpt from a post by a freelancer who is trying to explain how he balances his clients' concerns about confidentiality and his own need to work. Here, he is discussing non-compete clauses in contracts. This writer has a clearly articulated ethical position that he feels protects his clients' intellectual property while allowing him to seek clients.

Figure 1.3
A Post about the Ethics and Legality of Non-Compete Contracts

This is a clause that appears in many contracts in the state in which I do business: California. However, in our state, such a clause is completely unenforceable (by law) because it prohibits you from exercising your freedom to do business in a competitive market (I can't recall the exact legal terminology for this . . . but that's the idea). Most employers know this, but they leave such clauses in their contracts in order to deter you from taking on such clients.

This is how I handle the situation. First: Regardless of such a clause, I abide by a strict standard of ethics that does not allow me to work on two projects (for two different clients) that directly compete with each other *at the same time*. For example, last year, I wrote the online Help system for [product name]. Competitors of this product include [names of other similar products]. If at the same time, one of the competitor companies called me and asked me to work on the online Help for their [product name]—even just to edit one page of documentation—I would say "NO, absolutely not." However, if one of these companies called and asked me to work on some sales literature for a product that was COMPLETELY unrelated to the product I was documenting, I would have no problem doing that—because the two sets of documentation are completely unrelated and therefore my work poses no threat of exposure to either company. Another situation: once I completed the online Help (and the contract is up) for one company, then I am free to do business with any business I please (as long as the law continues to support free market practices).

THE MOST IMPORTANT THING to keep in mind if you find yourself in either of these two situations is to be careful NOT TO DIVULGE ANY PROPRIETARY IN-FORMATION to any other clients. And that's really what any client is concerned about. This means that you can bring your newly learned skills and knowledge on documentation process with you, but you CANNOT share with the client such information as: "Well, my last client decided not to have a section on Blah-Blah because they did market research that revealed it was counter-productive." That market research may have given your last client an edge in the marketplace and this information should absolutely not be shared with another client.

Figure 1.4 is an excerpt from a technical communicator who is describing her approach to including safety warnings on her company's products. The writer distinguishes between her ethical and legal obligations regarding protecting her company from liability claims. Liability is the subject of Chapter 9.

Figure 1.4
A Post about Ethics and Liability

I've been working on labels for a product lately, so I've been giving this situation quite a bit of thought. I found the Valujet article [an article about the 1997 crash of a commercial jet due to the explosion of oxygen canisters in the cargo compartment] to be quite thought-provoking, because my company is working on a product that has the potential to cause physical injury, if misused. It's *very* unlikely to happen, but it could happen. So I've been thinking about how to handle this in the documentation.

Marketing people tend to want to downplay the potential hazards of a product. Legal people want to make sure that all necessary regulations are being followed and that the company won't be sued. So there's all sorts of regulatory and other legal verbiage that goes onto the product. But it's legal stuff that most people never read, so it goes onto a small label in tiny print. There are hazard warnings there too (in three languages), but they are hidden in 5 point type. The marketing people are happy, because there are no obvious dangers to make potential customers nervous. And the legal people are satisfied because if something did happen, we can point to the product and say "See, it was clearly labeled."

To my mind, just being covered "legally" isn't good enough. We also have an ethical responsibility. What those oxygen canisters needed (and the instructions for disposing of them) was some kind of clear warning on a label big enough to read. Something on the order of "DANGER: These devices can cause explosions and fires" (accompanied by an explosion symbol of some kind). Maybe no one would have paid attention, and the accident might still have happened, but it seems to me that if the dangers had been explained more clearly in the documentation, there'd have been a better chance that someone would notice.

I'm thinking of adding a section to our manual called "Potential Hazards," where we can describe potential hazards honestly.

Figure 1.5 is an excerpt from a technical communicator writing about the use of frames in Web sites. This issue is discussed in Chapter 11.

Figure 1.5
A Post about an Intellectual-Property Issue Related to the Web

One of the reasons why some people avoid using frames is that, depending on the way you use the frames, you can end up having your content hijacked without your company name.

A common use for frames is to put your company name and logo in a prominent place and have it stay there when the reader scrolls through the content. It looks good, keeps the company identity in sight at all times, and means you don't have to maintain company identity stuff on every document. The problem is that other sites can then link directly to the content, and leave your company identity off, sometimes even substituting their own. There have been suits over that very prank, but I don't know the outcome, if any. It's not relevant to me—I'm not about to make my content vulnerable to such theft, and I'm not about to steal like that.

Hijacking a page into a frame to make it look like your own without the consent of the page's owner is a fairly risky proposition. I'm sure nobody here is unprofessional enough to do it, but there are plenty of pranks that the owner of the hijacked page could pull, making the frameset look very silly. For example . . . a sadistically chosen graphic, to say nothing of the possibilities that JavaScript presents.

But for a professional, the only response is to simply use a frame breaker JavaScript like the one that John posted.

These excerpts, and others from TECHWR-L, suggest a very broad range of ethical issues on the minds of technical communicators. Most prominent are dilemmas about dealing fairly with clients regarding confidentiality; about loyalty to employers who are asking the communicator to lie or mislead in product information; about being honest with job applicants regarding working conditions at the company. There are also many posts about intellectual-property issues, including the ownership of samples written by employees; about the proper way to cite trademarks and abide by copyright laws; and about the ethics and legality of copying information from Web sites.

A second point that comes through clearly in TECHWR-L posts is that many technical communicators are not experienced in thinking about ethics. Many do not distinguish between ethical and legal issues: if a practice is legal, it is by definition ethical (this idea is discussed in Chapter 2). Many appear to think only pragmatically about serious ethical issues. For instance, one communicator writes that you shouldn't lie in a job interview about something that can get you in trouble if the boss later discovers it. Another communicator writes that you shouldn't claim another person's writing sample as your own because you might mistakenly present that sample to its real author. These and many other communicators do not discuss whether a practice is right or wrong.

Most of the technical communicators who write posts to TECHWR-L about ethics, who respond to the ethics cases in the STC magazine *Intercom*, and who attend presentations on ethics in training sessions and professional conferences are sincerely interested in acting ethically and expanding their understanding of ethics as it relates to their profession. Unfortunately, most technical communicators did not study ethics extensively in college, and most employers do not offer sophisticated, comprehensive training in the subject. A new technical communicator is much more likely to be sent for two days of training on a new software application than two hours of training on the company's ethical code. This emphasis, understandable as it may be, accounts, at least in part, for many technical communicators' incomplete understanding of ethics.

To summarize, the two factors that motivate efforts to improve the quality of our thinking about ethics and technical communication are that ethical problems are common and important in our working environment, and that we all can improve our thinking about ethics. As I discuss in Chapter 2, studying ethics can have three practical results:

- *It can help us think more clearly and more sensitively.* Reading about ethics helps us learn how to think through ethical dilemmas more effectively.

- *It can help us explain our views articulately to others.* As communicators, we are often involved in explaining policies to others. Studying ethics helps us learn how to construct clear arguments.

- *It enables us to advance in our ethical thinking.* Although the development of our own ideas about ethics is a complex phenomenon linked to experience and age, studying ethics can help us understand the shortcomings of our ideas about ethics and refine them.

The first major point I want to make is that ethics is a practical matter for technical communicators, who are paid to act in the real world and are citizens. My intent in this book is to focus on the practical side of ethics. By this I do not mean that I will produce a flowchart showing how to resolve ethical dilemmas. Such flowcharts, plentiful in the literature, are, in my view, impractical because they are simplistic. What I do mean is that I hope to provide a clear and concise description and analysis of the issues that are necessarily part of a sensitive understanding of any kind of ethical dilemma. The practical study of ethics requires, ironically, a willingness to do some abstract thinking and a tolerance for significant levels of ambiguity.

RESEARCH ON TECHNICAL COMMUNICATION
AND ETHICS

The research on ethics and technical communication probably includes more than 100 major items (depending on how the terms *ethics* and *technical communication* are defined). Because this body of research is fairly large, I will provide only an overview. My goal in this section is to try to describe the major topics, perspectives, and challenges remaining for researchers of this complex and multidisciplinary topic, focusing on how my approach extends and diverges from the existing research.

Let me start by listing three sources that are extremely useful for anyone interested in studying this topic. Figure 1.6 describes an anthology and two review articles that provide a starting point for interested readers.

Figure 1.6
Three Sources that Provide an Introduction to the Topic of Ethics and Technical Communication

Technical Communication and Ethics (1989), a brief anthology of articles edited by R. John Brockmann and Fern Rook. This collection includes more than a dozen essays, largely from *Technical Communication* (the STC journal), on subjects including the influence of business, science, and medical contexts; ethics and rhetoric; and pedagogy. Also included are the codes of conduct of professional associations in five communication fields. The collection is limited in that most of the articles are brief, and many are out of date, but it is a useful collection, especially for those interested in the early debates about whether ethics is related to technical communication.

The bibliographic essay "Ethics and Technical Communication," by Stephen Doheny-Farina, in *Technical and Business Communication: Bibliographic Essays for Teachers and Corporate Trainers* (1989), edited by Charles H. Sides. This essay is broader ranging than the Brockmann and Rook anthology, providing clear summaries of much of the existing research, but, like the anthology, it is largely out of date.

The bibliographic essay "Technical Communication and Ethics," by Scott P. Sanders, in the volume *Foundations for Teaching Technical Communication: Theory, Practice, and Program Design* (1997), edited by Katherine Staples and Cezar Ornatowski. Concentrating on the articles that have appeared since the Doheny-Farina essay, Sanders classifies the research into three categories—practical, philosophical, and rhetorical—pointing out the merits and demerits of each. Sanders's article is the best introduction to the scope and complexity of the recent research on ethics and technical communication.

One challenge that becomes apparent immediately to anyone studying ethics and technical communication is the lack of consensus on the meaning of the word *ethics*. To some writers, ethics refers to the study of questions about right and wrong and how they relate to human conduct. This definition, which derives from the philosophical study of ethics, is the one I use in this book (I discuss this in much more detail in Chapter 2). Other writers see ethics as tied to *ethos*, the Greek term used by Aristotle and usually translated as the character of the speaker or writer. Still others see ethics as an indeterminate concept related to the composing process, involving the dynamic of the relationship created between the writer and the reader as they create a text.

Some writers decline to define the term. For instance, Dombrowski (1994), in a bibliographic essay, comments that defining ethics is "problematic" and therefore "I will not argue for a single, particular, consistent definition of ethics because to confine myself to a single definition would impede consideration of alternate perspectives and definitions" (p. 182). In an article reporting survey results about ethical dilemmas, Dragga (1996) also declines to define ethics: "Notice that I offer no definition of the word *ethical:* instead of testing the ability of the respondents to apply a given definition of ethics, the survey tries to determine how the respondents themselves define the word *ethical* within the seven document design situations" (p. 258). What Dragga gains in avoiding the messiness of defining the term he perhaps loses in validity, since he asks his respondents to comment on each ethical dilemma by ranking the decision on a five-point scale from "completely ethical" to "completely unethical" but neither defines the word nor asks his respondents to do so.

I hope to show in the rest of this section on research that the community's failure to settle on a reasonably precise definition of ethics has led to significant problems, for the writers as well as the readers of the research. For readers interested in philosophical ethics, it can be quite frustrating to spend time searching for a particular article about ethics and technical communication, only to discover that the author is really discussing public relations or an abstract point about rhetoric, completely unrelated to human conduct. For researchers themselves, the lack of a consensus on what *ethics* means complicates the process of formulating clear research questions and thereby retards the process of writing insightful scholarship.

I would classify the research on ethics and technical communication into two categories: advice on techniques for communicating clearly and honestly, and theoretical discussions of the relationship between ethics and rhetoric.

Research on Communicating Clearly and Honestly

The articles and chapters in this category are among the earliest in our literature, but examples of this category are still being written today. The important characteristic of this category is that the writer assumes (or argues briefly) that the technical communicator's responsibility is to present information clearly and honestly. Rather than explaining why the communicator is obliged in this way or examining complex situations in which it might be preferable, necessary, or customary to be less than candid, the writer simply presents advice on how to use language or graphics clearly and honestly. If there is a philosophical foundation for the advice, it is implicit or indistinct, usually amounting to no more than a cursory statement that sometimes a company will ask the communicator to compromise his or her personal ethical standards but that the communicator should resist.

Examples of research of this type are J. C. Young's 1961 essay, "Responsibilities of Writers and Editors to Readers" and Louis Perica's 1972 essay, "Honesty in Technical Communication." In "Ethics and Rhetoric in Technical Writing," H. Lee Shimburg (1978) urges his readers to avoid imprecision and ambiguity in their writing. Herbert Michaelson's "How An Author Can Avoid the Pitfalls of Practical Ethics" (1990) focuses on avoiding the sins of omission, ambiguity, and bias in engineering writing. Sigma Xi, The Scientific Research Society, published *Honor in Science* (1986), a booklet that recommends that scientists not delete aberrant data or invent corroborating data.

Research of this type can also take the form of case studies. An example is Lisa Tyler's (1992) discussion of the Exxon Valdez, which includes advice on avoiding legalistic language. In addition, research of this type can offer advice on creating clear and honest graphics. John Bryan's "Seven Types of Distortion: A Taxonomy of Manipulative Techniques Used in Charts and Graphs" (1995) and Nancy Allen's "Ethics and Visual Rhetorics: Seeing's Not Believing Anymore" (1996) are representative examples.

Although many studies in this category cover familiar territory, urging writers to avoid biased, vague, and imprecise language, some articles explore more sophisticated concepts of language use. For example, Kathryn Riley's "Telling More Than the Truth: Implicature, Speech Acts, and Ethics in Professional Communication" (1993) explains how the linguistic concept of implicature can lead to misleading communication even though the communicator has not written anything literally untrue. Dan Jones, in *Technical Writing Style* (1998), includes a chapter on the ethics of style, concentrating on doublespeak and bureaucratese.

In addition to these articles urging writers to communicate clearly and honestly, most textbooks, handbooks, and other guides for students and professionals include similar advice. Allen and Voss's *Ethics in Technical Communication: Shades of Gray* (1997) is full of advice on being clear.

In describing this category of research as assuming a fairly simple philosophical background and providing well-worn advice, I am not suggesting that this research is pedestrian, illogical, wrongheaded, or useless. The philosophical backing of this research, although largely implicit, is valid: the most common dilemma faced by technical communicators is probably the conflict between the organization's desire to shade the truth (on the basis of a shallow and unexamined utilitarian reasoning) and the communicator's desire to be candid (on the basis of the Golden Rule). And if the advice in this research is largely repetitive, that is most likely an indication that the problems examined in the research persist, and therefore the authors think the advice is still necessary. As new technology changes the shapes of familiar problems of clarity and dishonesty—as in issues of navigation in hypertextual media—researchers will begin to offer appropriate advice. Word for word, this practical research provides the most useful insights for students and professionals who wish to improve the ethics of their communication.

Research on Technical Communication and Rhetoric

For the last two and a half millennia, perhaps the biggest question in rhetoric has remained the same: What is the proper relationship between communication and truthfulness? Is communication merely a set of techniques for persuading an audience to accept a particular version of reality, or is communication inextricably related to telling the truth? This question was at the heart of the difference between Plato and Aristotle, and it has not yet been resolved.

For Plato, a speaker must be a virtuous person, because the purpose of communication is to reveal truth. Truth can be determined only through rational discourse, the dialectical method displayed in Plato's dialogues, and it can be communicated only through honest speaking. For Aristotle, by contrast, rhetoric is an instrumental faculty, a means of making a persuasive case about reality. Although in his *Ethics* (trans. 1953) Aristotle describes his ideas of ethics as human excellence and the exercise of virtue, he does not address the question of truth in the Platonic sense of eternal, immutable reality. For Plato, reality is the unchanging truth of ideal Forms in Heaven; for Aristotle, reality is a web of connections between people in families and in larger communities. For Plato, communication provides glimpses of truth; for Aristotle, communication is the skill of persuasion (see Chapter 6 for more on Aristotle).

In an excellent brief history of rhetoric from classical times through the present, Nan Johnson (1984) explains how the different perspectives of Plato and Aristotle occupied the Roman rhetoricians Quintilian and Cicero, with Quintilian taking a position close to Plato's and Cicero taking a position close to Aristotle's. (See Richard Lanham's "The Q Question" [1988] for an interesting look at the viability of Quintilian's ideas.) The debate about rhetoric and truth interested rhetoricians through the Renaissance and the modern period. Today, Aristotle's position dominates. Modern rhetorical theory sees truth as a human construct, a collection of ideas, opinions, and mores that are created by a culture that inhabits a particular time and place.

Johnson (1984) argues persuasively that not only are rhetoric and ethics viewed as distinct fields, they are studied differently: "[P]ragmatic definitions of ethos and aims for rhetoric dominate rhetorical education while concepts of virtuous ethos and moral rhetoric are advanced only in theory" (p. 112). According to Johnson, efforts by rhetoricians such as Richard Weaver and Wayne Booth to "restore a balance between pragmatic and objective ideals as a basis for rhetorical theory and practice" (p. 113) have been overwhelmed in the rhetorical community by postmodernism, which emphasizes the power of particular, local context. Postmodernism rejects outright the concept of coherent ideologies that would permit belief in an unchanging truth.

In technical communication, the debate about the relationship between rhetoric and truth-telling has taken a somewhat different form. Carolyn R. Miller's landmark 1979 essay, "A Humanistic Rationale for Technical Writing," focuses on the role of the technical communicator. The Platonic viewpoint is represented by logical positivism, the early 20th-century theory that valued empirical science at the expense of nonmeasurable phenomena. To the logical positivist, reality is separate from a person's perception of it. Reality is out there, it is solid, and it can be measured and understood if we use accurate instruments and think clearly. The technical communicator serves, to use the term from the STC "Code for Communicators," as a bridge between the scientist or engineer (who understands scientific reality) and the reader (who doesn't). The job of the technical communicator is to write clearly and thus to remove the sources of noise from the communication channel, enabling the reader to receive and interpret scientific truth accurately. The technical communicator, in other words, is a butler.

(The writings of the Vienna Circle scholars, who were the core of the movement called *logical positivism*, were considerably more complex and subtle than this summary suggests, but for the purpose of this argument, the summary provides a clear contrast.)

Miller (1979) proposed a different model for the technical communicator: an Aristotelian rhetorician. The technical communicator does not merely deliver a message; rather, he or she is a creative rhetorician who assesses the audience, gathers data, interprets it, selects the appropriate information, and shapes it into a coherent, articulate document that meets the audience's needs. This document represents the communicator's creative interpretation of a point of view.

In proposing this model, Miller (1979) drew on a rich body of literature in the philosophy of science called *social constructionism*. The single most influential text in social constructionism is Thomas Kuhn's *Structure of Scientific Revolutions* (1970). Kuhn argued that the history of Western science is the story of the life and death of paradigms. A paradigm is an accepted theory, such as the idea that the Earth is the center of our solar system, or the idea that the sun is. A paradigm is proposed by a scientist, then supported by corroborating evidence from other scientists. Today, for example, we "believe in" Einstein's theory of relativity; that is, we think it offers better explanatory power than any rival theory.

At some point, however, a scientist presents evidence that seems counter to the prevailing paradigm. For some years or decades, the new scientist is dismissed by the leaders of the community. Eventually, these defenders of the current paradigm die off and are replaced by younger scientists, who are more tolerant of iconoclastic theories. At this point, there is a paradigm shift; the community discards the old paradigm and adopts a new one. The new paradigm matures, then ages, and is eventually replaced by a newer one.

Kuhn's (1970) idea, at first glance, seems obvious, for everyone knows that old science is constantly being replaced by new science. But Kuhn's idea is powerful in that it underscores the extent to which science is a human, social, interpretive activity. Science is a mythology, a system of beliefs in which people create, refine, and discard ideas about reality. Science is built on a foundation of reasonable guesses. Through professional conferences, scientific journals, e-mails, and hallway discussions, scientists propose their versions of reality, and the version that best explains the observable world becomes the paradigm. Scientific truth is what the smartest people in the community have agreed is true. In other words, science is Aristotelian and rhetorical, not Platonic and true.

Miller's (1979) call for us to see technical communication as a rhetorical activity has been enormously influential, and it is now the reigning paradigm of our field. Ornatowski (1992) argues persuasively, for instance, that the first step in empowering our students to make ethical choices on the job is to see technical communicators not as technicians whose job is to write clear, impersonal text but as full-fledged rhetoricians. Philip Rubens (1981) also comments that we need to abandon the idea that we write objective, unbiased prose. We are rhetoricians, and we need to reintroduce our voice into our writing. Barton and Barton (1981) describe a similar social-constructionist model of technical communication.

However, the irony in our community's thinking about technical communication and ethics is that while the victory of the rhetorical view of technical communication enables us to admit ethics as a legitimate subject, it simultaneously devalues ethics by reducing it from a fundamentally important subject to just another human construct. In the older paradigm, in which the technical communicator was the bridge between the writer and the reader, the technical communicator was merely a technician, but ethics was solid and stable. Although the technical communicator's responsibility was limited—tell the truth, be clear, stay out of the way—the scientist or engineer who created the information was responsible for living up to the ethical responsibilities of his or her professional code.

Now, however, the rhetorical paradigm gives the technical communicator ethical responsibility, but at the cost of the solidity and stability that ethics used to enjoy. As I try to show in Chapter 6, the controversies about the validity of different approaches to ethics were at least as heated in earlier decades of the twentieth century as they are now, but philosophers and the general public in earlier decades seemed to share a stronger belief in the usefulness and practicality of ethics in daily life.

Much of the recent rhetorical research on technical communication and ethics makes it difficult to see ethics as a vital, important aspect of technical communication. Three problems dominate:

- Ethics is conceived so broadly that it loses its connection to the study of values and conduct.
- Ethics is conceived as a critique of capitalism.
- Ethics is equated with *ethos*.

I discuss these three problems in the following paragraphs.

The problem of an overly broad definition of ethics is seen when ethics is equated with audience analysis or some other aspect of the composing process. Ethics becomes the effort to work cooperatively with an audience. Gregory Clark (1987) writes, "If ethics is understood to be an agreement about what people together are attempting to accomplish, then the failure of cooperation that occurs when people attempt to work together on the basis of principles and purposes that differ can be understood as a failure of ethics" (p. 190). The ethical communicator should try to talk with his or her readers to learn their needs, but when such discussions are not possible,

an ethical communicator must anticipate such an exchange as if it were actually occurring, enacting it imaginatively while preparing the communication, so that the final document still reflects the kind of shared understanding that would have resulted from such interaction had it actually taken place. This perspective on ethics requires technical communicators to do more than address their audiences; they must, in the process of communicating, adapt their own understanding of the information to accommodate the knowledge, needs, and abilities of their audiences as they perceive them in a process of cooperation and collaboration by proxy. (p. 194)

Paul Dombrowski (1994) sees even more elasticity in ethics, arguing that communication embodies ethics because it involves language. "Contemporary rhetorical theory holds that language, and all knowledge constituted and mediated by language, always inescapably embodies, represents, and propagates a world view and therefore a system of values. Thus science and technology embody ethics by virtue of their rhetoricity" (p. 184). The problem with this view is that every human interchange "embodies" ethics. On the next page of his essay, in discussing Frank Lloyd Wright, Dombrowski describes the great architect as a boy building a windmill, then watching the wind blow it down. "This experience taught Wright the need to conform to the laws of Nature. . . . He learned, in effect, the ethics of Nature" (p. 185).

In other research, ethics is described as a political, economic, and social ideology that stands opposed to capitalism. In his article on Nazi rhetoric, Stephen Katz (1992) argues, reasonably, that technology can take on an ethos of expediency—rationality, efficiency, speed, productivity, and power—and can thereby create its own undesirable ethical appeal. Sometimes, however, researchers go significantly further than Katz by arguing that technical communication is inherently unethical because it is the communication of capitalism, which is itself unethical. One statement of this thesis is by Susan Wells (1986), who writes that "a technical writer would not be shaken by a critique that his or her work served domination. A discipline founded on the principle of service is not ashamed to be of use" (p. 247). The most forceful statement of this view is that of Dale L. Sullivan (1990), who states that "teaching the standardized formats and forms means teaching the technological mindset, and, thus, enculturing students into the military-industrial complex" (p. 377). By teaching workplace writing, we are supporting an oppressive social and economic system that subordinates people to "the technological imperative" (p. 379). In this way, technical communication is "the rhetoric appropriate for slaves—those barred from making decisions about the ends, those whose decision-making authority is restricted to determining the most efficient means of obtaining predetermined ends" (p. 380).

Although Sullivan's (1990) essay can be criticized rhetorically and logically as an unsuccessful argument, the real problem it presents is that it removes ethics as a topic of discussion and exploration. People in the working world cannot be ethical communicators because they have already been ethically compromised by their decision to work for corporations. We are back where we were 30 years ago, when technical communicators couldn't be ethical because they were technicians.

The best rejoinder to the essay by Sullivan and the others that see ethics as ideology is Carolyn R. Miller's (1989) "What's Practical about Technical Writing?" Miller argues that the prudent course is the middle ground between, on the one hand, offering training programs for industry and, on the other hand, teaching students to reject the values embodied in capitalism. Miller argues that we should understand "practical rhetoric as a matter of *conduct* rather than of production, as a matter of arguing in a prudent way toward the good of the community rather than of constructing texts" (p. 23).

A third category of research equates ethics with *ethos*. Often these essays offer little that can be of practical guidance for students or professionals. Martin and Sanders (1994) are representative when they write, "By ethics, we mean the representation of *ethos*, or character, in a text" (p. 149). The composing process, they continue, begins its "circularity of continual re-currence, the internal shuttling of consciousness whereby we hope to com-pose a text that offers as effectively as possible a literal space in which the intentionalities of the writer and the reader may complement each other, creating a community of consciousness, that community being the basis of effective communication" (p. 151). Marshall Kremers (1989) offers a similar take on ethics:

I am using the term *ethics* in the traditional sense derived from classical rhetoric. For Aristotle, the word *ethos* means character, and to fully develop one's character was to engage in the discussion of shared values in terms of the debate of public issues. Thus, *ethical thinking*, or *reasoning*, means consciously discussing problems in the context of personal and shared values. (p. 58)

Leaving aside the oversimplification of claiming that Aristotle's views rep-resent the whole of classical rhetoric, this definition of ethics seems particu-larly toothless, for being ethical requires nothing more rigorous than engaging in a discussion. How a person acts after the discussion is, appar-ently, irrelevant.

Essays such as these that equate ethics with *ethos* and then go on to speak abstractly about shared values, negotiating, and accommodating have started to appear in the literature only in the last decade or so. Before that, most researchers saw ethics and *ethos* as related but not synonymous. John Brockmann (Brockmann & Rook, 1989), for example, introducing the STC anthology on ethics, argues sensibly that ethics does not encompass all manner of communication between people. In justifying the decision not to include in the anthology any articles on plain language, he comments that the "identification of plain language with ethical language mistakes the outward signs of ethics, plain language, for ethical actions" (p. v). Jack Grif-fin (1989) explains that equating ethics and *ethos* might derive from an ety-mological accident:

Sometimes the term "ethos" is confused with "ethics" because translations of Aris-totle use the latter in the phrase "ethical appeal," which concerns the ethos of a com-municator. Ethos is the public character produced by " . . . the argument from authority," the argument that says in effect, "Believe me because I am the sort of per-son you can believe." As crucial as ethos is to rhetoric, however, it is, as a number of writers have pointed out, not ethics. (p. 64)

The most detailed and compelling argument that ethics is not the same as *ethos* is George Yoos's "A Revision of the Concept of Ethical Appeal" (1979). Yoos suggests that Aristotle's "emphasis on feigned *ethos* raises seri-ous moral questions about his notion of ethical appeal" (p. 42). The prob-lem is that, for Aristotle, "ethical proofs" are only tenuously connected with reason. Although Aristotle does give lip service to having a good case in persuasion, his emphasis is on the potency of *ethos* to persuade in and of itself. He makes no pretense that having good reasons is always the strongest means of persuasion. (p. 45)

Yoos writes that *ethos* without good reasons, without *logos*, "has little to recommend it morally or rationally, for it is immoral to pretend that you are being rational when in fact you know that you are not" (p. 45). Ethical appeals (that is, appeals based on *ethos*) become merely emotional appeals. Yoos argues for a model of ethical appeal "defined by ethical factors that affect an audience's perceptions of the appeal, not by reference to perceptions of the speaker" (p. 54). In other words, the speaker or writer must earn his or her "ethical appeal" by presenting good reasons—not just any reasons, or bad reasons—for the audience to believe in his or her credibility. (For a discussion of the "good reasons" rhetoricians Karl Wallace and Wayne Booth, see Marie Secor's "Recent Research in Argumentation Theory" [1987].)

To summarize this discussion of research on technical communication and ethics, the articles and chapters that discuss techniques for presenting information clearly and honestly offer practical advice that students and professionals can put into practice quickly and easily. These articles, however, do not address how to consider the ethical dilemmas that technical communicators routinely face. The research that defines the technical communicator as a rhetorician (rather than a technician) accurately portrays the day-to-day work of a technical communicator. However, much of this research also fails to provide any insights into ethical decision-making. Instead of offering useful suggestions about how to confront ethical dilemmas, this research defines *ethics* so broadly and abstractly that the word loses all reference to technical communication. Too often, these articles drift off into the rhetorical ether on empty clichés about negotiating meaning with the audience.

THE ARGUMENT OF THIS BOOK

In this first chapter, I have discussed a number of aspects of the relationship between technical communication and ethics, as revealed in the ongoing conversations of practitioners and in the research literature. I have tried to suggest ways in which my own perspective both aligns with and differs from the existing discussions.

At this point, I want to explicitly state the five premises on which I have based the argument of this book:

- Because technical communicators practice their craft in the real world, the relationship between ethics and technical communication should be viewed not as an abstract theory but as a practical art. By this I do not mean that we need a simple flowchart explaining how to resolve ethical dilemmas. On the contrary, I believe strongly that such heuristics are useless. What we need are clearheaded discussions of the dilemmas we face as communicators. A practical approach to ethics and technical communication acknowledges that ethical issues can be very complex, and that intelligent, well-meaning people can often reach very different conclusions about the proper course of action in a particular case. As ethicist Robert Solomon (1992) comments, "The aim of ethics, whether for students or seasoned executives, is not to 'teach the difference between right and wrong' but to make people more comfortable facing moral complexity" (p. 4).

- Although ethics is intimately related to rhetoric, the traditional definition of ethics—as the study of values and proper conduct—is logically prior to the concerns of rhetoric, which is the study of the art of communicating effectively. The question "Should I tell the truth?" must be addressed before the question "How do I tell the truth?" This is not to suggest that a person can determine his or her ethical position without the use of words; obviously, language is essential in thinking and communicating with others to derive a position. I mean only that a person typically devises a position before presenting it. Certainly, the process of expressing a position often leads a person to reexamine and revise it. But in most cases, deriving a position and expressing it are logically separate, even though they can be instrumentally related. For this reason, although the research on how to communicate honestly and clearly is necessary because it helps technical communicators root out practices that unintentionally foster misleading or unclear writing, the ethical concerns faced by communicators have little to do with the difficulty of implementing techniques for being clear and honest. Those techniques are easy to implement. Rather, the ethical concerns have to do with analyzing a complex rhetorical situation and determining how best to implement those techniques.

- The most sophisticated and most practical thinking about ethics—values in action—derives from the long heritage of philosophical ethics. I want to be clear that I am not saying that traditional ethical systems offer effective problem-solving techniques. All the traditional systems are seriously (some would say *fatally*) flawed and incomplete, as I try to show in considerable detail in Part I of this book. But the literature on the traditional ethical approaches offers the most penetrating analysis of their strengths and weaknesses. We all understand what the Golden Rule says, but unless we think about it long and hard, we are unlikely to understand what the Golden Rule does not say, or does not say well. Reading the ethicists and scholars helps us understand the rich interplay among the different values that have animated and permeated our civilizations for centuries. This understanding in turn helps us to think more clearly about the ethical issues we face. A number of articles in our literature, such as that by Wicclair and Farkas (1989), address philosophical ethics, but none of these articles devotes more than a few paragraphs or, at most, a few pages, to philosophical ethics.

- Business ethics offers a rich literature that can help us understand the relationship between ethics and technical communication. Rubens (1981) asks the question in the title of one of his articles, "Reinventing the Wheel? Ethics for Technical Communicators." He argues that, as we start thinking seriously about ethics and technical communication, we should look at related communication fields such as journalism and mass communication to see how they have built a research agenda on ethics. Rubens is right. However, we should not restrict ourselves to related communication fields. We should also study business ethics, the discipline that focuses on issues of the workplace, including privacy, discrimination, truth in advertising, and obligations to employers, employees, customers, and the environment. The most typical and most intractable ethical conflict inherent in organizational contexts is between an organization's shallow, unexamined use of utilitarian thinking (reflected in the motivation to reduce costs by laying off employees or to shade the truth in product information) and an individual's own subjective, rights-based thinking (reflected in the desire to safeguard the rights of the employee himself or herself or of the customer). This conflict is precisely the conflict frequently faced by technical communicators, as argued by several technical-communication scholars. Two decades ago, Powledge (1980) called this the "double-agent problem." More recently, Bryan (1992) described the "slippery slope" down which many technical communicators might slide when they try to balance their obligations to write both honest technical information and marketing materials.

- Thinking about ethics is most effective when it is conducted openly and involves all the stakeholders. An article by Dragga (1997) reports on interviews the author conducted with a nonscientific sample of technical communicators. Of the 48 communicators Dragga interviewed, 33 reported that, at least sometimes, they talked with colleagues as part of the process of resolving ethical dilemmas. That's the good news, because the colleague often challenges the person's understanding of the ethical issue or suggests other obligations or approaches to consider. The bad news is that 27 communicators report that, at least sometimes, they decide by themselves. (The categories are nonexclusive.) Talking with one or two other people is useful, but in an ideal situation, all the other stakeholders—those people whose interests might be affected—participate in the discussion, and the discussion is conducted publicly. A public discussion reduces the chances that some stakeholders' interests are ignored or that inaccurate facts or flawed arguments are tolerated. In the discussion of ethical decision-making that I present in Chapter 7, I focus on the theory of discourse ethics, which is built on the principles of open, free discussion.

This book is based on these five premises.

Part I, "Ethical Decision-Making," surveys several of the major themes that have formed the basis of philosophical ethics in the Western world from classical Greece through the present day. This part culminates with my own synthesis of these ideas. My approach to ethical decision-making consists first of deciding what is the most ethical course of action, then deciding what is the most ethical *available* course of action. I favor a flexible, nonhierarchical approach that draws on three values of foundational ethics—rights, justice, and utility—and a contemporary idea, the ethic of care. Although none of these four values by itself provides a satisfactory formula for ethical decision-making, together they form a coherent set of interests or priorities that must be considered in any systematic examination of an ethical dilemma. I argue further that this examination needs to be conducted in an open, public setting that enhances the possibility that all stakeholders' views are heard.

Following is a brief overview of the contents of the book.

Chapter 2, "Thinking About Ethics," establishes some basic principles that are necessary for thinking about ethics seriously, including the relationship between ethics and general morality, characteristics of rational thinking, and general principles of blameworthiness. In this chapter, I critique common arguments against thinking about ethics, including subjectivism and relativism. Finally, I examine the arguments against studying ethics in organizational settings.

Chapter 3, "Rights," examines three main ideas established by the German philosopher Immanuel Kant: that principles have to be supported by good reasons, that they must apply consistently to everyone, and that people must be treated as ends and not merely as means. Kant's theory, though seriously flawed as a monolithic approach to ethics, remains the most compelling formulation of the Golden Rule.

Chapter 4, "Utility," examines the ethical theory that an action is good to the extent that it produces good effects. Utilitarianism is a fundamentally important ethical approach, in part because it is the philosophical basis for the capitalist system within which technical communication operates.

Chapter 5, "The Transition from Foundational Theories," examines three philosophers from the first third of the 20th century who permanently changed the direction of Western ethical thought. G. E. Moore discredited hedonism (the belief that pleasure is the sole good), the value system that was at the heart of utilitarianism, thus reviving the ancient idea that there is no Truth, no stable body of thought that can provide a single, correct answer to every ethical dilemma. W. D. Ross offered a flexible, commonsense revision of Kant's rights theory by arguing that, in a given situation, a person's actual duty might conflict with his or her theoretical duty. And John Dewey espoused the values of empiricism by urging that ethical principles be studied to determine whether they in fact lead to good outcomes. If they do not, they should be revised or discarded altogether.

Chapter 6, "Contemporary Approaches to Ethics," focuses on the basic tenets of the ethic of care, virtue ethics, and postmodernism. The ethic of care, with roots in feminist theory, proposes an ethical system that values those practices that support care for the needy. Virtue ethics, a revival of Aristotelian virtue ethics, is based on the idea that the person, not the action, is the appropriate focus of attention. Virtue ethics addresses the question, "What qualities ought we to try to instill in people to enable them to act well?" Postmodern ethics is not a normative ethic at all; it does not provide guidelines for appropriate action. In fact, it rejects categorically the idea that there can be a value system or a normative ethic.

Chapter 7, "Toward an Approach to Ethical Decision-Making," briefly reviews two contemporary approaches—John Rawls's theory of justice and Jürgen Habermas's discourse ethics—then presents my own approach. By examining two well-known cases, I try to show that my approach enables a person to reach sensible, sensitive conclusions about ethics.

Part II, "Issues and Cases," focuses on those issues that are of particular concern to technical communicators. In Part II, I examine these issues through the lens of the ethical approach developed in Part I. Part II begins with Chapter 8, "Truthtelling in Product Information." In this chapter, I argue for a limited paternalistic approach: the writer is ethically obliged to provide accurate technical information that the reader could not be expected to discover. However, the writer is not obliged to provide nontechnical information that the reader could be expected to discover.

Chapter 9, "Liability and the Duty to Instruct and Warn," surveys the evolving legal attitude toward liability, focusing on the ethical and legal responsibilities of the technical communicator. I present practical guidelines that the technical communicator can use to reduce both the incidence and severity of injuries and the manufacturer's exposure to liability suits.

Chapter 10, "Ethical Relativism and Multicultural Communication," surveys the literature on technical communication and multiculturalism, critiquing the latent ethical relativism in much of it. I adapt from business ethics a framework for dealing with multicultural issues, arguing that the technical communicator is obliged not to reinforce patterns of discrimination but is not obliged to actively counter such discrimination.

Chapter 11, "Intellectual-Property Issues," focuses on copyright, patent, trademark, and trade secret issues. I concentrate on evolving practices related to digital information, including such issues as deep linking, improper framing, and misleading metatags in Web pages.

Finally, Chapter 12, "Codes of Conduct," describes the strengths and weaknesses of codes, distinguishes between professional codes and corporate codes, and offers guidelines for creating and distributing them.

2

Thinking About Ethics

In Chapter 1, I tried to establish that ethics is an important topic for technical communicators to think about. I argued, first, that technical communicators frequently face ethical dilemmas because of the nature of the profession and, second, that our thinking about ethical questions is often less clear than it might be.

To think about ethics, we first need to accept the premises that ethical insights are not necessarily intuitive, that they do not derive from divine intervention, and that they require a rigorous use of logical argumentation. Thinking about ethics requires that we examine our premises, that we test the logic of our arguments, and that we use evidence effectively.

In addition to these "technical" matters, we must be willing to approach debate with an open-minded spirit of inquiry. We must accept that other people of good faith will see things differently, and that the most challenging ethical dilemmas will probably remain unresolved despite our best intentions.

In this chapter, I outline basic principles necessary for productive thinking about ethics. The remaining chapters of this book, which will focus on the content of discussions about ethics, are based on the foundation laid in this chapter.

The basic principles presented in this chapter serve as rules of the road for thinking about ethics. This chapter addresses three topics:

- General principles of ethics, including the relationship between ethics and general morality, characteristics of rational thinking, and general principles of blameworthiness.

- Arguments against thinking about ethics, including such attitudes as subjectivism and relativism. After presenting each of these arguments, I offer counterarguments.

- Arguments against thinking about ethics in an organizational setting. Because most technical communication is carried out in an organizational context, arguments against thinking about ethics in organizations—arguments such as that the capitalist system is the best insurance against unethical actions or that our system of laws is a more appropriate framework than ethics—need to be confronted if our subject is ethics for technical communicators.

GENERAL PRINCIPLES ABOUT ETHICS

What is ethics? How does it differ from morality? What is the purpose of studying ethics? These are the questions I address first in this section. Next, I argue that the principal characteristic of thinking about ethics is that it is rational. I discuss two arguments often cited in opposition to this idea: that conscience is a sufficient guide and that religious values should take precedence over rational thinking about ethics. Finally, I describe a basic approach to the subject of blameworthiness. Because the most basic purpose of ethics is to provide guidance in determining conduct, it is necessary to establish right away the two conditions under which a person can be held ethically blameworthy for a wrong action. I also discuss the several excusing and mitigating factors that are crucial in assigning blame.

What Is Ethics, and Why Should We Study It?

In popular use, *ethics* and *morality* are synonyms. They both mean the study of right and wrong. For most philosophers, however, the terms are fairly distinct.

Morality refers to a society's set of beliefs and mores about appropriate conduct. In a particular society, for example, the bulk of the population might believe in a particular religious faith, such as Buddhism; might believe that it is the family's responsibility to care for its aged parents in its home; and might believe that polygamy is wrong. A person does not formulate his or her own morality; the morality of the society or culture already exists when that person is born, and that morality does not await the individual's approval or disapproval. And although it is true that a society's moral standards can be changed by the efforts of an individual, such change is neither common nor rapid.

Ethics, however, concerns the individual's thinking and conduct about matters of right and wrong. Whether a person thinks it permissible to lie under certain circumstances, whether it is the individual's responsibility to give money to charities, whether it is permissible for a company to mislead when advertising its products—these and many related kinds of questions relate to an individual's ethics. And, of course, what a person actually does—the actions the person takes or refrains from taking or chooses not to take—is fundamental in discussing that person's ethics.

What, then, is the relationship between morality and ethics? In most cases, people's ethics are derived to a greater or lesser degree from their society's morality, as it is transmitted by their parents and the society's institutions. In a society with a strong attachment to the Roman Catholic Church, for instance, many people's individual ethical codes will be based on the teachings of that church. Many individuals in that society—perhaps even most—might believe that abortion is always wrong. If asked why they think that, they might reply that they learned that from their church, or even that God said so.

Whereas a society's set of moral standards is likely to remain unchanged for decades or even centuries, an individual's ethical views are likely to change quite dramatically over a lifetime. Psychologist Lawrence Kohlberg (1981) articulated three basic stages of ethical development.

- *The preconventional stage.* Children exist in this first stage. Children are aware of the words *right* and *wrong*, but they see ethics as a matter of reward and punishment. Children believe that hitting another person is wrong because their parents say so and will punish them for doing it.

- *The conventional stage.* In this second stage, a person sees ethics in terms of group norms. Murder is wrong because it is illegal, or because the church says it is wrong. According to Kohlberg, most adolescents are in the conventional stage, and many people never progress beyond this stage.

- *The postconventional stage.* In this stage, which Kohlberg also called the *autonomous* or *principled* stage, people see right and wrong in broader terms. Murder is wrong not because it is illegal but because it deprives the victim of the most basic human right. A person in the postconventional stage examines the society's morality, approving of some of its implications and disapproving of others. Most people never reach the postconventional stage.

In general, a higher-stage ethical sense is likely to be superior to a lower-stage one, because in moving from one stage to the next, a person is moving away from a selfish perspective to a more selfless one. In addition, a person is adopting more sophisticated, abstract thinking. However, it is not always true that a particular person's higher-stage thinking is superior to another person's lower-stage thinking. For example, a man in stage two who identifies with a hate group's morality would be considerably less advanced than he was as a child, when he was afraid to hurt people for fear of punishment. (For an overview of Kohlberg's ideas, as well as those of his critics, see Lickona [1976].)

This book is about third-stage ethical thinking, with particular application to technical communicators. However, it is necessary to answer a fundamental question at this point: What exactly is the purpose of thinking about ethics? There is no empirical evidence that doing so makes someone a better, more ethical person. If it is true that most people will never reach Kohlberg's third stage, anyone who does think critically about ethics is going to be swimming upstream anyway. In addition, isn't there the danger that the result will be negative, that an individual's third-stage thinking might be inferior to most people's second-stage thinking? These are serious questions.

The answers to them are simple. We should think seriously about ethics because doing so can have several important effects:

- *Studying ethics can help us think more clearly and more sensitively.* Although it is true that the world would be a much better place if everyone treated other people as they would like to be treated, and if everyone refrained from lying, real-world problems usually are so complicated that the platitudes offer no clear solution. For example, on the one hand, a motorcyclist should have the freedom to ride without a helmet. After all, it's the motorcyclist's own head. On the other hand, the state often finds itself assuming the costs of treatment, rehabilitation, and long-term financial support for people with severe head injuries. Only by thinking critically about the ethics of helmet laws can we hope to derive a reasonable, sensitive position on it.

- *Studying ethics enables us to explain our views articulately to others.* People in the working world are constantly having to make decisions about challenging ethical issues involving such questions as whether to move a plant overseas, whether to monitor employees' e-mail, and whether to offer benefits to same-sex partners. Deriving a position is one challenge; explaining it effectively to the affected parties—the stakeholders—is another challenge. Studying ethics helps a person frame the argument, for ethical thinking is reasoned thinking.

- *Studying ethics enables us to advance in our ethical thinking.* If we were all to stay at the conventional stage, we would never improve the quality of our society's morality. For example, racism and sexism still exist, in society at large and in the workplace, even though both forms of prejudice have, to a large extent, been outlawed. Today, a number of corporations permit employees to receive benefits for their unmarried partners or their same-sex partners, but most corporations do not. Will we look back on this situation in a century the way we now look back on slavery? I don't know. However, the only reasonable way to approach the issue is by discussing it, and that requires that we think about it and present arguments.

Rational and Nonrational Thinking

The central distinguishing characteristic of thinking about ethics is that it is rational. That is, effective thinking about ethics involves making claims that are supported by clear, valid reasoning and appropriate evidence.

Ethicist Manuel Velasquez (1998) sees three important aspects of effective thinking about ethics:

- *The argument must be structured logically.* That is, the structure of the argument must be correct, with true premises and valid links from premises to conclusions. The argument must be free of logical fallacies, such as *non sequiturs* or hasty generalizations.
- *The evidence used in support of the claims must be accurate, relevant to the context, and comprehensive.* In making a claim, a person must use evidence that is factually accurate and relevant to the issue being discussed. In addition, the person must present as much evidence as possible. Of course, the person making a counterclaim must also offer accurate, relevant, and comprehensive evidence.
- *The ethical principles used in the argument must be applied consistently.* In one sense, *consistency* refers to noncontradictoriness. For instance, it would be contradictory to believe, at the same time, the following two ethical principles: that it is everyone's duty to help the poor and that all people have the right to do what they wish with their own property. In a second sense, *consistency* means that ethical principles have to be applied equally to all people. Suppose, for example, that two people perform the same job with the same level of competence, but that one of the two is rich and the other is poor but has many dependents. It would be inconsistent to pay the poor person more than the rich person, because the factor that distinguishes the two people—their needs—is irrelevant in determining salary.

The idea that thinking about ethics must be rational would seem simple enough, but two objections to this idea are voiced frequently:

- *Religious value systems supersede nonreligious value systems.* The question of the relative merits of rational inquiry and religious value systems is at least as old as the ancient Greeks. In Plato's *Euthyphro*, Socrates asks Euthyphro to think about whether an act is right because God wills it or whether God wills it because it is right. Plato favors the second interpretation, but not everyone then or now does. Without getting into the complexities of Plato's argument, I would say at this point that because some people do not believe in God at all, and because those who do believe in God do not always agree about what God wills, relying on the revelation of God as the independent source of wisdom about human affairs offers no certainty. To which holy book are we to turn in seeking to determine God's will? To which passage?

- *A person's conscience is an appropriate guide in ethical dilemmas.* However, if we believe that a person's conscience is a product of genetic inheritance and environment, the same two factors that influence a person's ability to get along in society, we ought to be skeptical that most people's consciences are alike or similarly well developed. Even if we believe that our consciences are not developed by genetic inheritance and environment but rather reflect God's commandments, a quick look at the daily newspaper suggests clearly that something can go very wrong between God's commandments and some people's actions.

Using rational argumentation in thinking about ethical problems does not ensure that we will derive logical and clear insights, and it does not ensure that we will derive insights with which everyone, or even most people, would agree. The mere fact that intelligent people of good will continue to hold very different views about numerous ethical questions attests to that. In the Western world, the history of significant disagreements is now two and a half millennia old and counting. But, as James Rachels (1985) comments, "The fact that rationality has limits does not subvert the objectivity of ethics, but it does suggest a certain modesty in what can be claimed for it" (p. 30).

Still, regardless of how much we might despair of our ability to untangle difficult ethical dilemmas using the tools of rational argumentation, we have yet to find a better alternative. Perhaps the surest way to demonstrate our collective reliance on rational argumentation is to talk with someone who believes that there is some other, better approach to resolving ethical dilemmas. If that person says, for example, that individual conscience is a better guide than rational argumentation, you can simply ask "Why?" If the person offers a reason, he or she has unwittingly demonstrated a belief in the value of rational thinking. If the person says "No reason; I just think that," it's probably best to stop the conversation there anyway.

Principles of Blameworthiness

In devising the ground rules of rational argumentation about ethics, philosophers have established general principles about the circumstances under which a person should or should not be held accountable for performing a wrong action or for failing to perform a right action. These principles are referred to as the *theory of blameworthiness*. Although the word *blameworthiness* has an unusual or even slightly comical sound, the theory is critically important in discussing ethics. If, for example, a car goes out of control on a city street, injuring a pedestrian, because the driver had a heart attack, most people would say that the driver should not be blamed. However, if the driver knew he had a heart condition, his driver's license had been revoked, and he drove anyway, most people would say that he was to blame.

Ethicists have established several general principles to help sort through particular cases in which blameworthiness needs to be established. A person is to blame for a wrong action if he or she knowingly and freely performed it or brought it about (Velasquez, 1998). (In addition, a person is to blame for knowingly and freely failing to perform or prevent an action when failing to perform it or prevent it was wrong.) The key concepts here are *knowledge* and *freedom*.

If, for instance, the manufacturers of a drug do not know that the drug can have serious side effects—that is, if they lack the necessary knowledge—they are not to blame for these side effects. Many tobacco manufacturers have tried to avoid blame by arguing that they never knew that smoking is inherently dangerous. (Some tobacco manufacturers still deny that smoking is dangerous.) Similarly, a person or organization that lacks the freedom to prevent a wrong action is not to blame for it. For instance, if a computer manufacturer made a good-faith effort in its product documentation to explain to its customers why it is a bad idea to rest a drink on top of the computer case, it is not to blame if a customer spills a drink into the computer case and thereby damages the computer. Lack of knowledge and lack of ability are referred to as *excusing conditions,* for they excuse a person or organization from any ethical responsibility.

However, there are several situations in which ignorance or inability do not excuse a person or organization from blame. Obviously, if an officer in a company tells his staff not to alert him to any dangers involved in using the products the company makes, that officer is to blame for any resulting injuries. Similarly, if the officer fails to take reasonable measures to determine whether the product is dangerous, that officer is to blame. If a worker injures other workers by not paying attention while on the job, he is not excused from ethical responsibility, because it is a condition of his job that he pay attention.

The concept of blameworthiness is not black and white, however (Velasquez, 1998). There are four *mitigating* factors that decrease a person's or organization's blameworthiness:

- *Uncertainty.* If a person is uncertain whether an action is wrong because the facts are unclear or because the question of the relationship between the facts and the relevant ethical standard is unclear, that person's blameworthiness is mitigated. For instance, if a person works for a company that is submitting a bid on a project and unintentionally learns that the chief competitor's bid will be substantially higher, that person could tell management about the competitor's bid, and management could adjust its own bid upward to increase its own profit while still undercutting the competitor. Would doing so be wrong? The person in this situation might honestly be unsure how to answer this question.

- *Difficulty.* If doing the right thing is difficult, because the person is under some duress, the person's blameworthiness is mitigated. For example, a person might knowingly perform a wrong action, believing that if she fails to take that action she will be fired and thereby lose her medical benefits. If she is the sole support of several dependents who rely on her medical benefits, and one of the dependents requires constant medical care that she would be unable to afford without the benefits, her blameworthiness is mitigated.

- *Involvement.* If a person is part of a team that together performs a wrong action, that person's blameworthiness is mitigated. For instance, an engineer who fails to object to a plan to carry out a wrong action is thought by many ethicists to be less blameworthy than he would have been if he were the sole agent of this same wrong action. However, some ethicists do not agree with this position. Rather, they argue that an individual with a small role in an action has as much responsibility as the sole agent would, especially if that person's job explicitly requires taking responsibility for preventing harm. For instance, an engineer who does not take every possible step to prevent the construction of a bridge that he feels is potentially unsafe is fully blameworthy because as a Professional Engineer he took a pledge to prevent precisely this sort of unsafe situation.

- *Seriousness.* If the wrong that a person commits or permits is minor, that person is less blameworthy than if the wrong is major. Taking an action that leads to injury or death obviously is more blameworthy than taking an action that leads to a minor financial loss. The problem, of course, lies in determining whether a loss is major or minor.

ARGUMENTS AGAINST EXAMINING APPROACHES TO ETHICS

"When in Rome, do as the Romans do." "Who am I to impose my standards of right and wrong on others? Don't they have a right to their own opinions?" "If everyone just looked out for their own interests, we wouldn't have to worry about ethics." "*Right* and *wrong* are merely words we use to express approval and disapproval. They have no real meanings." These and similar statements—some centuries old, others quite modern—suggest arguments that it is meaningless, wrongheaded, or futile to think about ethics. None of these statements are absurd or trivial; all of them are serious challenges. In this section, I present four such arguments, explaining the principal reasons that most philosophers have rejected them. Figure 2.1 lists the major arguments discussed in this section.

Figure 2.1
Four Arguments against Examining Ethics

Subjectivism	The belief that all statements about ethics are simply the speaker's opinion.
Emotivism	The belief that all statements about ethics are not really statements because they cannot be verified empirically and are not definitions.
Ethical egoism	The belief that people should act only in their own self-interest.
Ethical relativism	The belief that the morality of a culture is correct in that culture.

Subjectivism

Subjectivism is the belief that all statements about ethics merely reflect the speaker's opinion. Ethics is simply a matter of opinion, much like taste in food or movies. One person thinks abortion is always wrong; another person thinks that abortion is not always wrong. One person likes vanilla ice cream; another prefers chocolate.

In fact, ethical questions are like matters of opinion in one way: neither can be resolved to everyone's resolution the way that a triangle can be proven to be or not be a right triangle. Chocolate ice cream cannot be "proven" to be better than vanilla, and the pro-choice position cannot be "proven" to be better than the pro-life position.

However, the fact that matters of taste and questions of ethics cannot be resolved objectively does not mean that the two are similarly important and that therefore we should not attempt to think about ethical matters. Statements about ethical matters—statements such as "Industrial espionage is acceptable"—are not like statements about matters of taste, because whereas it makes no difference whether one person prefers vanilla ice cream to chocolate, it can make a great deal of difference whether one person thinks industrial espionage acceptable or unacceptable. If a person thinks that industrial espionage is acceptable, he or she might carry out industrial espionage on the job or might work to influence legislation that encourages industrial espionage. Subjectivism is incorrect because ethical questions matter.

Emotivism

Emotivism is a variation on subjectivism. Whereas subjectivism holds that statements about ethics are merely matters of opinion, emotivism holds that statements about ethics are not really statements at all. State-ments about ethics are in fact imperatives in disguise. A speaker who says "Abortion is wrong" is really urging us to disapprove of abortion, as he or she does.

Although emotivism can be traced back to the 18th-century Scottish phi-losopher David Hume, its chief proponent was A. J. Ayer, whose book *Lan-guage, Truth, and Logic* (1936) created a firestorm in the philosophical community. Ayer argued nothing less than that there is no field such as eth-ics, because ethical statements are literally meaningless. Ayer proposed the *verification principle,* by which a statement is to be considered meaningful under either of only two conditions: (a) The statement can be proven or disproven by means of sense data. Thus, the statement "The speed of light is 186,000 miles per hour" is a meaningful statement, as is "The speed of light is 186 miles per hour" or (b) The statement is a definition ("A bachelor is an unmarried man"). However, a statement such as "Pleasure is the only good" is literally meaningless, for it contains no information. It merely re-flects the speaker's desire to experience pleasure and to urge others to do so as well.

Our experience as humans tells us that emotivism cannot be true. It is simply not the case that the only kind of meaningful statements are defini-tions and empirically verifiable statements. Certainly, a person who says "People from other countries are not as good as people from my country" may well be urging us to mistreat people from other countries, as emotivism holds. But that person is also making a claim about reality, and in doing so can be held responsible for the quality of that claim. In this case, the quality is low; that is, nothing in the speaker's statement provides good reasons for agreeing that people from other countries are not as good as people from the speaker's country. In other words, the statement is not a reasoned argument. The speaker has not provided good reasons for us to agree with the statement. This is the point at which emotivism breaks down, for by definition an emotivist cannot distinguish "good reasons" from "bad reasons," because the words *good* and *bad* have no meaning, for they are neither verifiable by sense data nor definitions.

Again, as is the case with subjectivism, an emotivist literally cannot make a rational argument that emotivism is valid. The best an emotivist can do is express the emotion "Hooray for emotivism!"

Egoism

There are two very different forms of egoism: *psychological egoism* and *ethical egoism.* When discussing ethics, people sometimes rely on psycho-logical egoism, sometimes on ethical egoism. To understand the challenge of egoism, it is necessary to discuss each variety separately.

Psychological egoism is a descriptive theory, not a normative ethical theory. That is, psychological egoism is an attempt to describe how people act. Psychological egoism holds that people act only in what they perceive to be their own self-interest. People are just selfish. Most obviously, people spend money on their own pleasures rather than giving their money to help others. But even when a person appears to be acting altruistically—when, for example, he risks his life to save a stranger in a burning building—he is really doing an act that gives him pleasure. He was looking for publicity or a reward, or he did it because he couldn't live with himself if he hadn't taken the action. Either way, according to psychological egoism, he is doing what he wanted to do.

Even when a person does something that is not in her best interest—when, for example, she persists in smoking cigarettes when she knows doing so is dangerous—she is still acting according to psychological egoism because she is acting according to her *perceived* self-interest. She may be wrong about her real self-interest, but psychological egoism doesn't say that everyone acts wisely, just that everyone acts only in his or her own perceived self-interest.

If psychological egoism is an accurate description of how people live, the study of ethics is irrelevant, for there is no reason to offer theories of appropriate conduct if everyone is wired to act selfishly. But is psychological egoism accurate?

The clearest rejoinder to it is by James Rachels (1986). If I help others, at some cost to myself, that action is precisely the definition of unselfishness. The fact that I want to do it does not mean that the only reason I want to do it is to please myself. I also want to help others, or I would not have done it. The problem with psychological egoism is that it reduces a complex of motivations to a single motivation. The result is that any voluntary action is deemed selfish because the person willed it.

By contrast with psychological egoism, *ethical egoism* is a normative ethical theory. That is, it is a prescriptive statement: people should act only in their own self-interest. We have no obligation to act in others' interests. If doing so works to our own advantage, the act is justified; if doing so does not act to our advantage, it is not justified. Three arguments are commonly presented to justify ethical egoism:

- *Helping others is ineffective or inefficient.* Only the individual knows his or her own best interest; therefore, any attempt I might make to help you is bound to fail or at least be ineffective. The argument "Let's stop giving each other Christmas presents; we only buy the wrong things anyway" fails. While it is true that you probably don't know exactly what kind of clothing a poor family needs when winter is approaching, there are plenty of agencies to which you could contribute money that would in fact find out exactly what that family most needs.

- *Helping others is offensive.* It undermines their dignity. In some cases, yes, but in other cases, no. It would be difficult to argue that providing food relief to starving people is an affront to their dignity. What could affirm their dignity more than to help them stay alive?

- *Acting selfishly facilitates cooperative relationships in society.* Society relies on each person's acting in his or her own self-interest. The merchant who treats his customers fairly is merely an ethical egoist; his motivation is to gain the reputation for fair dealing and thereby increase his business. But ethical egoism wouldn't explain why the merchant treats *all* customers fairly. If, for example, the merchant knows that he can take advantage of a particular customer who will never realize he has been cheated, ethical egoism calls for the merchant to do so. He could become the cab driver who charges the unwitting Japanese tourist $1,400 for the half-hour ride into Manhattan from the airport. Admittedly, there are some cab drivers who do so, but many more do not, and not merely because they are afraid they will be caught. Some people feel that you should do an honest day's work for an honest day's pay because it's the right thing to do, not because altering the time clock could get them fired.

Perhaps the most compelling reason to reject ethical egoism is that other people have the same rights that we do. While it would be unrealistic to expect that most people will heed the dictates of their religion and treat others like themselves, we all *should* do so. We should advance the interests of others, not over our own interests, but *in addition to* our own interests, because others are people too. Chapter 3 in this book examines Immanuel Kant's arguments for this position.

Relativism

Perhaps the most popular objection to the study of ethics is represented by relativism. As is the case with egoism, there are two forms of relativism: *cultural relativism* and *ethical relativism.*

Cultural relativism, a descriptive theory, states that different cultures have different moral codes. In one culture, infanticide is permissible; in another, it is not. In one culture, polygamy is permitted; in another, it is not. Cultural relativism came of age in the early decades of the 20th century, when sociologists and cultural anthropologists explored indigenous cultures around the world, cataloging and describing the practices that differed so much from those of developed Western cultures.

By contrast, *ethical relativism* is a normative ethical theory. It holds that the morality of a particular culture is in fact correct in that culture. Therefore, infanticide is moral in a culture that approves of it but immoral in a culture that doesn't. The implication of ethical relativism is that there is no such thing as ethical universalism; no practice is in fact immoral in all cases, apart from its context. According to ethical relativism, it makes no sense to say, for instance, that abortion is wrong, whereas it does makes sense to say that abortion is wrong in a country in which it is outlawed.

The implications of ethical relativism for technical communicators are profound. For instance, ethical relativism would support the contention that a practice is correct in one organization because that is the way the organization operates. If the organization believes that presenting inaccurate information in product documentation is permissible under all circumstances, an employee would have no justification for questioning the practice.

Ethical relativism has far broader implications than this example suggests. Business ethicists have debated for decades the complex problems faced by multinational corporations. When an organization based, say, in Germany operates a facility in Nigeria, should the moral principles of the home nation or the host nation apply? Or should the organization follow whatever principles generate the greatest profit? Whatever principles seem to be the most ethical? Whatever principles current management wishes to follow? The issues can have far-reaching effects involving such factors as environmental pollution, worker safety, and the general living standards of workers. In addition, issues of fairness are involved, because the major reason most corporations operate facilities in host countries is to take advantage of significantly lower wages in the host country. The issue of ethical relativism and multinational corporations is large and complex; I treat it in detail in Chapter 10.

In responding to the challenge of relativism, philosophers generally accept the validity of cultural relativism but deny that cultural relativism in any way entails ethical relativism.

In accepting the validity of cultural relativism, philosophers generally point out that the wide variety of practices seen in different cultures around the world often says more about the demands of living in the particular cultures than it does about differing views about morality. The Eskimo practice of abandoning old people to death by exposure is a commonly cited example. Although the typical person from a developed Western culture recoils in horror at what seems like a cruel and immoral practice, an anthropologist would explain the practice as a rational response to the harsh conditions of Eskimo life: the Eskimos do not have enough food to support their elderly after their productive years are over. Therefore, the elderly are sacrificed so that the unproductive young can survive. From this perspective, the Eskimo practice reflects local customs that have developed in response to the particular needs of that culture; the practice does not represent disregard for the elderly. From this perspective, philosophers argue that the differences in cultures across the globe reflect differing mores rather than differing moralities. All cultures that have been documented share a set of core values that include telling the truth and forbidding the murder of other members of the culture.

Even apart from this point about how cultural differences do not necessarily represent essential differences in morality, most philosophers reject the idea that cultural relativism entails ethical relativism. This rejection focuses on two major points:

- *It can be impossible to determine what a culture believes.* Although it might be fairly easy to list the core beliefs held by the members of a particular small tribe living in isolation in Borneo, it is considerably more difficult to make sweeping statements about large, pluralistic societies. For instance, do people in the United States approve of abortion? Well, perhaps under some conditions, if the polls are to be believed, but not under all conditions. If it is impossible to determine whether a culture approves, say, of late-term abortions when the mother's health is at risk, it would therefore be impossible to say whether such abortions are right or wrong.

- *Cultural relativism does not logically entail ethical relativism.* Even if every person in one culture thinks infanticide is right and every person in another culture thinks infanticide is wrong, there are other options than to conclude that both cultures are right: only one culture could be right, or neither culture could be right. In other words, the fact that one culture believes that infanticide is right says only that this culture believes that infanticide is right. It doesn't show that the culture's belief is reasonable.

Although ethical relativism is attractive in that it rejects ethical imperialism, it can lead to some paradoxical conclusions. For one thing, ethical relativism involves a logical inconsistency. Ethical relativism is based on the premise that a culture's beliefs are binding on only those people in that culture. But as soon as someone has a belief about what is appropriate behavior for people *outside* their own culture, ethical relativism breaks down. For example, fundamentalist Muslims believe it is unacceptable for anyone in any culture to blaspheme. Is it therefore the case that it is unacceptable for anyone in any culture to blaspheme? Or is it acceptable for an atheist in New Jersey to blaspheme, if the atheist's own culture permits blasphemy? Or is the atheist bound by the beliefs of the fundamentalist Moslem in Tunisia?

Ethical relativism is also vulnerable to two other logical paradoxes. First, the same practice could be right in one context and wrong in another. For instance, an ethical relativist would have to admit that slavery was ethical in, say, Mississippi in 1859 but unethical in Mississippi today. But why would slavery today be any more abhorrent than it was then? Second, the ethical relativist would have to admit that he should not try to change other people's beliefs about a practice—either people in another culture or people in his own culture—because whatever a culture believes is by definition right. There could be no evolution in a culture's thinking because whatever is is right. But, obviously, ethical positions do change. If ethical relativism is valid, the only explanation for this change would be spontaneous ethical mutation.

ARGUMENTS AGAINST EXAMINING ETHICS IN ORGANIZATIONAL SETTINGS

Several of the arguments against examining ethics in organizations are clearly derived from the more general arguments against examining ethics in any context, those arguments presented in the previous section. For instance, the argument that business is a game that is played according to its own rules is really a specific instance of ethical relativism. Other arguments presented in this section relate more to the specific context of business itself, and how that context relates to human nature. For instance, the argument that ethics is best served by pure capitalism derives from the utilitarian argument that people are the best judges of what they like, and capitalism is the best system for satisfying those desires.

Regardless of the pedigree of the four ideas discussed here, it is necessary to confront them directly before beginning a more detailed look at individual approaches to ethics.

"Ethical" Really Means "Legal"

One argument against studying ethics in organizational life is that the legal system is a better framework for codifying matters of conduct. If a practice is legal, it's ethical. This position is attractive in that the law is rooted in the real world and ensures a level playing field: your company and my company both have to abide by the same laws, despite any differences we might have in our views of ethics. Indeed, in most cultures, law and morality are closely related; the law reflects, to a greater or lesser degree, that culture's morality. The law spells out what practices are permitted and not permitted, and what penalties are to be imposed on a person who violates the law.

However, there are three major problems with this approach:

- *The law is not the same thing as morality, and some laws are immoral.* In addition to such obvious examples from the past as laws permitting slavery or discrimination against people of certain ethnicity or religious beliefs, the case could be made that some current practices are legal but immoral. For example, many thoughtful people feel that "employment at will"—the practice that enables employers to fire workers at will, without having to show cause—is wrong. It is also perfectly legal to sell an expensive life-insurance policy to an elderly person who has no dependents, but most people would consider the practice unethical.

- *Laws conflict from place to place.* Given the size and growth rate of the global economy, it would seem logical to ask, "Whose law?"

- *The law is very slow.* Many aspects of intellectual-property law, for example, do not reflect the complexity of current technologies, especially regarding digital information on the Internet. Years or perhaps decades will pass before law catches up with our culture's evolving ideas about the ethics of using and distributing digital information.

For these reasons, most ethicists believe it is not satisfactory to use law as a substitute for ethics in organizational settings.

Ethics Is Best Served by Pure Capitalism

This argument is a form of ethical egoism that dates back to Adam Smith's *Wealth of Nations* (1776): capitalism is the best system for bringing about an ethical society because it ensures that companies produce what the public wants, and do so in the most efficient manner possible. To the extent that companies strive for profits without the distraction of ethical questions, then, the greater will be the benefit to society. Smith's famous phrase for this effect is "the invisible hand" of capitalism.

Some of the problems associated with this viewpoint are spelled out by Velasquez (1998):

- It assumes that markets are perfectly competitive, but this is never the case. Is the business software market perfectly competitive, or does one company pursue monopolistic practices?

- It assumes that all efficiencies benefit the public, but such practices as deceptive advertising, bribery, and price fixing do not.

- It assumes that all people are members of the buying public, but this not the case. Many people do not participate in the market economy.

- It assumes an underlying premise—that people should work to benefit those people who participate in markets—without proving it. A different premise—that people should work to benefit all people—might be more ethical.

An Employee Is Merely an Agent of the Principal

This viewpoint holds that it is the role of an employee to set aside his or her private ethical beliefs and serve the interests of the employer. The most famous statement of this viewpoint is Milton Friedman's 1970 essay, "The Social Responsibility of Business Is to Increase Its Profits" (1996).

Friedman argues that the employee is an agent of the employer and therefore is obliged to work toward fulfilling the employer's aims, restricted only by the dictates of law and general ethical custom. If the agent works to advance his or her own aims, such as by offering higher wages than the market requires or by reducing pollution more than the law requires, he or she is in effect imposing an unfair tax on the organization's owners and employees, as well as on the consumers of the organization's products or services. Only elected civil servants have this taxation privilege. A person who wishes to run his or her own business of course has the right to pursue any business strategy, including one that allows for "social responsibility," as do people who work in such not-for-profit institutions as hospitals or schools. However, the business of a business is to make money for its owners.

Does an agent retain no ethical rights? If an employer demands that an agent perform an action that is legal but that the agent thinks is unethical, is the agent ethically obliged to do so? This question is not easy to answer. There simply is no rule that states what may be demanded of an employee, just as there is no rule outlining the options of an employee who is forced to carry out an action that he or she considers unethical. The courts frequently hear cases in which an employer demands that a worker carry out an act but the worker refuses; the employer argues that the organization is fully justified in making the demand, and the worker argues that the demand is unreasonable. The fact that such cases are not resolved within the organization, and that sometimes the organization wins the court case and sometimes the worker wins, suggests that there is no general answer to the question about precisely which rights a worker retains when employed as an agent.

One common rejoinder to Friedman's perspective on agency is the stakeholder theory, articulated by Evan and Freeman (1993). Corporations do not exist solely to benefit the owners, they argue. Rather, corporations have six stakeholders: owners, management, employees, suppliers, customers, and the local community. Each stakeholder bears certain responsibilities and enjoys certain rights. The purpose of the corporation is to benefit all the stakeholders, not just the owners. Evan and Freeman call their approach Kantian, in that an employee is not merely an agent of the employer, but rather a stakeholder who retains all rights of autonomy by virtue of being human. This principle is discussed in more detail in Chapter 3 in this book.

Business Is a Game with Its Own Rules

Finally, some argue that business is a game with its own rules, and that so long as all participants understand and abide by those rules, nobody is victimized. This viewpoint is articulated most forcefully by Albert Carr, in his 1968 essay, "Is Business Bluffing Ethical?" (1993).

Carr's (1993) argument is that business is more like poker than it is like religion. In poker, we don't expect players to tell the truth; we expect them to bluff and mislead. That is how the game is played. Therefore, the main argument that business bluffing is unethical—that it is unethical because it deprives people of accurate information on which to make informed choices—is irrelevant. When you go to buy a used car from a dealer, you expect him to try to mislead you about the condition of the car. Although some forms of deception, such as turning back the odometer, are illegal, many others are permitted. And since you know that the dealer will try to mislead you by bluffing, you bluff, too. The one who bluffs better wins in the transaction.

That business bluffing is common is not contested, and Cramton and Dees (1996) are probably correct in remarking that even the most compelling argument that honesty and trust are superior to dishonesty and distrust in business practices is unlikely to be effective. Business bluffing is of course common, but to argue from that fact that business bluffing is ethical because everyone knows that it occurs is simply a *non sequitur*. If people were able to choose whether to be treated honestly or dishonestly when they entered into a business negotiation of some sort, few would choose to be treated dishonestly. This fact is just one obvious rationale for concluding that business bluffing is unethical. Other points—such as that bluffing raises the costs of business transactions, that it hurts the most vulnerable people, and that it drives some people out of the market altogether—also support the same conclusion.

Therefore, it makes sense to work toward practical measures to reduce the prevalence of business bluffing, as Cramton and Dees (1996) argue in their essay on negotiating, rather than argue that the prevalence of business bluffing justifies the practice.

The following chapters in Part I discuss some of the major approaches to ethics that have dominated Western thought. Chapter 3 focuses on the concept of rights, as articulated by perhaps the most influential ethicist in the Western tradition, Immanuel Kant. Although Kant's ideas on rights have been criticized and amended frequently over the last two centuries, they form a permanent contribution to the field.

3

Rights

In the essay "On the Supposed Right to Lie from Altruistic Motives," Immanuel Kant (1724–1804) presents the hypothetical Case of the Inquiring Murderer: you are approached by a man who claims that a murderer is looking for him. The man runs away; you see him go into his house. A few moments later, the murderer comes up to you and inquires whether you have seen the man. Should you tell the murderer where the man went? Kant argues that you should, because you should never tell a lie. Perhaps the intended victim has slipped out of his house, Kant argues, and the murderer will not find him. Or perhaps the murderer will be apprehended by neighbors and thus be prevented from killing the man. But if you were to lie and say that the man is not at home, the murderer might come upon him somewhere outside his house and kill him. Therefore, it is your duty to tell the truth, regardless of the circumstances.

It is hard to accept that the author of "On the Supposed Right to Lie from Altruistic Motives" is arguably the most influential thinker in the tradition of Western ethics, despite his atrocious reasoning about the absolute duty to tell the truth under all circumstances. In his major work on ethics, *Foundations of the Metaphysics of Morals* (1785), Kant codified a basic principle of ethics: that ethical laws are universalizable; that is, they apply to everyone, including oneself. In addition, he systematized the ancient commonsense idea that all people have the right to be treated with respect, for by their very existence all people possess dignity.

In this chapter, I discuss Kant's major contribution to ethical thinking: the argument that individual rights are fundamentally important. I also survey some of the major limitations of his thinking and explain why his ideas on duties and rights remain influential two centuries after his death.

REASONS AND EXPLANATIONS

One statement of Kant's basic thesis about ethics is that, in deciding how to act, we require reasons, not explanations. In other words, we need to justify our actions, not merely explain the factors that lead us to choose them. This point requires a brief explanation of the two major contemporary theories of human action: rationalism and empiricism.

Rationalists held that all knowledge is derived from the exercise of reason and is independent of any particular person's own experience. Because reason deals with ideas that exist outside time and space, it offers an objective view of the world. By contrast, empiricists argued that knowledge is derived from sense experience. The most famous statement of empiricism is David Hume's (1888): "Reason is, and ought to be, the slave of the passions, and can never pretend to any other office than to serve and obey them" (p. 415). And because we can be certain only of what we have experienced, we are limited to our own individual perspective. The most radical empiricists believed not only that all knowledge is subjective, but also that there cannot be any assurance even of our own existence.

Trained as a scientist, Kant rejected the extremes of rationalism and empiricism, for although he believed strongly in the importance of rational thought, he thought the mind had to have ideas, derived from experience, to think about. For Kant, rational thought without the substance derived from experience is meaningless, and experience without the conceptualizing power of reason is blind. Kant argued in his *Critique of Pure Reason* that neither reason nor experience alone can provide knowledge; we need the structuring capacity of reason and the content of experience to create knowledge.

As Roger Scruton (1982) explains, Kant saw this duality reflected in the essential irony of human existence on earth: just as knowledge derives from experience and reason, human existence is simultaneously part of causal necessity and yet separate from it. On the one hand, the world in which humans live is a web of causal events: nature works according to cause and effect, the realm of sciences such as physics, biology, chemistry, and geology. On the other hand, we exercise free will by using our reason—if we so choose. In *The Foundation of the Metaphysics of Morals,* Kant sought to explain how humans can—and should—exercise this freedom.

THE CONCEPT OF MAXIMS

This insistence that people must produce reasons, not explanations, for their actions is what John Silber (1968) has called the Copernican revolution in ethics. Kant held that all previous attempts to define a material object or condition as being good were inadequate; only by defining first the laws governing correct action can people be truly liberated. These laws Kant called *maxims.*

A maxim is a general principle that governs how we act. For example, it is wrong to lie; or, we should help people in need if we can. Feldman (1978, pp. 99–100) makes four useful points about Kant's views on maxims:

- *Maxims are general, not particular.* A maxim is a general principle that we use to guide our actions in particular cases. For example, it is wrong to lie. A maxim does not take the form, "When it's Tuesday, a little after noon, and I'm hungry, I think I'll make myself lunch."

- *We often act without formulating or examining a maxim.* Much of the time, we act without taking the time to think through the bases of our current situation; we have to act quickly. Therefore, we simply act.

- *We often formulate inaccurate maxims.* Usually, when we have to act quickly, only after the fact do we have the leisure to examine the maxims that might have guided our decision. Often, we rationalize our action by positing an honorable maxim, one that puts a good face on our decision. For instance, if we did something to hurt the interests of a person whom we don't like, we rationalize our action by telling ourselves that the person deserved it.

- *The same action can be explained by different maxims.* Kant's example is the butcher who is honest with his customers. One maxim that might motivate his honesty is that people deserve to be treated honestly. Another maxim might be that honesty is the best policy: he will earn a reputation for honesty that will increase his business. Fundamental to Kant's theory is that the maxim a person uses in selecting a course of action is critical in determining whether the action has moral value.

This is merely common sense, and Kant was forthright in asserting that his ideas about ethics were quite simple. In fact, he argued, early in the *Foundations,* that the common person is superior to the sophisticated philosopher in understanding ethics: the average person "knows well how to distinguish what is good, what is bad, and what is consistent or inconsistent with duty" (pp. 403–404). Unlike a philosopher, the average person will not be distracted by "a mass of irrelevant considerations." In discussing ethics, it is best "to acquiesce in the common rational judgment, or at most to call in philosophy in order to make the system of morals more complete and comprehensible and its rules more convenient for use . . . "

(p. 404). Philosophers systematize and explain ethical systems, but they are unlikely to have reached unique insights about right and wrong.

Kant articulated a philosophy that called for acting according to maxims based on reason, not according to what he considered the baser motive of pleasure. He wanted to create a philosophy of moral law that would exist independent of the world of the senses. To the argument that we need practical moral guidelines grounded in real-world situations, Kant responded that precisely because the world is so full of contingencies, we need a reasoned approach separate from the contingencies.

Foundations begins with the assertion that "Nothing in the world—indeed nothing even beyond the world—can possibly be conceived which could be called good without qualification except a *good will*" (pp. 392–393). The good will is the will to act from duty, according to reason, not according to desires or inclination. Other goods—intelligence, wit, fortune, and so forth—can be misused by an unethical person. Only an action *based on* duty—the good will—is of moral worth. An action that merely is in accord with duty carries no moral worth. Therefore, the butcher who is honest because it is right to be honest is demonstrating moral worth, whereas the butcher who is honest in order to increase his business demonstrates no moral worth because he is not acting from duty.

To clarify the distinction between acting from reason and acting from some other motivation, Kant introduced two terms: *hypothetical imperative* and *categorical imperative*. A hypothetical imperative is a descriptive statement about the contingent world. It takes the form of "If you want to accomplish *x*, then do *y*"; for instance, "If you want to publicize your business, put up a Web site." A categorical imperative, however, is a description of how we should act regardless of the world of contingency. A categorical imperative takes the form "Do *y*"; for example, "Tell the truth." A categorical imperative is an absolute; it does not admit qualifications, explanations, or exceptions.

In *Foundations*, Kant offered a number of different versions—or, as he called them, formulations—of the categorical imperative, of which the first two provide his vision of the form and content of an ethic based on rational principles.

FIRST FORMULATION OF THE CATEGORICAL IMPERATIVE

Kant's model for the form of this ethic is contained in the first formulation, "Act only according to that maxim by which you can at the same time will that it should become a universal law" (trans. 1969, p. 421). Kant supported this universalizability formulation with four examples of how to use it to analyze whether an action would be ethical or unethical:

The Suicide

A man in despair due to "a series of evils" wonders whether it would violate his duty if he committed suicide. Kant argues that it would, because of the maxim it would entail: "For love of myself, I make it my principle to shorten my life when by a longer duration it threatens more evil than satisfaction. But it is questionable whether this principle of self-love could become a universal law of nature. One immediately sees a contradiction in a system of nature whose law would be to destroy life by the feeling whose special office is to impel the improvement of life." (p. 422)

But why does the principle of self-love necessarily impel the improvement of life? As Feldman (1978) points out, Kant has not proved that self-love has any function at all. In addition, he has not proved that self-love must have one, and only one, purpose. The truth could be that self-love impels us to continue living when life is pleasurable and to cease living when it is not.

The Lying Promise

A man in need wishes to borrow money, even though he knows he will not be able to repay it. But if he were to admit this, nobody would lend him money. It would be wrong to act according to the maxim underlying this action: "He immediately sees that it could never hold as a universal law of nature and be consistent with itself; rather it must necessarily contradict itself. For the universality of a law which says that anyone who believes himself to be in need could promise what he pleased with the intention of not fulfilling it would make the promise itself and the end to be accomplished by it impossible; no one would believe what was promised to him but would only laugh at any such assertion as vain pretense." (p. 422)

Kant's reasoning here is invalid, for he assumes that everyone who makes a promise does so falsely. But as long as most people fulfill their promises, the concept of promising will survive. In fact, the credit-card industry and the mortgage-loan industry have always absorbed a certain percentage of false promises. Ethicist John Boatright (2000) points out that whereas a world without promises is less desirable than the present world, there is nothing in Kant's argument to show that a world without promises literally could not exist.

The Rusted Talents

A man with a talent decides to devote himself to pleasure rather than develop this talent. Kant argues that it is impossible to imagine such a world: "But he cannot possibly will that this should become a universal law of nature or that it should be implanted in us by a natural instinct. For, as a rational being, he necessarily wills that all his faculties should be developed, inasmuch as they are given to him for all sorts of possible purposes." (p. 423)

Kant has not shown that we are under any obligation to develop our talents. Basketball fans are undoubtedly glad that Michael Jordan chose to develop his basketball talents, but can we say that he was obliged to do so? Did he not have the right to go to graduate school or open a business upon graduating from college? A second problem with Kant's example is that he says that people are obliged to develop *all* their talents. Michael Jordan has considerable talent for baseball, but those who witnessed his brief baseball career probably would reject the idea that he was obliged to develop that talent. More likely, they would have preferred that he continue to develop his basketball talent.

The Failure to Aid Others

A man who is well off decides not to help people in need: "Now although it is possible that a universal law of nature according to that maxim could exist, it is nevertheless impossible to will that such a principle should hold everywhere as a law of nature. For a will which resolved this would conflict with itself, since instances can often arise in which he would need the love and sympathy of others, and in which he would have robbed himself, by such a law of nature springing from his own will, of all hope of the aid he desires." (p. 423)

But what if the man never finds himself in need? Or, if he finds himself in need, he does not wish assistance from anyone?

The four examples of the first formulation of the categorical imperative are ineffective because of their brevity and lack of precision. Grassian (1981) clearly summarizes the problem:

When Kant tells us that we should do only what we can will that everyone else do, what exactly is the force of the "can" here? Does it mean what we *can logically* will (that is, what it is possible to conceive), or what is *scientifically possible for us to* will (that is, what is consistent with "the laws of nature"), or what we can *rationally will*, or merely what *we would desire as a matter of psychological fact*. Kant himself does not clearly say and what he does say points in different directions. (p. 81)

But as Boatright (2000) points out, the principal value of Kant's first formulation is that it stipulates that for ethical judgments to be valid, they must be consistent; if we are to defend an action of ours, we must be prepared to defend the same action if someone else, or, indeed, everyone else, were to do it.

SECOND FORMULATION OF THE CATEGORICAL IMPERATIVE

Kant's first formulation of the categorical imperative, then, is "Act only according to that maxim by which you can at the same time will that it should become a universal law." The only way that such a maxim can exist is if all people have the same ends. Obviously, there is no instrumental good, such as money or pleasure, that all people seek; some people take little interest in money, and everyone has different pleasures. To Kant, the only good that links all people is humanity itself: personhood. The second formulation of the categorical imperative stipulates this relationship: "Act so that you treat humanity, whether in your own person or in that of another, always as an end and never as a means only" (p. 429).

Although Kant believed that the three formulations of the categorical imperative were almost identical, his second formulation is, in my view, the most clear, the most compelling, and the most far-reaching. At first glance, there seems nothing particularly unusual about the idea that we should treat ourselves and others not only as means but also as ends. After all, the Golden Rule—"Do unto others as you would have them do unto you" (Matthew 7:12)—is fundamental not only to Christianity but also to Judaism, Confucianism, Islam, and Buddhism.

However, Kant rejected the idea that he was merely restating the Golden Rule (p. 430n). For one thing, the Golden Rule, unlike the categorical imperative, does not mention duties to oneself; it only discusses duties to others. In addition, it calls only for reciprocity; that is, we should treat others as we wish to be treated. It does not contain the content of the categorical imperative: that people must be treated with respect. A person who is content to be treated poorly is entitled to treat others poorly.

Perhaps the most significant difference between Kant's second formulation and the Golden Rule is that the Golden Rule can be interpreted as a hypothetical imperative, that is, if you want people to treat you well, you should treat them well. The bedrock of Kant's ethics is that the categorical imperative does not consider such contingent reasoning. We should treat people as ends and not merely as means not because doing so would make our lives easier but because it is the right thing to do.

In his second formulation, Kant is arguing that we should treat all people as fully rational creatures, that is, as entities that possess ethical autonomy. The world of experience (nature, for example) is ruled by cause and effect; we know what causes rain, and what it causes. But only humans possess free will: the ability to act in accord with their reason, overruling all contingent motives such as convenience, pleasure, and material gain. The central and unique characteristic of humans is, for Kant, this ethical autonomy. And this second formulation provides a clearer rationale for the example of the man who would borrow money knowing that he cannot repay it:

he who intends a deceitful promise to others sees immediately that he intends to use another man merely as a means, without the latter containing the end in himself at the same time. For he whom I want to use for my own purposes by means of such a promise cannot possibly assent to my mode of action against him and cannot contain the end of this action in himself. (p. 430)

Kant was fully aware that he could not prove his central contention—that humans possess free will—or the idea that this contention justifies the concept of the categorical imperative. "But why should I subject myself as a rational being, and thereby all other beings endowed with reason, to this law? I will admit that no interest impels me to do so, for that would then give no categorical imperative" (p. 449).

Admitting the apparent circularity of his position—because we are free, we are compelled to act in accordance with the categorical imperative—Kant argues that actually there is no conflict: the fact that he cannot prove his contention does not invalidate the contention, just as our imperfect vision of an object does not define or constrain the object itself. The distinction between the world of sense and the world of reason explains our inability to "prove" the categorical imperative: we exist simultaneously in both worlds and cannot see clearly enough to recognize the reality of this idea apart from the way it affects us.

This rationale might seem like sophistry, but Kant's second formulation of the categorical imperative is ultimately simple and powerful. The reason that we should not lie when we communicate is not that we can get in serious trouble (although that is true) but that we would be treating our readers and listeners as means only: as customers or as subordinates or bosses, but not as people. If we are to treat them as people, we must be honest and forthright so that they can exercise their own rational autonomy.

A new cliché sums up this idea effectively: empowerment. If our boss wants us to lie about the capabilities of the software we are advertising by describing a feature that will (perhaps) appear in the next update, we are ethically obliged to empower our readers by telling them the truth: that we hope to include that feature in the next update. Then we have enabled them to make a rational decision on whether to buy the product. Of course, logic then requires that we also offer to send them that update, free, when it is available, and to guarantee when it will be introduced and offer a specified refund if we do not meet that deadline. If we are not willing to do so, then we cannot logically expect them to buy the present product.

Kant's second formulation of the categorical imperative thus stipulates that, if we are to treat others as ends, we have to accord them their full dignity, which means that as communicators we have to write and speak truthfully, in the broadest sense of the word. And if we are to treat *ourselves* as ends rather than as means only, then we must view ourselves not as technical communicators—technicians whose job is to turn out documents that please our supervisors—but as humans who sometimes create technical communication. Thus, we owe it to ourselves, as well as to our readers and listeners, to be truthful.

Many commentators have corroborated Kant's own admission that there is no way to prove the second formulation of the categorical imperative. Pepita Haezrahi (1969), for instance, is among the most pungent in remarking that "We might be inclined to sympathise prompted by some obscure feeling of its sublimity, did not Kant fall back from this emotional vantage to a particularly unsatisfactory piece of reasoning in lieu of proof" (p. 292). In a similar critique, Feldman (1978) asks why it would not be equally plausible for Kant to argue that pleasure, not humanity, is the intrinsic good, the ultimate end.

Still, Kant's second formulation is a useful starting point in ethical deliberations; if a course of action seems ethically satisfactory except that it violates a person's human dignity, the technical communicator ought to think carefully before proceeding. Admittedly, the idea that we must treat people—ourselves and everyone else—with full human dignity is commonplace and cannot answer every question. And it is too general to be rendered in a flowchart. Yet Kant makes an eloquent case that rational duty is ethically superior to the contingency of the world of experience, that it is more important for us as technical communicators to treat ourselves and others as persons in possession of full human dignity than to perform the expedient act. In a world that often seems intent on taking the opposite position, Kant's idea is compelling, if ultimately unproved and unprovable.

THIRD FORMULATION OF THE CATEGORICAL IMPERATIVE

Kant's third formulation of the categorical imperative is "the idea of the will of every rational being as a will giving universal law" (p. 432). This formulation encompasses the main idea of the first formulation (the universalizable law) and the idea of the second formulation (treating people as ends and not merely as means).

Here, Kant is offering his most subtle argument: "A rational being belongs to the realm of ends as a member when he gives universal laws in it while also himself subject to these laws. He belongs to it as sovereign when he, as legislating, is subject to the will of no other" (pp. 433–434). It is imperative to act from duty not because that is what we want to do but because as rational beings we are obliged to create universal laws that govern all people's actions, including our own. Because all humans are rational, we all will the same laws, and these laws, by definition, apply to all humans. We achieve autonomy by formulating and acting from these laws.

And what is it that justifies the morally good disposition or virtue in making such lofty claims? It is nothing less than the participation it affords the rational being in giving universal laws. He is thus fitted to be a member in a possible realm of ends to which his own nature already destined him. For, as an end in himself, he is destined to be legislative in the realm of ends, free from all laws of nature and obedient only to those which he himself gives. Accordingly, his maxims can belong to a universal legislation to which he is at the same time also subject. (p. 435)

By subjugating themselves to this universal law, people become sovereigns in this realm of ends.

CONCLUSION

Figure 3.1 summarizes the discussion of Kant's three formulations of the categorical imperative.

Figure 3.1
Kant's Three Formulations of the Categorical Imperative

First Formulation: "Act according to that maxim by which you can at the same time will that it should become a universal law." This formulation is often called the universalizability formulation; for ethical values to be valid, they must be consistent for all people.

Second Formulation: "Act so that you treat humanity, whether in your own person or in that of another, always as an end and never as a means only." This is Kant's noncontingent version of the Golden Rule.

Third Formulation: "A rational being belongs to the realm of ends as a member when he gives universal laws in it while also himself subject to these laws. He belongs to it as sovereign when he, as legislating, is subject to the will of no other." This formulation is Kant's summary of the first and second formulations, stressing a universal realm in which people live according to self-created rules derived from reason.

Until we achieve this "possible realm of ends," we are caught in the middle position, existing partly in the world of sense, partly in the realm of reason. Just as there are lower animals that have no capacity for reason and live exclusively in the world of sense, Kant holds open the possibility that there are other beings, somewhere in the universe, who possess a holy will. Such beings would not need a categorical imperative, for they would always act purely from reason.

The dilemma for humans is that we are an impure combination of lower animals and gods. As such, we cannot describe the transcendental world of pure reason. Kant remarks, in a moving passage near the end of *Foundations*, that he cannot explain how subservience to a universal law grants freedom.

Certainly I could revel in the intelligible world, the world of intelligences, which still remains to me; but although I have a well-founded idea of it, still I do not have the least knowledge of it, nor can I ever attain to it by all the exertions of my natural capacity of reason. This intelligible world signifies only a something which remains when I have excluded from the determining grounds of my will everything belonging to the world of sense in order to withhold the principle of motives from the field of sensibility. I do so by limiting it and showing that it does not contain absolutely everything in itself but that outside it there is still more; but this more I do not know. (p. 462)

Human reason constantly seeks to understand its own origins and its own necessity, and we as humans have to be content to understand the nobility of this search. Yet the search, although necessary, is doomed to failure, because we are tied to the world of senses, because we are not pure reason. "And so we do not indeed comprehend the practical unconditional necessity of the moral imperative; yet we do comprehend its incomprehensibility, which is all that can be fairly demanded of a philosophy which in its principles strives to reach the limit of human reason" (p. 463).

As I suggested in mentioning Kant's essay "On the Supposed Right to Lie from Altruistic Motives" at the start of this chapter, Kant has been subject to more criticism—and more withering criticism—than almost any other ethicist. The respected business ethicist Robert Solomon (1992) has even gone so far as to call Kant "a kind of disease in ethics" (p. 114). Kant is indeed vulnerable to criticism on six bases:

- *His ideas are insufficiently precise.* While his final comments on how we can only comprehend the incomprehensibility of the realm of ends are eloquent, they are not particularly helpful. Whenever he tries to explain how his ideas would work in the real world, as in the four examples of the first formulation of the categorical imperative, he falters.

- *His concept of free will is assumed, not proven.* The basis of his argument is that we are all totally free, and that only actions derived from good will have moral worth. But we know that a person's mind is determined, to a large degree, by heredity and environment. Does it make sense that when a person who derives pleasure from doing good deeds does a good deed, that act is of no moral worth, whereas when a person who doesn't want to do a good deed performs one, that act is of great moral worth? The person who enjoys doing good might not have free will to determine his or her own makeup, yet Kant is discounting the value of that person's actions.

- *His ideas are subject to numerous counterexamples and paradoxes.* On the question of treating people as ends and not merely as means, would it be wrong or right to attempt to dissuade a person from doing an evil deed? Attempting to do so would seem to be the right thing, yet the attempt would in itself prevent the person from exercising his own autonomy as a legislator. Kant does not address the paradox of the person who, say, hates black people and would be happy to have everyone else hate them, too.

- *He believes that only humans have rights.* People have rights because they are rational creatures. Other animals are only of instrumental value, therefore, and do not have rights. Nonanimal living things similarly have no rights.

- *He doesn't account for special relationships.* Kant advocates treating all people the same, yet in our lives we have special obligations to friends and family members. Most people would think that we have a greater obligation to care for these people than for people with whom we have no special relationship. (The ethic of care is discussed in Chapter 6 in this book.)
- *He ignores conflicts of rights.* Your right to buy and develop a piece of property can conflict with my right to see the mountain beyond it. Kant does not address the question of adjudicating such conflicts.

All this being said, his three main ideas—that principles have to be supported by reasons, that they must apply consistently to everyone, and that people must be treated as ends and not merely as means—remain powerful as general ethical guidelines. Kant provided an eloquent argument that people must act consistently, according to reason, and must respect the rights of all people. Even though he failed to provide rational proof of these ideas or explain clearly how they might be applied in addressing real problems, Kant succeeded in articulating the most fundamental principle of ethics, the one principle that undergirds all ancient and modern approaches to ethics. Kant's idea of a person's right to be treated as a person and not a thing, an idea so clearly tied to the most fundamental Judeo-Christian tenet, retains its powerful pull on our sense of moral conduct.

For technical communicators, Kant's dictum that people must be treated as ends and not merely as means is still the single most significant ethical touchstone. If a technical communicator is being pressured to include misleading information in a documentation set, the simplest and most profound question she might ask herself is this: If I did so, would I be treating my readers as people (as ends) or as customers (as means)? Does the reader have the right to honest information? The answer to this question—from the perspective of ethics, at any rate—is obvious. Certainly, there are other questions the technical communicator might ask, answers to which can help in making a decision. But neglecting to ask the question about the reader's rights invalidates the decision-making process.

The next chapter considers utilitarianism, the main rival foundational approach to ethics. Utilitarianism, which holds that the important criterion in judging an act is not the good will of the agent but the tangible results of the act, could not be further from Kantian rights.

4

Utility

If Kantian rights, with its emphasis on treating people fairly, as people and not as things, is one tower of traditional Western ethical thought, utilitarianism is the other. Utilitarianism shifts the focus from analyzing the motives and character of the agent to assessing the outcomes of the action: Is the action likely to produce more good than any other possible action would? The likely effects of the action, not an adherence to an abstract rule or maxim, are the standard of utilitarianism.

Although philosophical discussions of utilitarianism are as technical and complex as similar discussions of Kantianism, the average person is immediately comfortable with the broad outlines of utilitarianism. This is not surprising, for utilitarianism is the philosophical foundation of capitalism, which holds that the best way to ensure the creation of the greatest social utility is to encourage both producers and consumers to pursue their own self-interest. Producers will offer the best products and services they can at the lowest cost possible to still earn a profit, and the consumer will search for the best value. This dynamic relationship is portrayed in the supply-and-demand curve. Through the workings of this system of enlightened self-interest, the whole society will prosper as more and more goods and services are made available to consumers.

More specifically, utilitarianism is seen as the intellectual engine of a common business calculation: the cost/benefit analysis. The manufacturer decides whether to start a new product line by weighing the amount of pleasure that might be gained (profits if the product succeeds) against the amount of pain that might be incurred (losses if the product fails). A supplier decides whether to bid on a proposal by comparing the potential profits from a successful bid and the actual costs of writing an unsuccessful bid. A large company considering whether to shut down an unprofitable plant calculates the benefits of cutting costs, as well as the expenses of shutting down, the costs of retraining and relocating employees, and the damage to the affected community and to the company's reputation. Utilitarianism is the ethics of pragmatism and common sense.

Although utilitarianism is the ethic of the modern capitalist system, it is among the oldest approaches to ethics in Western thought. Contemporaries of Socrates in ancient Greece first expressed one of the central ideas of utilitarianism: that people are motivated by the desire for pleasure, and that pleasure is the chief good. The idea that the best way to evaluate the goodness of an action is to look at its effects was added later. A modern version of utilitarianism was developed by the Scottish philosopher David Hume in the 18th century.

In this chapter, I focus on the ideas of two major proponents of utilitarianism—British philosophers Jeremy Bentham and John Stuart Mill—as well as on a contemporary formulation called rule utilitarianism. My goal is to describe and critique the major forms of utilitarianism.

JEREMY BENTHAM AND THE HEDONISTIC CALCULUS

In his 1789 book *Introduction to the Principles of Morals and Legislation*, Jeremy Bentham (1748–1832) sought to reform the British legislative and legal systems by presenting what he saw as a rational system of ethics. The prevailing approach to ethics in Bentham's day was a natural-laws doctrine articulated most forcefully by John Locke. According to the natural-laws viewpoint, people were intended to live in accord with certain natural laws ordained by God and revealed through the inner light of conscience. Bentham totally rejected the natural-laws approach, calling it "nonsense on stilts," a mere attempt to justify irrational preferences and prejudices.

Bentham critiqued those aspects of current social and legislative policy that he believed revealed these prejudices. For instance, he asked whether it made better sense to outlaw a sexual practice between consenting adults because it was an abomination against God or to determine whether the practice itself actually had good effects or bad effects. Why did people who committed sexual offenses face great legal penalties, he asked, whereas businessmen who caused great misery through fraud receive only token punishment? Does it make sense to mete out severe penalties when we find a practice highly offensive to our moral sentiments but light penalties when we consider a practice only slightly offensive?

According to Bentham, the whole fabric of English public institutions and public life was a hodgepodge of irrational, contradictory moralistic prejudices presented as reflections of a divine law. What was needed, he argued, was a system of evaluating acts, not agents. In the opening sentences of his book, he presented the concept that is the foundation of modern utilitarianism:

Nature has placed mankind under the governance of two sovereign masters, *pain* and *pleasure*. It is for them alone to point out what we ought to do, as well as to determine what we shall do. On the one hand the standard of right and wrong, on the other the chain of causes and effects, are fastened to their throne. They govern us in all we do, in all we say, in all we think: every effort we can make to throw off our subjection, will serve but to demonstrate and confirm it. In words a man may pretend to abjure their empire: but in reality he will remain subject to it all the while. The *principle of utility* recognizes this subjection, and assumes it for the foundation of that system, the object of which is to rear the fabric of felicity by the hands of reason and of law. Systems which attempt to question it, deal in sounds instead of senses, in caprice instead of reason, in darkness instead of light. (1789/1948, pp. 1–2)

Note three things about this passage:

- Bentham presents a theory of value (the hedonistic idea that pleasure is the only good and pain the only evil) as well as a theory of normative ethics (that we ought to act in such a way as to increase pleasure and decrease pain).
- The two ideas are causally linked. That is, the normative theory of conduct is based on the theory of value. The reason we ought to act as he dictates is that this is the way people are wired: we all seek to increase our pleasure and decrease our pain. As discussed in Chapter 2, Bentham's theory of value is called psychological egoism.
- Nowhere is there a mention of rights, duties, or God. Ethicist James Rachels (1986) describes this as the most revolutionary aspect of Bentham's contribution: "Morality is no longer to be understood as faithfulness to some divinely given code, or to some set of inflexible rules. The point of morality is seen as the happiness of beings in *this* world, and nothing more; and we are permitted—even required—to do whatever is necessary to promote that happiness" (p. 81).

Bentham's Utilitarianism

The spirit of Bentham's work is suggested by his very next sentence: "But enough of metaphor and declamation: it is not by such means that moral science is to be improved" (1789/1948, p. 2). He then presents his formal definition of the principle of utility:

By the principle of utility is meant that principle which approves or disapproves of every action whatsoever, according to the tendency which it appears to have to augment or diminish the happiness of the party whose interest is in question: or, what is the same thing in other words, to promote or to oppose that happiness. (p. 2)

As he develops his thesis, Bentham introduces one other point, which is also fundamental to all varieties of utilitarianism: ethical action requires positive effects not just for the agent performing the act but also for all people affected by the act.

How are people to be encouraged to act according to this utilitarian idea? Bentham argued that although the legislator ought to consider only one criterion—the pleasure or pain produced by an act—there are in fact three other "sanctions" that influence people's behavior:

- the *political* sanction: the way the person is treated by the legal system that dispenses penalties
- the *moral* or *popular* sanction: the way the person is treated within his or her community
- the *religious* sanction: the way the person is treated, in this life or the afterlife, by a "superior invisible being" (1789/1948, p. 25)

To determine the right action, therefore, requires understanding how much pleasure and pain the possible actions will cause. Bentham believed that it is possible to measure pleasure and pain quantitatively. To this end, he proposed a *hedonistic calculus,* by which seven criteria are measured:

- intensity
- duration
- certainty or uncertainty
- propinquity or remoteness
- fecundity (the chance that the act will be followed by sensations of the same kind)
- purity (the chance that it will not be followed by sensations of the opposite kind)
- extent (the number of people affected by it)

To determine whether an act is right, a person must perform the following five steps:

1. Assess the first six criteria for the person most directly affected by the act, usually the agent.

2. Consider the *extent* of the act; if the act affects more than one person, carry out the analysis for all the affected people.
3. Tally the positive and negative effects of the act.
4. Carry out the same procedure for the alternative acts.
5. Compare the relative utility of the alternative acts.

The one act that has the highest positive effects (or the lowest negative effects) is the right act to perform.

Problems with Bentham's Utilitarianism

The principal allure of utilitarianism is that it seems consistent with the way most of us make many decisions in our daily lives. We add up the potential advantages and disadvantages of our alternative actions and choose the one that we think will do the most good. Even when we base our decision-making on abstract principles, such as when we support a political candidate who represents our views on, say, school prayer or gun control, we are working within a utilitarian framework. We donate money to the candidate's campaign or take other steps that we hope will increase the candidate's prospects, for we believe that electing the candidate will have the most positive effects for us and for others.

Still, Bentham's formulation of utilitarianism has been criticized from a number of different perspectives. There are two major criticisms of Bentham's logic in developing his version of utilitarianism:

- *Hedonism is a flawed theory of value.* It is not intuitively obvious that the only thing we value is pleasure. We value many things, including virtues, knowledge, and friendship, and although these things give us pleasure, they are not reducible to pleasure. If we like playing the piano, we try to find time to play the piano, an activity that gives us pleasure. We do not say that we want to achieve pleasure and therefore we need to do something to achieve it. Bentham could not prove that hedonism is a correct—or *the* correct—theory of value. His argument that it is an unprovable first principle is uncomfortably close to the kind of intuitionism that he criticized in Lockean natural law.

- *Utilitarianism makes an illogical leap from psychological hedonism to normative altruism.* To say that people are interested in their own welfare is one thing. To derive from this the statement that we ought to act to improve everyone's welfare is quite another. Why, exactly, should we care about other people? Why not just do what is in our personal best interest, particularly if no one is likely to find out about our selfishness? Utilitarianism offers no support for the normative principle of helping others.

In addition, there are three major criticisms of Bentham's utilitarianism based on its failure to consider other ethical concerns.

- *Utilitarianism seems to violate our commonsense ideas about special relationships.* When we make a promise to a friend, we ought to keep that promise, unless something very important prevents us from doing so. The reason we ought to keep the promise is not that breaking promises would diminish that person's trust in us or diminish people's faith in the practice of promising. The reason we ought to keep a promise is that it is the right thing to do. (In Chapter 5 in this book, we will see that W. D. Ross presents just this argument in criticizing utilitarianism.) Similarly, we have a special obligation to care for our dependents, even if our money could provide greater assistance to needier people. (Chapter 6 discusses the ethic of care, which focuses on the ethical obligations that characterize special relationships such as those between family members and friends.)

- *Utilitarianism seems to violate important ideas about justice.* Migrant workers in many parts of our country labor under terrible conditions, yet from a utilitarian perspective, using migrant workers creates a great deal of utility, making inexpensive foods available to millions of people. Similarly, slavery would pass the utilitarian test, for although it creates significant pain for some people, it creates significant pleasure for many more. There is nothing logically incompatible between great injustice for some people and great utility for others.

- *Utilitarianism seems to violate important ideas about rights.* A person's most important right is to life itself. When a person becomes sick or injured and cannot offer anything "useful" to the world, utilitarianism offers no rationale not to simply kill that person. In fact, utilitarianism provides numerous reasons, some of which are compelling, for killing the person, including making more effective use of medical resources.

Finally, there are three main criticisms leveled at the concept of the hedonistic calculus:

- *The hedonistic calculus is unworkable because the effects of most acts are unmeasurable.* The seven criteria Bentham presents are merely abstractions that suggest some of the ways we think about future effects of acts. There is no reasonable unit of measurement. How, precisely, does a person empirically measure the positive or negative effects of spending a dollar on an ice cream cone, selecting a graduate school, or getting married?

- *The hedonistic calculus is unworkable because we cannot see into the future.* In idle moments, most adults try to identify the precise points in their lives when they made fateful decisions, for good or ill, that determined how their lives have unfolded. Most of the time, they realize that when they made those important decisions, they certainly did not anticipate what the effects would be. Everyone's life is a surprise.

- *The hedonistic calculus is unworkable because it is impractical to carry out.* To the extent that it is to be a logical, empirical way to make decisions, it must be able to be performed easily and quickly. Bentham conceded that it cannot: "It is not to be expected that this process should be pursued previously to every moral judgment, or to every legislative or judicial operation. It may, however, be always kept in view: and as near as the process actually pursued on these occasions approaches to it, so near will such process approach to the character of an exact one" (p. 31). In fact, the hedonistic calculus is nothing more helpful than the advice, "When you need to make an important decision, think carefully about your options."

Although Bentham was the first philosopher to present utilitarianism as a formal approach to ethics, its greatest and most influential exponent was John Stuart Mill (1806–1873).

JOHN STUART MILL'S UTILITARIANISM

Mill's definition of utilitarianism is close to Bentham's. Actions are "right in proportion as they tend to promote happiness; wrong as they tend to produce the reverse of happiness. By happiness is intended pleasure and the absence of pain; by unhappiness, pain and the privation of pleasure" (1863/1971, p. 18). Like Bentham, Mill insisted that by happiness he was referring to the happiness of all people affected by an act, not just that of the agent.

In his exposition in *Utilitarianism*, published in 1863, Mill differs from Bentham in two major ways:

- *Pleasures have a qualitative dimension.* There are higher pleasures, generally intellectual and social, and lower pleasures, principally associated with our appetites.
- *Different "sanctions" serve to enforce good conduct.* External sanctions include fear of punishment by the state, as well as love of God or fear of His retribution. As Mill wrote, "if men believe, as most profess to do, in the goodness of God, those who think that conduciveness to the general happiness is the essence or even the only criterion of good must necessarily believe that it is also that which God approves" (p. 32). The internal sanction is conscience: "a feeling in our own mind; a pain, more or less intense, attendant on violation of duty, which in properly cultivated moral nature rises, in the more serious cases, into shrinking from it as an impossibility" (p. 32). Our conscience, whatever its origin, is shaped by our upbringing, especially our religious and secular education.

Problems with Mill's Utilitarianism

Mill's book, more elegant than Bentham's and devoted entirely to ethics, has been subject to considerable critical examination. In discussing these critiques, I will concentrate on those directed toward Mill's own exposition, although there is some overlap between the criticism of Mill's book and Bentham's.

- *"The greatest good for the greatest number" is ambiguous.* The idea that the right action is the one that produces the greatest good for the greatest number combines two concepts: amount of pleasure and number of people affected. This combination leads to problems in determining the right act in a given situation. Using an example that Mill himself mentions, should we tax everyone at the same rate, or should we use a graduated rate? Two rival schemes could be devised that produce exactly the same total balance of pleasure and pain. A low, flat rate would produce a tremendous amount of pleasure for a small group of people (the rich), and a small amount of displeasure for a larger group (everyone else). A steeply graduated rate would produce great displeasure for the rich and considerable pleasure for everyone else. In such cases, utilitarianism offers no useful guidance.

- *The discussion of qualitative pleasure is muddled.* A persistent criticism leveled against all utilitarians from the Greek Epicureans through his own contemporaries was that the focus on pleasure is "a doctrine worthy only of swine." Mill argued that of course there are higher pleasures, "of the intellect, of the feelings and imagination, and of the moral sentiment," as well as lower pleasures, "those of mere sensation" (p. 18). Obviously, the higher pleasures are superior to the lower, not only for extrinsic reasons (they last longer, they are safer, and so forth, in a Benthamite way) but also for intrinsic reasons. In a famous passage, Mill writes that "[i]t is better to be a human being dissatisfied than a pig satisfied; better to be Socrates dissatisfied than a fool satisfied. And if the fool, or the pig, are of a different opinion, it is because they only know their own side of the question. The other party to the comparison knows both sides" (p. 20). This qualitative approach has been criticized on logical grounds: the person who seeks the higher pleasure is doing so either because of a preference for that pleasure (in which case the notion of quality is irrelevant, and we are back to the pig philosophy), or despite a preference for the lower pleasure (in which case the facts refute utilitarianism).

- *The defense of psychological hedonism is unclear.* In making the point that it is impossible to prove first principles, such as that pleasure is people's sole aim, Mill wrote a passage in *Utilitarianism* that has received more withering criticism than any other: "The only proof capable of being given that an object is visible is that people actually see it. The only proof that a sound is audible is that people hear it. . . . [T]he sole evidence that anything is desirable is that people do actually desire it" (p. 37). This last assertion is more damaging than a mere slip of the pen; it undercuts the hedonistic theory of value. It simply makes no sense to assert that the fact that people desire something proves that it is desirable. People desire many undesirable things, such as heroin.

- *The discussion of the motives for altruism is vague.* Just as Bentham had trouble making the leap from psychological hedonism to a normative theory of helping others, Mill can provide only vague statements to support his contention that people will seek the welfare of others. A good up bringing and an enlightened educational system will carry most of the burden. And the Golden Rule and the injunction to love your neighbor as yourself "constitute the ideal perfection of utilitarian morality" (p. 24). "Laws and social arrangements" will work to encourage people to see the link between their own individual aims and those of the greater society.

A Further Note About Utilitarianism and Justice

I want to mention here one other aspect of Mill's discussion of utilitarianism: his discussion of utility and justice in Chapter V of his book. In my brief overviews of Bentham and Mill, I have made the point that a central criticism of utilitarianism is that it fails to account for the principle of justice. This criticism is often stated by way of parable. Let's say, for example, that there is a riot brewing that is likely to lead to the deaths of numerous innocent persons. The crowd believes that a particular man named Smith has committed a great wrong, but you, as chief of police, know that Smith is in fact innocent. Do you arrest and publicly punish Smith—if necessary by executing him—in order to quell the riot and thereby prevent the deaths of numerous innocent persons, or do you defend Smith and risk the deaths of the innocent persons? According to utilitarianism, it is argued, it is right to prosecute and, if necessary, execute Smith because doing so will result in the least amount of evil.

Mill's discussion of justice does not directly address this kind of question. Rather, Mill characterizes justice as

a name for certain moral requirements which, regarded collectively, stand higher in the scale of social utility, and are therefore of more paramount moral obligation, than any others, though particular cases may occur in which some other social duty is so important as to overrule any one of the general maxims of justice. (pp. 56–57)

For instance, Mill writes, to save a life it might be a duty to steal or compel a physician to give care to an injured person. But Mill's example—to steal to save a life—does not address the hypothetical case involving the question of whether to prosecute one innocent person to save the lives of other innocent persons. In addition, it does not address the larger question of how to reconcile a quantitative approach to utility with the common-sense notion of justice.

In an excellent book on utilitarianism, Anthony Quinton (1973) argues that while Mill does not in fact adequately address some of the major critiques about utility and justice, and that some hypothetical dilemmas are probably unresolvable by any ethical system, in some ways utility is more consistent with justice than some critics contend. Quinton uses a hypothetical case involving 100 people and 100 oranges. Utilitarianism offers no opinion on whether it is more just to give each person one orange or give all the oranges to one person. But, argues Quinton, if we apply the economic principle called diminishing marginal utility, utilitarianism seems less vulnerable.

To use the example of the oranges, assuming the oranges are to be used as food, giving one to each person clearly produces more good than does giving 100 oranges to one person. This is because, in the first case, each of the 100 persons will benefit from the single orange, whereas in the second case, one person will benefit from one or perhaps a handful of oranges but will receive little benefit from the rest of them.

Similarly, the principle of diminishing marginal utility seems to show that utility is consistent with common notions of justice when it is applied to the question of taxation. Mill argues, as I mentioned earlier, that it is difficult to determine whether a flat tax is more just than a graduated tax. But diminishing marginal utility suggests that a graduated tax is more fair, for a person of limited means needs each of his or her dollars more than a billionaire needs each of his or her billions.

Of course, the question of needs is not the only way to look at justice. There is also the question of desert. Say the billionaire worked extremely hard, came up with several brilliant ideas, and in general did everything smart in amassing his fortune. Is it just that he be asked to support millions of people who don't work as hard, don't have any great ideas, and have missed many opportunities to improve their economic lot? It could be countered that a lot of the billionaire's success might be attributable to his intelligence, which is the result not of his efforts but of his genetic inheritance. Therefore, a least a part of his massive fortune should be redistributed through a graduated tax.

This kind of discussion gets into fundamental questions about whether justice consists of distributing goods equally or according to need, effort, accomplishment, or some combination of these factors. Such questions of course cannot be addressed adequately in a brief look at utilitarianism. I think it is reasonable, however, to conclude that justice is a complex, not a simple concept, and if utilitarianism does not seem to accommodate our commonsense notions of justice, we might ask whether any other approach, or the lack of an approach, does a better job.

This is precisely the point that Mill makes several times in his book. A critic should feel responsible, he argues, not only for pointing out the limitations of utilitarianism but also for asking whether a rival ethical theory better meets the objection.

It is not the fault of any creed but of the complicated nature of human affairs, that rules of conduct cannot be so framed as to require no exceptions, and that hardly any kind of action can safely be laid down as either always obligatory or always condemnable. . . . There exists no moral system under which there do not arise unequivocal cases of conflicting obligation. . . . they are overcome practically, with greater or less success, according to the intellect and virtue of the individual; but it can hardly be pretended that anyone will be the less qualified for dealing with them, from possessing an ultimate standard to which conflicting rights and duties can be referred. (p. 30)

Or, as Mill put it in another passage, "There is no difficulty in provoking any ethical standard whatever to work ill if we suppose universal idiocy to be conjoined with it" (p. 29).

Despite Mill's reasonable objection that utilitarianism should be evaluated not in a vacuum but in relation to other ethical theories, the number and force of the specific objections to utilitarianism were so great that by the middle of the 20th century, it seemed almost to have lost all credibility as a rational approach to ethics. Around that time, a new form of utilitarianism, called *rule utilitarianism*, was proposed as an alternative.

RULE UTILITARIANISM

Rule utilitarianism is an attempt to add the concept of rules to the existing concept of utility. In traditional utilitarianism, which is now often called *act utilitarianism*, a particular act is held to be the correct act if it will produce at least as much utility as any other possible act. By contrast, rule utilitarianism holds that an act is correct if it conforms with a rule that would produce the most utility. In other words, instead of asking whether the act itself would produce the most utility, rule utilitarianism calls for an additional step in the decision-making process: formulating a rule that would lead to the most utility, and then measuring the act against that rule.

For instance, you are walking on campus in early January, before the semester has begun. You want to cut across a lawn to save time, but you see a sign that says "Keep off the grass." If you were an act utilitarian, you would probably disregard the sign, because one person's walking on the grass would not hurt it. Besides, nobody else is on campus to see you, so your act would not encourage anyone to copy you. By contrast, a rule utilitarian probably would decide to heed the sign. The rule utilitarian's reasoning might be as follows.

First, what rule would apply here that would have the most utility? Three possibilities come to mind immediately:

1. People should always heed signs such as "Keep off the grass."
2. People should never heed signs such as "Keep off the grass."
3. People should make up their own minds on the basis of the specific situation.

Rule 2 seems obviously wrong, for it would lead to serious damage to the lawns on campus. Rule 3 seems attractive, but you worry that it would encourage some people who don't care about the lawns to walk wherever they like. Other people would see them and decide that there is no point in their not walking across the lawn. Rule 3, then, would likely lead to serious damage to the lawns. Therefore, you conclude that Rule 1 is the best rule to follow.

Second, what act follows logically from the rule that you think is most appropriate? In this case, you should not cut across the grass, even though doing so would not in itself ruin the grass or encourage others to act in such a way that would ruin the grass.

The distinction between act utilitarianism and rule utilitarianism, then, is that act utilitarianism asks the question, What is likely to happen if I do this act? Rule utilitarianism asks, What is likely to happen if everyone were to do this act?

Strengths of Rule Utilitarianism

Rule utilitarianism appears to have three main strengths:

- *It seems to address the justice and rights problems.* A central problem with act utilitarianism is that it does not adequately address concerns for justice and rights. If an act has the best utility, that is the correct act to perform, regardless of whether it violates principles of justice or rights. Rule utilitarianism incorporates a Kantian universalizability. You are obliged to translate the individual act into a universal maxim, then determine what the maxim tells you to do in the particular situation. For this reason, rule utilitarianism is much less likely to violate principles of justice or rights.

- *It seems to address the hedonism problem.* A central problem with Bentham's version of utilitarianism is that the hedonistic calculus is not shown to be a valid theory of value. In addition, it is not a workable plan. Mill's utilitarianism also offers no reason to believe that pleasure is the sole motivating force in human behavior. Different philosophers have offered numerous versions of rule utilitarianism that address this problem. Some propose what is called *ideal rule utilitarianism*, in which the word *ideal* is used to suggest a nonhedonistic theory of value, one that encompasses many different qualities. (Chapter 5 in this book discusses G. E. Moore's contributions in developing a nonhedonistic theory of value.) Other philosophers describe a *preference rule utilitarianism*, in which hedonism is replaced by a kind of algebraic x. That is, what is valuable for each individual is what he or she prefers.

- *It seems to address measurement problems.* An important set of problems with act utilitarianism concerns measurement: determining how to measure the utility of abstract entities and how to foresee the likely results of an act. Rule utilitarianism appears to eliminate the process of measuring utility altogether, substituting instead the simpler process of determining what history tells us about how people act. We do not have to try to figure out what is likely to happen in this particular case; all we have to do is ask ourselves how people have acted in cases such as this. For instance, in the case of walking across the lawn, we know from many similar kinds of cases that a certain number of people are going to do whatever they want anyway; if we explicitly tell people to use their own judgments and make their own decisions, chaos—and the destruction of the lawn—is the likely result.

The Central Problem with Rule Utilitarianism

Because rule utilitarianism is a set of different approaches rather than a single approach, there have been, and continue to be, numerous technical studies that critique the details of the various versions. For instance, it is clear that rules can conflict, offering little of practical value for a person needing to make a decision.

By far, however, the most prominent criticism of rule utilitarianism is that it is really act utilitarianism in disguise. This theory, of which David Lyons (1965) is the strongest spokesperson, holds that rule utilitarianism is fatally flawed in that the person facing the dilemma is likely to create a narrow "rule" that violates the interests of justice and rights. For instance, in the case of whether it is right to walk across a lawn, in violation of a policy that forbids it, I offered three possible "rules": always follow the policy, never follow the policy, and make up your own mind. I claimed that a rule utilitarian would likely choose "always follow the policy" and conclude that it is wrong to walk across the lawn.

However, there is another rule that the rule utilitarian might have devised: "Follow the policy unless you are certain that violating it will maximize utility." If this were the rule, walking across the lawn would be the best possible act, because it would increase the utility for the person, without causing any bad effects. It is easy to see how rule utilitarianism can easily collapse into act utilitarianism. When a person creates a "rule" so narrow that it applies only to the specific situation he or she faces, the rule has no universalizing effect. For instance, "Follow the policy about not walking on the lawn unless it is January and there is nobody on campus to see you walking on the lawn." Given the universal human inclination to shine the most favorable light on what we really want to do, rule utilitarianism can become self-serving. Other people should stay off the lawn, but it's fine for me to walk across it, just this once.

Another prominent critic, J. J. C. Smart (Smart & Williams, 1973), argues that, on logical grounds, rule utilitarianism collapses into act utilitarianism. If a correct act falls under a rule, the rule has accomplished nothing that is not accomplished in act utilitarianism. If a correct act does not fall under a rule (that is, if the act is an exception to the rule) on utilitarian grounds the person is obliged to violate the rule. That is, following a legitimate rule when violating it would lead to greater utility runs counter to the goals of utilitarianism. Why not walk on the grass if doing so leads to greater utility? Adhering to the rule would be what Smart calls "rule worship." If we follow the rule in such a case, we are either choosing the act that will lead to less utility or we are saying that it is impossible that a human can ever rightly conclude that breaking a rule would be best.

CONCLUSION

The philosopher Victor Grassian (1981) argues that rule utilitarianism fails, just as act utilitarianism does, because it does not provide for an *independent* source of moral considerations. If the person facing the dilemma constructs the rules by which the alternative acts are to be weighed, there can be no certainty that the interests of justice and rights will be protected. He uses the case of a mad bomber who has been captured by the police. The bomber brags to the police that he has planted a bomb that will soon explode, killing many innocent people. Are the police justified in torturing the bomber to learn the location of the bomb before it explodes? Grassian argues that nothing in rule utilitarianism says no. While many people might think that this conclusion is acceptable in the case of the mad bomber, far fewer would think it acceptable, for example, to quarantine or kill people with AIDS, although these acts would likely have some positive effects.

Utilitarianism is the philosophy of contingency; that is, in assigning value to an act according to the good or harm that it does, without an overriding principle that rules out certain actions unconditionally, it fosters an atmosphere in which all actions are ethically negotiable. Perhaps the most graphic example of this shortcoming in utilitarianism is the case of the Ford Pinto (Strobel, 1980). Utilitarian thinking enabled the Ford Motor Company to decide to use the faulty gas-tank design on the Pinto; according to Ford's accountants, the $11 savings per car was a greater benefit than the cost of the liability claims that would have to be paid to the expected number of burn victims and their beneficiaries. Lacking a principle that said it is wrong—unconditionally—to use the riskier design when it was certain to lead to many more injuries and deaths, Ford executives used utilitarian reasoning to justify an unethical act.

A utilitarian could object that the problem in the Pinto case was not that utilitarianism is flawed but that the Ford executives applied it poorly. Had Ford executives correctly calculated utility, they would have seen that using the safer design was the correct act. A safer design would have led to less bad publicity; in fact, progressive executives could have used safety as a selling point in their advertising. (Lee Iaccoca, Ford's president at the time of the Pinto case, went on to become president at Chrysler, where he became a leading proponent of airbags, which he touted in his advertising.)

Admittedly, clear-headed thinking about utility can lead to decisions that prevent some of the more obvious violations of justice and rights, but philosophers like Grassian are right when they claim that there is nothing inherent in any form of utilitarianism that will ensure that rights and justice are considered in the decision-making process.

For the technical communicator, the strengths and weaknesses of utility as an ethical theory are apparent. Consider the simple hypothetical example raised at the end of Chapter 3: a technical communicator is being pressured to include misleading information in a documentation set. What would a utilitarian analysis of the dilemma look like?

The technical communicator would analyze, for every stakeholder, the positive and negative results of each possible response. Possible responses include going along with the manager, refusing to go along, attempting to talk the manager out of it, trying to reach some sort of compromise, and going over the manager's head. Possible stakeholders include the communicator himself or herself; managers, owners, and suppliers of the company; people in the community in which the company is located; and customers.

The obvious problem with utility—that it does not accommodate issues of justice and rights—is apparent here. Even if there are many good reasons to give in to the manager (including the communicator's job security, the economic benefits to the company and the community if the product succeeds, and so forth), there is still something missing: providing misleading information violates the customer's right and is unfair.

One way to save utility as a reasonable ethical theory is to follow Mill's lead by incorporating "sanctions" into the calculation. Leaving aside questions of religion, we can suggest another powerful sanction: self-respect. If providing misleading information in a documentation set strikes the communicator as wrong, even though there are a dozen reasons to recommend it, he or she will pay a heavy price for going along with the manager. To use the term from economics, going along would lead to significant *disutility* for the communicator. And since utilitarianism requires that the good and bad results of every possible response, for every stakeholder, be examined, the technical communicator's personal discomfort with the option of going along is a powerful reason not to do so.

Whether we consider this argument as redeeming utility (at least to some extent) or being mere sophistry, the result is the same. One way or the other, we cannot escape thinking about rights and justice. Therefore, despite the considerable attractiveness of utility, it cannot exist as a coherent ethical principle without some consideration of rights and justice.

The next chapter considers the assault, in the first third of the 20th century, on the towering theories of utility and Kantian rights. The transitional figures of Moore, Ross, and Dewey pinpoint the fatal flaws of the foundational theories. None of the three, however, can describe a coherent theory that effectively replaces utility or rights. We see emerging, in the transitional figures, the broad outline of a nonfoundational ethic.

5

The Transition from Foundational Theories

Western ethics in the 19th century was dominated by the towering figures of Kant and Mill. Kant argued that ethics must be based on the categorical imperative, the idea that we must act only in a way that we could will to be a universal rule. On the basis of the categorical imperative, Kant proposed an ethic built around individual rights. Mill's theory of utilitarianism argued that actions are good only to the extent that they promote the general welfare. For the utilitarian, the ethical intent, which Kant called "good will," was irrelevant; results were what mattered.

Despite the clear differences between the approaches of Kant and Mill, they were essentially similar in one crucial way: they were foundational approaches. By calling these approaches *foundational* I do not mean that they offered step-by-step instructions on how to resolve particular dilemmas. Neither system was intended to be an ethical computer that processed input and yielded a correct answer. Neither Kant nor Mill argued that his approach was an algorithm.

Yet each approach was self-contained in that it offered a distinct theory of value that functioned as an ethical touchstone, intended to enable a person to think through the complexities of a particular case and determine the most appropriate course of action. A person who understood the approach, knew the facts of the case, and could think clearly could, after some deliberation, reach a reasoned and reasonable conclusion about what to do.

The three figures discussed in this chapter—G. E. Moore, W. D. Ross, and John Dewey—together represent a radical new direction in ethical thought.

Moore saw himself as a utilitarian, but not a hedonistic utilitarian like Mill. Whereas Mill's theory of value held that pleasure is the only good, Moore argued that many different things could be good, and that it is impossible to argue logically that one thing is good and another is not. In removing the theory of value from Mill's approach, Moore revived an ancient, radical idea: there is no Truth, no unchanging hierarchy of values that can be used to derive a single, correct answer to every imaginable ethical question.

In attacking Moore and utilitarianism in general, W. D. Ross offered a commonsense revision of the Kantian categorical imperative. Whereas Kant argued that there is only one categorical imperative, Ross argued that there are in fact a number of different duties to which all people are subject, and that, in a given situation, there is likely to be a conflict between two or even more of them. In such a situation, the individual must determine the actual duty that should govern his or her actions. Implicit in this approach are two ideas: that the process of ethical deliberation is inherently uncertain, and that individuals can never be certain that they have chosen the correct action. By removing certainty, Ross was moving in the same direction as Moore.

The most radical break from the 19th century was represented by the American pragmatist John Dewey. Essentially a utilitarian, he believed that results were what mattered, but to call him a utilitarian would be to overlook the originality of his contribution to ethics. In place of the self-contained approach of Mill, he substituted rational empiricism and experimentation. We need to apply scientific methods to problems of value and ethics, Dewey argued, to determine what kinds of actions in fact lead to good outcomes. If the values and ethics don't, we should revise them or throw them out altogether. Perhaps Dewey's greatest contribution to ethics is that in championing the scientific method, he moved ethics away from solitary thought experiments, not only those of Kant and Mill but also those of Moore and Ross. In Dewey's world, ethics is clearly an activity linked to social change, not merely a matter of personal decision-making. As a result, thinking about ethics is an activity carried out in group settings.

In this chapter, I describe the main contributions of Moore, Ross, and Dewey, explaining how their work both changed the way ethics was conceived and anticipated the fluidity and indeterminacy that characterize our contemporary approaches to ethics.

G. E. MOORE AND THE INDEFINABILITY OF "GOOD"

G. E. Moore's *Principia Ethica* (1903) was a landmark book in the history of ethics, for in critiquing utilitarianism, Moore radically redefined the terms of the debate about what is good. He could be thought of both as the last ethicist of the 19th century and as the first thinker of the 20th-century movement called analytical philosophy.

Part of Moore's impact on readers in 1903, as well as his continuing appeal, derives from the force of his personality. His first words in his first major work are the following:

It appears to me that in Ethics, as in all other philosophical studies, the difficulties and disagreements, of which its history is full, are mainly due to a very simple cause: namely to the attempt to answer questions, without first discovering precisely *what* question it is which you desire to answer. I do not know how far this source of error would be done away, if philosophers would *try* to discover what question they were asking, before they set about to answer it. . . . But I am inclined to think that in many cases a resolute attempt would be sufficient to ensure success; so that, if only this attempt were made, many of the most glaring difficulties and disagreements in philosophy would disappear. (1903, p. vii)

So much for the ethical theorists of the previous two millennia in Western civilization: they simply didn't try hard enough.

But this quotation is not just bravado. It introduces Moore's main thesis: that our thinking about ethics has been muddled because we have failed to frame clear questions to answer. To Moore, the two main questions that ethicists ought to answer are the following: What is good, and how ought we to act to bring about good? The first question is an attempt to determine what has intrinsic value, that is, what is good in and of itself. The second question is an attempt to determine what has instrumental value. That is, what are the right actions that will lead to the creation of the most good? What are our duties?

So far, there is no indication that Moore's thinking is significantly different from that of any other utilitarian. Mill, for example, distinguishes between intrinsic value (happiness, which is derived from pleasure) and instrumental value (acting in such a way as to increase the general amount of happiness). Yet in Moore's discussion of the concept of good, we see the beginning of contemporary ethical thinking. He begins his argument by discussing the three senses in which we use the word *good*:

- *As a general, nonethical adjective.* For instance, we speak of a good restaurant or a good automobile. In such cases, we are not discussing ethics.
- *As a matter of examples of things that are good.* For example, we could say that pleasure is good, or keeping promises is good.
- *As a matter of definition.* What is the meaning of the word *good*?

Moore is uninterested, of course, in the first sense of the word. The second sense of the term—finding examples of things that are good—is of considerable interest to him and does in fact occupy the bulk of his book. But he is most interested in the third sense of the word *good:* the definition of the word itself. Moore's book is an argument that unless we understand what we mean when we use the word, we will not be able to think clearly about how to act well, for we will be unable to understand that which we seek. For this reason, he begins with a definition of *good.*

What then, is the definition of *good*?

> my answer . . . may seem a very disappointing one. If I am asked "What is good" my answer is that good is good, and that is the end of the matter. Or if I am asked "How is good to be defined?" my answer is that it cannot be defined, and that is all I have to say about it. (p. 6)

At first glance, this might seem like an inauspicious beginning for a revolution in ethics. Yet his brief explanation of this idea has had a tremendous influence on the course of 20th-century thinking about ethics.

To explain his thinking, Moore uses as examples two other words: *yellow* and *horse. Good* is a simple notion, like *yellow*. By contrast, *horse* is a complex notion.

When we think of yellow, we are thinking of things that are yellow, such as lemons or traffic lights or pieces of paper that are yellow. Although we know that the word *yellow* can be defined by reference to its physical characteristics—the specific wavelength that gives light the color we call yellow—in general usage, the term refers to our perception of the yellowness of something. Yellowness cannot be described to someone who has never seen something that is yellow. In this sense, yellow is a simple notion. It cannot be broken into smaller concepts.

A horse, however, is a complex notion. That is, a horse is a thing that is composed of many different elements and notions. It is an animal with a certain size and shape and texture, and it consists of certain organs working together in a unique way. And it has a certain color.

The difference between a complex notion and a simple notion is that a complex notion is composed of many simple notions. The result of an analysis of any complex notion, such as a horse, a table, or a computer, is a set of simple elements, each of which is a property of a complex notion but cannot itself be reduced to simpler notions. Simple notions, therefore, are the atoms of ethics. Simple elements cannot be defined because they have no parts. The notion *good* "is one of those innumerable objects of thought which are themselves incapable of definition, because they are the ultimate terms by reference to which whatever *is* capable of definition must be defined" (p. 10).

Another way to look at the simplicity of *good* is to say that it *is*, but that it does not *exist*. Goodness is a part of many complex notions, but it does not exist as an entity by itself. As Moore states, you cannot hold goodness in your hands; it doesn't exist in time. It exists only as a property of some other thing.

So far, this is perhaps interesting but not particularly illuminating. The big advance, the idea that might be said to begin the transition away from foundational approaches to ethics, is the following brief passage:

If we start with the conviction that a definition of good can be found, we start with the conviction that good *can* mean nothing else than some one property of things; and our only business will then be to discover what that property is. But if we recognize that, so far as the meaning of good goes, anything whatever may be good, we start with a much more open mind. (p. 20)

Thus Moore attempts to undermine the central argument of utilitarianism. His argument is subtle, for he is not dismissing the utilitarian idea that an action is good if it serves to promote the greatest happiness for the greatest number. Moore doesn't disagree that happiness is a good, and that pleasure is a means to achieve happiness. Rather, he writes, " . . . I quarrel only with the reasons by which [hedonistic utilitarians] seem to think their conclusions can be supported; and I do emphatically deny that the correctness of their conclusions is any ground for inferring the correctness of their principles." (p. 62)

The central fallacy of utilitarianism, as of any other ethical theory that seeks to define good, Moore calls the *naturalistic fallacy*: the fallacy of attempting to define the non-natural (good) by reference to a natural phenomenon (pleasure, happiness, keeping promises, and so on).

When you commit the naturalistic fallacy in arguing that some natural phenomenon such as pleasure is the meaning of *good*, you cannot be proved wrong. If you say *good* is pleasure and someone else says *good* is desire, neither can prove the other wrong. Moore uses this analogy: one person says a triangle is a circle, and another person says a triangle is a straight line. "What is proved is that one of us is wrong, for we agree that a triangle cannot be both a straight line and a circle: but which is wrong, there can be no earthly means of proving, since you define triangle as straight line and I define it as circle" (p. 11). Of course, as in this case, both can be wrong. To say that *good* is *pleasure* is to say that *pleasure* is *good*, which is to say that *pleasure* is *pleasure*. This is not an argument but a tautology.

The most obvious example of the naturalistic fallacy, Moore argues, is committed by Mill when he argues that pleasure can be shown to be desirable because people do desire it, just as we know that something is visible because people can see it. Moore's comment: "Well, the fallacy in this step is so obvious, that it is quite wonderful how Mill failed to see it. The fact is that 'desirable' does not mean 'able to be desired' as 'visible' means 'able to be seen.' The desirable means simply what *ought* to be desired or *deserves* to be desired" (p. 67). (See Shaw [1995] on how others have pointed out the problem in Mill's argument, and Hudson [1980] for a defense of Mill against Moore.)

In explaining his concept of the indefinability of *good*, Moore was fully aware that he might be accused of intuitionism, the belief that moral rules are self-evident. After all, if anything can be good, who is to say that any particular person's definition of good is wrong. Moore's argument is subtle. He denied that he was an intuitionist, although he asserted that the truth of a proposition of an object being good is indeed self-evident. Here, Moore addresses the question of self-evident propositions: That a proposition is self evident

means properly that the proposition so called is evident or true, *by itself* alone; that it is not an inference from some proposition other than *itself*. The expression does *not* mean that the proposition is true, because it is evident to you or me or all mankind, because in other words it appears to us to be true. That a proposition appears to be true can never be a valid argument that true it really is. . . . The *evidence* of a proposition to us is only a reason for *our holding it* to be true: whereas a logical reason, or reason in the sense in which self-evident propositions have no reason, is a reason why *the proposition itself* must be true, not why we hold it so to be. . . . We must not therefore look on Intuition, as if it were an alternative to reasoning. Nothing whatever can take the place of *reasons* for the truth of any proposition: intuition can only furnish a reason for *holding* any proposition . . ." (1903, pp. 143–144)

This distinction might be too subtle for most readers; on most days, it is for me. In addition, Moore's argument is made more complex than it need be by his choice of the term *self evident*, a term that focuses on the process by which a person comes to the proposition rather than on the nature of the proposition itself. Had he used a term that more precisely suggested his real meaning, a term such as *arational proposition* or *unverifiable proposition* or *initial proposition*, he would have made his job easier.

Moore was fully aware that for his thesis to be of any value, he would have to be more precise about what things are good. His statement on this question is characteristically pungent:

Once the meaning of the question is clearly understood, the answer to it, in its main outlines, appears to be so obvious, that it runs the risk of seeming a platitude. By far the most valuable things, which we know or can imagine, are certain states of consciousness which may be roughly described as the pleasures of human intercourse and the enjoyment of beautiful objects. No one probably, who has asked himself the question, has ever doubted that personal affection and the appreciation of what is beautiful in Art or Nature, are good in themselves; nor if we consider strictly what things are worth having *purely for their own sakes*, does it appear probably that any one will think anything else has *nearly* so great a value as the things which are included under these two heads. (pp. 188–189)

At first glance, Moore's discussion of how we ought to act as a means of bringing about good will strike many readers as reasonable but not particularly interesting. He argues that most commonsense rules about behavior—such as telling the truth, respecting other people's property, and the like—are usually valid guides to proper behavior, so long as they are generally followed in society and seem likely to lead to an ordered civilization that permits people to pursue their own notions of good. A person should violate a commonsense rule about behavior only after extremely careful thought. There are two reasons for calling for great caution:

- The actual outcomes of any particular act are so difficult to predict, even in their broadest outlines, that following a general rule is almost certainly more likely to produce more good than violating it would, for the simple reason that it has worked in the past.
- The individual is not in the best position to carry out an objective analysis of his or her own situation. Most individuals tend to see reasons that they should violate the rule, even though the rule is reasonable for others to follow.

The question of what is the right action to take in any particular case is an empirical question that, theoretically, can in fact be answered:

any answer to it *is* capable of proof or disproof—that, indeed, so many different considerations are relevant to its truth or falsehood, as to make the attainment of probability very difficult, and the attainment of certainty impossible. Nevertheless the *kind* of evidence, which is both necessary and alone relevant to such proof and disproof, is capable of exact definition. (pp. viii-ix)

"The utmost, then, that Practical Ethics can hope to discover is which, among a few alternatives possible under certain circumstances, will, on the whole, produce the best result" (p. 151). Ethics, then, is concerned with formulating very general approaches, not ironclad rules. In simple statements such as this, not in his grand rhetorical gestures or his statement of what classes of experiences are good, lies Moore's great contribution to the history of ethics.

In his preface, Moore stated that his central interest was in correcting the way people think about ethics, not in the details of where that thinking might lead. "I have endeavored to discover what are the fundamental principles of ethical reasoning; and the establishment of these principles, rather than of any conclusions which may be attained by their use, may be regarded as my main object" (p. ix). Moore's argument did provide a useful corrective to classical utilitarianism, for he separated it from hedonism. But in his central idea, the indefinability of good, he may well have unknowingly charted a direction for ethical thinking that has led to ideas of which he would thoroughly disapprove. Ultimately, despite Moore's attempts to prevent it, his position is vulnerable to charges that he is in fact an intuitionist.

W. D. ROSS AND THE DISCOVERY OF ACTUAL DUTIES

A measure of the influence of Moore's writings on other philosophers is suggested by the preface to W. D. Ross's *The Right and the Good* (1930), published 27 years after Moore's landmark text. In *The Right and the Good*, a frontal attack on Moore, Ross begins his preface with these words:

I wish also to say how much I owe to Professor G. E. Moore's writings. A glance at the index will show how much I have referred to him; and I will add that where I venture to disagree, no less than where I agree, I have always profited immensely from his discussions of ethical problems. (p. vi)

Moore had seen his mission as substituting for Mill's hedonistic utilitarianism a form of ideal utilitarianism: acts are good to the extent that they promote good. Ross saw his mission as substituting for Kant's unbending fidelity to duty a more flexible framework that admitted the possibility of conflicting duties. In arguing his case, Ross often criticized Moore's utilitarianism, using the same kind of argument that Moore used in critiquing Mill.

Ross does not dismiss the idea that promoting good is in itself intrinsically good. How could anyone? In fact, Ross's statement about intrinsic goodness is the following:

The first thing for which I would claim that it is intrinsically good is virtuous disposition and action, i.e. action, or disposition to act, from any one of certain motives, of which at all events the notable are the desire to do one's duty, the desire to bring into being something that is good, and the desire to give pleasure or save pain to others. (1930 p. 134)

Moore's main thesis thus constitutes motive number two in Ross's list, while another of his ideas is listed as motive number three. The main objective of Ross's book is to make the case that motive number one—doing one's duty—is in fact primary.

In arguing his case, Ross uses a number of tactics. One is straightforward assertion that whereas philosophers may think in abstract terms when they consider how to act, most of us don't:

When a plain man fulfills a promise because he thinks he ought to do so, it seems clear that he does so with no thought to its total consequences, still less with any opinion that these are likely to be the best possible. He thinks in fact much more of the past than of the future. What makes him think it right to act in a certain way is the fact that he has promised to do so—that and, usually, nothing more. That his act will produce the best possible consequences is not his reason for calling it right. (p. 17)

Keeping promises is one example of *prima facie duties*, Ross's term for those conditional duties that should motivate our actions, all other things being equal. If there is no overriding reason to the contrary, we should keep our promises. Ross's list of *prima facie duties* is the following:

- *fidelity*, such as to keep promises or tell the truth
- *reparation*, such as to offer compensation when you have wronged some-one
- *gratitude*, such as to perform services for people who have performed services for you
- *justice*, such as to work to prevent unjust distribution of costs and bene-fits
- *beneficence*, such as to help the needy
- *nonmalificence*, such as not to injure others
- *self-improvement*

However, our actual duty—what we ought to do in a particular situa-tion—is often hard to determine. Often we are subject to two or more *prima facie* duties at the same time. For example, you owe a friend $5, and you have the money to repay her. But you know she does not desperately need the $5, whereas there are needy people to whom the money would be very valuable. Ross's approach calls for you to think first of your most obvious *prima facie* duty: to repay the person who lent you money. You have entered into an implicit ethical contract with this person. Then you think of other relevant duties, in this case, the duty of beneficence. If the duty to help oth-ers seems to you—in this case—to be stronger than your duty to repay the lender, then you should follow the duty of beneficence.

To come to this conclusion, however, requires that the less-direct duty—the duty of beneficence, in this case—be significantly more compel-ling than the more direct duty. If, for example, you know that the $5 will en-able a homeless person to spend a night in a shelter rather than in an alley, the duty of beneficence might outweigh the duty of repaying a lender. If, however, you have no use for the $5 that is obviously significantly more compelling than repaying the lender, your duty is to repay the lender, for you have entered into the implicit ethical contract with that person.

When you make a decision to take one course of action, how can you be certain that you have done the right action? You can't. Thus Ross argues that the main shortcoming of utilitarianism is that

it ignores, or at least does not do full justice to, the highly personal character of duty. If the only duty is to produce the maximum of good, the question of who is to have the good—whether it is myself, or my benefactor, or a person to whom I have made a promise to confer that good on him, or a mere fellow man to whom I stand in no such special relation—should make no difference to my having a duty to produce that good. But we all are in fact sure that it makes a vast difference. (p. 22)

Ross uses analogies to support his contention that duty is more important than utility. For example, suppose that in fulfilling a promise to person *A* you would produce 1,000 units of good for her. But you alternatively could produce 1,001 units of good for person *B*, to whom you have made no promise. In all other respects, the two actions would have exactly the same consequences.

What, exactly, a promise is, is not so easy to determine, but we are surely agreed that it constitutes a serious moral limitation to our freedom of action. To produce the 1,001 units of good for *B* rather than fulfill our promise to *A* would be to take, not perhaps our duty as philanthropists too seriously, but certainly our duty as makers of promises too lightly. (p. 35)

Another analogy:

Few people would hesitate to say that a state of affairs in which *A* is good and happy and *B* bad and unhappy is better than one in which *A* is good and unhappy and *B* bad and happy, even if *A* is equally good in both cases, *B* equally bad in both cases, *A* precisely as happy in the first case as *B* is in the second, and *B* precisely as unhappy in the first case as *A* is in the second. (p. 72)

In response to the utilitarian idea that promise keeping is important because it encourages our general confidence that people will repay promises in the future, Ross asks:

if we suppose two men dying alone together, do we think that the duty of one to fulfill before he dies a promise he had made to the other would be extinguished by the fact that neither act would have any effect on the general confidence? Any one who holds this may be suspected of not having reflected on what a promise is. (p. 39)

Ross was well aware of the kind of criticism his thesis would elicit. One criticism is that he too often refers to what the "plain man" thinks, or "what we really think." The objection is that plain people often think very poorly, and "what we really think" might be wrong. Rather, the criticism goes, we should subject our current thinking to the light of theory. In other words, we should question what we really think rather than accept it *because* we really think it. Ross's response:

I would maintain . . . that what we are apt to describe as "what we think" about moral questions contains a considerable amount that we do not think but know, and that this forms the standard by reference to which the truth of any moral theory has to be tested, instead of having itself to be tested by reference to any theory. (p. 40)

Ross insists that reality is so complex that no single foundational principle can offer sure guidance, and that honest, intelligent people might differ in the decisions they reach about ethical dilemmas. But if Ross avoids the dogmatism and paternalism of foundational theories, he has done so by significantly limiting the scope of his inquiry. As ethicist Mary Warnock (1978) puts it, "It is difficult to imagine feeling very greatly exercised about . . . whether to slow down as we approach the main road in our car, or whether to return the book that we have borrowed" (p. 44).

JOHN DEWEY AND EXPERIMENTAL ETHICS

Writing about John Dewey's influence on philosophy in the first half of the century is difficult for two reasons. First, he wrote a tremendous amount; in an active career of some 70 years, he produced a bibliography more than 150 pages long. Second, Dewey was a synthetic thinker, one who saw interrelationships among many diverse topics. Science, history, anthropology, education, philosophy, social policy, educational theory—these broad subject areas occupied his writing in all his many books.

Still, for the purpose of demonstrating Dewey's role in the transition from foundational theories to contemporary approaches to ethics, one of his books, *The Quest for Certainty* (1929), provides a clear overview. Some 21 years before, he and James H. Tufts had written *Ethics*, a more technical work critiquing the works of prominent ethicists from the Greeks through Moore, Ross, and his own contemporaries, the logical positivists. But *The Quest for Certainty* is Dewey's real contribution to the evolution of ethical theory, for in this book he offers a thorough reconceptualization of Western ethics.

Along with William James and Charles Sanders Peirce, Dewey was a leader of the pragmatist movement in American philosophy. The main tenets of pragmatism included a belief in human evolution, in democratic processes, in problem-solving, and in the improvement of society through education. (See Campbell [1995] for an excellent introduction to pragmatism.) *The Quest for Certainty* (1929) exemplifies all these ideas.

In this book, Dewey explores a central intellectual theme in Western civilization: the valuing of contemplation over action. Knowledge and philosophy, the world of Being, have long been associated with the world of permanence, as exemplified by Platonic Forms. Action, the world of Becoming, has been associated with impermanence and death. Dewey sees two intellectual movements as primarily responsible for the split between knowledge and action: Greek philosophy and Christianity. Both movements were responses to the harsh and uncertain lives led by most people in antiquity. The world offered disease, war, hunger, and sudden death. Only ideas offered any certainty. Dewey's book calls for a radical revision of this binary opposition:

Our deprecatory attitude toward "practice" would be modified if we habitually thought of it in its most liberal sense, and if we surrendered our customary dualism between two separate kinds of value, one intrinsically high and one inherently lower. We should regard practice as the only means (other than accident) by which whatever is judged to be honorable, admirable, approvable can be kept in concrete experienceable existence. (p. 32)

For Dewey, the world of Being is here, it is now, and only we can define, create, and preserve what we value. "The thing which concerns all of us as human beings is precisely the greatest attainable security of values in concrete existence" (p. 35). Philosophy is not a narrow field for the recondite few; philosophy is the study of how we live, and, as such, we all ought to be philosophers.

Dewey believed it necessary to unite action and ideas, for the central human challenge was to create a moral society. Phrases such as "create a moral society" have lost most of their novelty, for they are today's political clichés. But in the first quarter of this century, most thinkers did not think of ethics in terms of practical action: using reason to analyze social problems, determine cause and effect, weigh alternative options, take action, then measure the results. While Bentham and Mill had always had social issues in mind as they wrote, their focus had remained on the individual making the choice of an appropriate action to take in a given situation. Dewey saw ethics not as an approach to individual decision-making, but rather as the broader field of directing group action toward the rational improvement of human society.

Dewey argued that we need to apply scientific methodology to the inquiry. He noted the irony that whereas we are perfectly willing to test and evaluate the objects of the material world, we will not do the same for the moral sphere of our lives, and that, as a result, our thinking about ethics has ceased to evolve. The goal of society should be growth and change, rather than the stagnation represented by a willingness to believe what our ancestors believed. Dewey believed that it is better to travel than to arrive, because "traveling is a constant arriving, while arrival that precluded further traveling is most easily attained by going to sleep or dying" (1922, p. 195).

To respond to the ossification of ethics, Dewey proposed that we study it scientifically, by which he meant that we should observe carefully whether "virtuous" actions lead to good outcomes and "vicious" actions to bad outcomes, then refine our definitions of virtue and vice accordingly. Living in the dawn of modern industry and science, Dewey sought to break the barrier that separated the phenomenal world and the spiritual world. He argued that we live in a world of constant change, a world in which our concepts of right—like our concepts of science—need to be evaluated and, if appropriate, revised. For Dewey, ethics was not a static body of law to which we must dedicate our actions, but rather an intellectual house that we build and live in; it should serve our needs. What constitutes goodness and rightness is what we today would call a situated, historical construct. Dewey's thought thus contains the seeds of an important tenet of postmodernism—the critique of deductivism of foundational theories—while retaining the essential framework of foundationalism: rationalism and goal orientation.

Dewey's work, so central to American philosophy in our century, has been subject to much criticism. One of his most persistent critics, Morris Cohen (1954), wrote that "Dewey is essentially one of those philosophers who, like Spinoza, impress the world with their profound simplicity" (p. 293). The problem with Dewey's ideas on ethics, Cohen argued, is that they are imprecise. Certainly, ethics must be related to public policy, and ethical education must originate in the home and the schools, but how precisely is Dewey's spirit of questioning, analysis, and experimentation to be implemented? The irony of Dewey, Cohen argues, is that the great spokesman for practical action (as opposed to abstract conceptualization) has not provided a coherent plan of action for realizing his ideas.

Cohen is not alone in arguing that Dewey painted with too broad a brush, but Dewey himself was indifferent to this charge. At the end of *The Quest for Certainty*, he wrote that "the nature in detail of the revolution that would be wrought by carrying into the region of values the principle now embodied in scientific practice cannot be told; to attempt it would violate the fundamental idea that we know only after we have acted and in consequences of the outcome of action" (p. 276). Bringing a scientific spirit to ethics would enable people to think of themselves as agents who have some control of their own destinies, who can enjoy "the fruits of a transforming activity." Philosophy and science need not be separate. Philosophy can be "a liaison officer between the conclusions of science and the modes of social and personal action through which attainable possibilities are projected and striven for" (p. 311).

CONCLUSION

Together, Moore, Ross, and Dewey significantly undermined the two prevailing orthodoxies: Kantian rights and utility. Figure 5.1 summarizes the contributions of the three.

Figure 5.1
The Major Contributions of Moore, Ross, and Dewey

Moore dispensed with the intellectual heart of utility when he eliminated the idea that hedonism is the essence of goodness. Without that idea, utility ceases to be a foundational ethical theory. It becomes, instead, a method of accounting.

Ross critiqued Kantianism by articulating the commonsense distinction between *prima facie* duties and actual duties. Ross's real contribution, however, might lie in his critique of utilitarianism as a foundational ethical theory. By stating clearly and memorably the basic power of duty and rights, Ross showed that an ethic that ignores duties and rights is seriously flawed.

Dewey questioned the basic premises on which the foundational theories rested. He asked his readers to consider whether ethical theories should be evaluated solely according to their logical coherence, or whether they should be tested empirically. In so doing, Dewey argued that the study of ethics should be not an intellectual exercise but instead a matter of public policy. Dewey introduced to ethics the idea of group decision-making.

Together, the three transitional ethicists introduced uncertainty, fluidity, and open discussion into what had been a realm of certain, solid theories articulated in the drawing room. In this way, these three transitional figures dispensed with the static value theories and decision-making procedures of Kant and Mill, which were meant to provide certain answers, substituting instead less-comprehensive approaches that were meant only to account for the complex realities of ethical decision-making.

For today's technical communicators, Moore's critique of utilitarianism is significant more for undercutting the intellectual dominion of utility than for offering a substitute. If we follow the implications of Moore's thinking, however, we can see at least the hollowness of the unexamined cost/benefit reasoning that lies at the heart of most utilitarian arguments offered in business. A careful reader of Moore will admit that profit and economic prosperity is a good but ask whether it is Good.

Ross's distinction between *prima facie* duties and actual duties will hardly seem like news to the working technical communicator. But I would suggest that this shows the extent to which Ross's commonsense ideas match those of the typical thoughtful person. Although as technical communicators we do not always keep our promises to our readers, keeping our promises is, most of us would agree, a *prima facie* duty, or, to use a modern cliché, the default value. Ross might not have invented that idea, but in cutting away the excesses of Kantian theory, he made that idea clear and reasonable.

Dewey discussed ethics at such a high level of abstraction that we cannot identify specific ideas or practices in the workplace that are attributable to him. Yet his idea of uniting ethics and social policy, of linking contemplation with action, is now the orthodox approach to ethical decision-making. A technical communicator or a manager who failed to discuss a serious ethical question with other people, who declined to solicit the views of all the stakeholders, would be seen not only as a novice in public relations but also as a fool.

The next chapter discusses several contemporary ethical approaches that rely on the ideas of these transitional figures: the ethic of care, virtue ethics, and postmodernism.

6

Contemporary
Approaches to Ethics

To this point, I have surveyed two very different approaches to ethics—rights and utility—that for many decades were considered the foundations of Western ethical thought. Kant proposed that an action is correct to the degree that it could be willed to be a universalizable law, and that we must treat ourselves and others as ends and not merely as means. Utilitarianism held that the likely effects of an action—the extent to which it would tend to increase the general happiness—determined an act's correctness. In addition, I have sketched the transitional thinking of three thinkers from the first third of the 20th century—Moore, Dewey, and Ross—who exposed some of the major weaknesses in the foundational theories, substituting more flexible, contextual approaches to ethical decision making.

Together, these transitional thinkers anticipated the approaches discussed in the present chapter. Here, I will describe the basic tenets of three contemporary approaches to ethics: the ethic of care, virtue ethics, and postmodern ethics.

In addition to the fact that all three approaches are being developed and critiqued today, they share another characteristic: each is nonprincipled. By this I mean simply that, unlike Kantianism or utilitarianism, these three approaches explicitly reject the notion that there can be a valid decision-making model.

The ethic of care is closest to the foundational approaches to ethics in that it proposes a coherent value system: those practices that support care are valuable. Virtue ethics takes a different tack. Rather than constructing a theory of value and decision-making model, virtue ethics is based on the premise that the agent—the person—is the appropriate focus of attention. Virtue ethics addresses the question, "What qualities ought we to try to instill in people to enable them to act well?"

Postmodern ethics is not a normative ethic at all. That is, it does not seek to prescribe a theory of value or provide guidelines for appropriate action. Instead, it is a metaethical theory, by which I mean a theory that analyzes and comments on the language of normative ethical systems. Although it is quite risky to summarize postmodern ethics, I think it is safe to say that it rejects categorically the idea that there can be a normative ethic. Postmodern ethics sees all foundational approaches—as well as any other approach that proposes a value system—as an exercise of a myth, what Lyotard calls a "grand narrative," by which a ruling elite subjugates the nonelite.

THE ETHIC OF CARE

In this section, I describe the ethic of care, first by explaining its general tenets, then by summarizing the work of Carol Gilligan, and finally by reviewing some of the major methodological and theoretical criticisms of her work.

One way to understand what is meant by an ethic of care is to look at the difference between two phrases: *caring about* and *caring for.* Joan Tronto (1989), a leading theorist of care ethics, explains that *caring about* suggests an abstract feeling about something; people can care about opera, baseball, religion, and so forth. By contrast, *caring for* suggests specific activities directed toward a particular person to satisfy that person's emotional, physical, or spiritual needs. *Caring for* implies both a person's attitude and motivation to help that particular person, as well as specific activities to provide that care.

Attempting to define the ethic of care, however, is significantly more challenging than attempting to define such foundational approaches as Kantian rights or utilitarianism, for two main reasons.

First, there is no single canonical text—no *Foundations of the Metaphysics of Morals* or *Utilitarianism*—to which we can all refer as a starting point for commentary. The ethic of care is a broad term that encompasses a wide variety of approaches, some of which are incompatible with others. And the research on care continues at a steady clip, with many commentators actively sifting through the voluminous literature and offering refinements.

Second, and more significantly, defining care immediately introduces perhaps the most significant and pressing theoretical problem regarding the whole study of care: Can an approach to ethics that is rooted in valuing particular relationships ever become a comprehensive approach that illuminates impersonal relationships? That is, can an ethic of care effectively address the kinds of relationships between strangers that are at the heart of concepts such as rights, duties, and justice? I discuss this question in some detail later in this section.

The major texts on the ethic of care share a foundation in the feminism of the late 1970s and the 1980s. As might be expected, they represent the broad range of viewpoints and the controversies that characterize feminist scholarship. Some commentators see care as a substitute for the fundamentally flawed foundational approaches to ethics; others see care as a complement to them, a kind of supplement or corrective. This split can be seen, for example, in a brief look at several essays in an anthology, *Explorations in Feminist Ethics* (Cole & Coultrap-McQuin, 1992). Mary Raugust (1992) opens her essay by commenting that one fundamental principle is that "Adding women's experiences to androcentric philosophical theories is not sufficient; an alternative way of knowing is demanded" (p. 125). By contrast, Charlotte Bunch (1992) argues that it would be wrong to dismiss or supplant traditional approaches, which, although flawed, have provided a reasonably solid foundation on which the personal relationships central to an ethic of care can be erected and maintained.

Characteristic of all approaches to an ethic of care, then, is a link to women's ways of perceiving moral questions, ways that emphasize creating and maintaining personal and familial relationships and deemphasize abstract principles of rights and justice. But if the various approaches to care all derive from feminist thought, they diverge markedly in their agendas. Some theorists seek to replace what they see as male-biased, impersonal ethical theories, while others seek to incorporate their insights and priorities into a larger ethic that addresses the needs of both the personal few and the impersonal many.

Perhaps the most productive way to understand the central tenets of an ethic of care is to look in more detail at the research of the most prominent exponent of the ethic, Carol Gilligan.

Gilligan's "Different Voice"

One work more than any other can be viewed as central for most people writing about the ethic of care. That book is Carol Gilligan's *In a Different Voice: Psychological Theory and Women's Development* (1982), which documents research studies she performed for her doctoral dissertation at the Harvard Graduate School of Education. In these studies, she performed three sets of interviews. In one set, she interviewed women who were facing or had faced the question of whether to have an abortion. In a second set of interviews, a longitudinal study, she asked 25 men and women college seniors for their views on resolving ethical dilemmas; she then reinterviewed them five years later. In the third set of interviews, Gilligan asked males and females, from age 6 to 60 years, for their views of rights and responsibilities.

In her research, Gilligan sought to examine and critique the work on moral development of Lawrence Kohlberg. As described in Chapter 2 in this book, Kohlberg argued that people's moral development progresses through three sets of stages, ranging from two preconventional stages to two conventional stages, then two postconventional stages. These six stages mark a person's growth from a purely egocentric, reward-and-punishment orientation toward a completely autonomous orientation in which the person creates an individual ethical orientation. Most people never progress beyond the middle two stages, Kohlberg stated, and he admitted that the sixth stage is purely hypothetical, for he never actually discovered anyone who had achieved it.

Gilligan's research program was a response to what she saw as a male bias in Kohlberg's highly influential research. For one thing, most of the people Kohlberg interviewed were males. Of more importance, however, was the premise on which the interviews were based. Kohlberg believed that a person's moral development could be measured by an ability to conceive of ethics from the perspective of abstract rights and justice, a viewpoint derived largely from the ethics of Kant. As a result, Kohlberg posed a series of hypothetical moral dilemmas to his interview subjects, such as the case of Heinz, whose wife is desperately ill and in need of some medicine. The pharmacist is selling the medicine at greatly inflated prices, which Heinz cannot afford. Does Heinz have a right to steal the medicine to save his wife's life? On the basis of his studies, Kohlberg concluded that most men were at stage four of his hierarchy, whereas most women were only at stage three.

Gilligan argued that Kohlberg's biases ensured that he would find what he sought. On the basis of her own research, she concluded that women speak "in a different voice" from men. Men think in terms of abstract, impersonal moral principles that value autonomy and focus on standards of justice and rights; men see other people as generalized. Women think more in terms of care and responsibility. Women see others as particular persons in their lives: parents, spouses, children, friends. They seek to create and maintain relationships, to prevent harm, to ensure that no one is left out. Women value empathy, compassion, and sensitivity. Women approach moral dilemmas first by providing care for the needy, and only then by turning to abstract principles. For men, applying the abstract principles *is* the appropriate response. Men see other people as worthy of our attention because they are humans; women see particular needy people in their lives.

Women speak in a voice that many men, including Kohlberg, simply do not hear. Those aspects of women's ways of thinking about ethics are not, despite Kohlberg's claims, defective, undeveloped, and deficient; nor are these ways of thinking intuitive or instinctual; rather, they are culturally formed, and they represent a significant strength.

Gilligan (1982) proposed her own three-stage model of moral development for women. In Gilligan's model, the First Level, orientation to individual survival, involves no explicit thinking about ethics. The woman (or girl) is interested solely in her own needs. The Second Level, goodness as self-sacrifice, is the conventional stage for most women. In this stage, the woman focuses on her role as a caregiver, and she wishes to avoid hurting others. The Third Level, the morality of nonviolence, involves a resolution of the conflict between selfishness and responsibility. Women at the Third Level see care—for others and for themselves—as a universal obligation. (See Brabeck [1993] for a full explanation and analysis of Gilligan's stages.)

In her own work, Gilligan acknowledges the strong influence of sociologist Nancy Chodorow (1978), who argues that differences in the moral development of boys and girls can be attributed largely to the fact that in all cultures, women are the primary caregivers of infants and young children. As a result, Gilligan (1982) notes,

relationships, and particularly issues of dependency, are experienced differently by women and men. For boys and men, separation and individuation are critically tied to gender identity since separation from the mother is essential for the development of masculinity. For girls and women, issues of femininity or feminine identity do not depend on the achievement of separation from the mother or on the progress of individuation. Since masculinity is defined through separation while femininity is defined through attachment, male gender identity is threatened by intimacy while female gender identity is threatened by separation. Thus males tend to have difficulty with relationships, while females tend to have problems with individuation. (p. 8)

Needless to say, Chodorow's thesis is controversial. Scholars are still trying to determine whether there are in fact real differences in the moral development or moral reasoning of males and females. (See Walker [1993] and Baumrind [1993] for two review articles that reach very different conclusions on this question.)

Gilligan's research on women's voices is a permanent contribution to the study of how men and women think differently. One measure of her influence is the extent to which Kohlberg himself has acknowledged her contribution. Kohlberg has written many times about Gilligan's research, and although his comments are not always consistent, in general he has admitted that her work describes an aspect of moral reasoning that his own research had ignored. Writing in 1984, he stated, "We admit . . . that the emphasis on the virtue of justice in my work does not fully reflect all that is recognized as being part of the moral domain" (p. 227). In that same work, Kohlberg writes that the phenomenon he was studying might more precisely be called "justice reasoning" than "stages of moral development" (p. 224).

Methodological Criticisms of Gilligan's Research

Gilligan's research is the subject of hundreds of critiques, from both inside and outside the feminist research community. Among the problems cited more frequently are the following three criticisms of her research methodology:

- *Her research sample was unrepresentative.* As Annette Baier (1987) points out, Gilligan's most famous study, the interview with women considering having an abortion, included only those women who were at that time grappling with that decision. "The clear-headed or at least the decisive women simply did not get into this study" (p. 48). Zella Luria (1993) criticizes Gilligan by pointing out that good samples must be stratified by age, social class, education, and method of recruitment. As she writes, "Twenty-nine women considering abortions in Boston may provide an important example of decision-making, but they cannot provide data on how men and women differ in such thinking" (p. 200). Tronto (1993), citing research on how people of different races and economic classes show different values that affect their ethical decision-making, argues that the "different voice" Gilligan heard might have social rather than psychological causes.

- *Her research was based on what women say they believe, not on how they act.* As John Broughton (1993) comments, "As long as Gilligan asks her subjects only what they think of themselves, and accepts what they say at face value, she cannot distinguish insightfulness from defensiveness, knowledge from wishful thinking, or fact from fantasy" (p. 134). Annette Baier (1987) makes this same point: both Kohlberg's and Gilligan's research have "looked at verbally offered versions of morality, at intellectual reflection on morality, not at moral development itself, at motivational changes and changed emotional reactions to one's own and other's action, reactions and emotions" (p. 48).

- *Her coding scheme was not explained in sufficient detail.* As Luria (1993) points out, "interviews that yield discursive data such as explanations, personal histories, and discussion of abstract questions require objective rules that categorize the respondents' texts" (p. 200). Yet Gilligan fails to explain her coding scheme in enough detail for the reader to understand whether this requirement has been met. In a detailed critique of Gilligan's coding, Broughton (1993) argues that a number of the respondents' excerpts in the book can be interpreted very differently than Gilligan interpreted them. Where Gilligan saw a particular subject's quotation as valuing a personal relationship, Broughton sees it as representing an abstract duty.

Broughton's questioning of Gilligan's reading of her subjects' interview statements broadens into a more theoretical questioning of her work, a questioning that persists.

Theoretical Concerns About Gilligan's Ethic of Care

One theme that appears often in the commentary about Gilligan and other advocates of an ethic of care concerns the question of whether the dualities suggested by the "different voice" theory in fact exist. Gilligan (1982) asserts, for example, that the hypothetical dilemmas that Kohlberg posed in his research, such as the case of Heinz, who must decide whether to steal in order to save his wife's life, are useful only in getting people to articulate abstract concepts such as justice and duty. For eliciting a woman's different voice—the valuing of particular relationships—hypothetical dilemmas are ineffective: "Only when substance is given to the skeletal lives of hypothetical people is it possible to consider the social injustice that their moral problems may reflect and to imagine the individual suffering their occurrence may signify or their resolution engender" (p. 100).

Gertrud Nunner-Winkler (1993) responds that Gilligan has it backwards. Kohlberg's hypothetical dilemmas, such as the Heinz case, are in fact highly contextual and particular, even though they are fictional. The whole premise of these hypothetical dilemmas is that context complicates a theoretical position. Of course, stealing is wrong, but so is failing to save your spouse's life. Among the major philosophers, only Kant would argue that Heinz has no right to steal to save his wife's life. (Stealing would be like lying, which, for Kant, is unconditionally forbidden.) According to Nunner-Winkler, Kohlberg "adopts a radical female position, however ironic this may sound" (p. 148), for in the Heinz example, he almost compels the interview subject to choose the violation of an abstract principle—"don't steal"—because of the contingency of his wife's illness.

A second common theoretical critique of Gilligan's duality of abstract/particular is that to the extent that care can be considered an "approach" to ethics, it becomes an abstraction. Mary Brabeck (1993) argues that, while of course the individual woman's decision whether to have an abortion, for example, requires attending to the particulars and the context, the very act of discussing that woman's dilemma involves a certain degree of abstraction. Commenting that ethics involves the study of what one ought to do, Brabeck writes that "a rational defense of the moral good reflected in each woman's individual judgment must attend to principles outside of one's experience or feelings about that experience" (p. 47). Gilligan's ethic of care, then, "is a universal abstraction of a concrete imperative which she argues ought to govern moral choice: inflict no harm, leave no one abandoned" (p. 47).

If Brabeck (1993) is right that care is itself an abstraction, proponents of an ethic of care are left with a difficult dilemma: either embrace subjectivism or explicitly define care as a foundational principle. Embracing subjectivism would seem unacceptable, for it would require saying that every person, regardless of the quality of his or her own ethical thinking, must make an individual decision about, first, whether to care for anyone and, second, how to provide that care. If that person chose not to exercise any care at all for his children or aged parents, for example, that would be his decision, a result of his analysis of the particular context. Presumably, this decision would seem unacceptable to the rational outside observer.

The other alternative, to give care the status of other normative theories such as Kantian rights or utilitarianism, would require the kind of abstraction that appears not to interest many proponents of care. How, precisely, can care be defined as an abstract principle and still retain its allegiance to particularity? Peta Bowden (1997) describes a more radical phrasing of the question: Can care even be considered a moral approach at all? Isn't care "somehow secondary, parasitic, or inferior to impartialist moral theories" (p.7)? After all, caring is encompassed within traditional approaches to ethics: it is a *supererogatory* act, that is, an act above and beyond the call of duty.

Another complication is the idea that care ultimately assumes an abstract theory; otherwise, we would all feel obliged to care equally for every other human on the planet. As George Sher (1987) puts it, in critiquing the abstract/particular duality as well as the principled/unprincipled and rights/responsibilities dualities, an ethic of care does not "require any exotic recasting of our familiar understanding of 'morally adequate'" (p.187). As he observes, "Women's moral judgments may be expressed in a different voice, but that voice echoes through some quite familiar rooms" (p. 179).

Some commentators do in fact argue that care needs to be raised to the metaethical level. Joan Tronto (1993) advocates that care be studied in its fullest political, social, and economic spheres. She articulates some of the major questions that will need to be addressed:

Where does caring come from? Is it learned in the family? If so, does an ethic of care mandate something about the need for, or the nature of, families? Who determines who can be a member of the caring society? What should be the role of the market in a caring society? Who should bear the responsibility for education? How much inequality is acceptable before individuals become indifferent to those who are too different in status? How well do current institutions and theory support the ethic of care? (p. 251)

For Tronto, such questions must be answered before care can be taken seriously as a rival to the established normative ethical theories.

Concerns About Marginalization

Those who question whether care can be thought of as a foundational principle express two common concerns: that care can lead to partiality and prejudice. Care can lead to partiality in that if we have a friendship with a coworker, for instance, and we need to recommend someone for a promotion, we might find it easy to favor our friend over a better qualified stranger. And care can lead to prejudice in that to the extent that we forge bonds with the people in our immediate context, we run the risk of devaluing those with whom we do not share a relationship, and those "outsiders" are likely to be different from us in terms of race, ethnicity, or any number of other factors. The flip side of care, in other words, can be clannishness.

By far, however, the most persistent criticisms of the ethic of care concern the fear that if we valorize care, which is associated with women, we will be contributing to their marginalization. We will be supporting the paternalistic economic, political, and social institutions that value and reward the abstract, impersonal activities of men.

Patricia Ward Scaltsas (1992) is one of many commentators who express concern that valorizing a women's voice plays into the hands of a sexist society. While scientists may have shown that the fact that women are the primary caregivers for children is a learned, cultural phenomenon rather than a biological one, that fact is too easy to overlook. It too easily can become an argument that women care for children because that is what they are good at, and by implication, men are good at holding positions of authority in the working world. As Eve Browning Cole and Susan Coultrap-McQuin (1992) write, this culture demands that the "sensitive and caring woman support, nurture, and reproduce the bruised male warrior and his scions" (p. 5).

Linda K. Kerber (1993) states the danger in terms of the two voices of feminism: "one that claimed for women the natural rights of all human beings, and one that claimed that women were different from—and, usually better than—men" (p. 105). Social forces of subjugation will find it convenient to concede the point about women's difference from men, then use it as a rationale for limiting women's options to those activities to which they are better suited than men, namely caring. Tronto (1993) writes that care is ultimately a conservative perspective, for "as long as women's morality is viewed as different and more particular than mainstream moral thought, it inevitably will be treated as a secondary form of moral thinking" (p. 246). A different voice justifies and reinforces the existing sexual division of labor. Scaltsas (1992) echoes many commentators when she argues that associating care with women "may be seen to indicate *inability* to conduct abstract thinking" (p. 17).

Perhaps the strongest opponent of the notion of a different voice is Julia T. Wood (1994), who sees the injunction to care as "potentially paralyzing" (p. 13). Gilligan "essentializes" women; she gives them a single, overarching nature, that of caregivers who watch the kids, freeing the men to go out into the world. Wood quotes Jean Baker Miller's observation that "in our culture 'serving others' is for losers, it is low-level stuff" (p. 120). Dianne Roamin (1992) comments that her friend Mildred Dickemann, an anthropologist, read Gilligan's book and called it "the same old tune, sung upside down" (p. 35).

Part of the problem in discussing the issue of marginalization is that Gilligan (1982) is not as clear as she might be on the question of whether, or to what extent, care is associated with gender. At some points in her work, she claims that care is not essentially gender-related. "The different voice I describe," Gilligan writes,

is characterized not by gender but theme. Its association with women is an empirical observation, and it is primarily through women's voices that I trace its development. But this association is not absolute, and the contrasts between male and female voices are presented here to highlight a distinction between two modes of thought and to focus a problem of interpretation rather than to represent a generalization about either sex. (p. 2)

But the title of Gilligan's book, *In a Different Voice: Psychological Theory and Women's Development,* suggests that there might be some truth to Wood's comment (1994) that Gilligan herself is speaking in two voices: that of the scholar and that of the partisan. In a reply to her critics, Gilligan (1993) wrote

I am well aware that reports of sex differences can be used to rationalize oppression, and I deplore any use of my work for this purpose. But I do not see it as empowering to encourage women to put aside their own concerns and perceptions in thinking about what is of value and what constitutes human development. (p. 214)

Gilligan's choice of words here—the scholarly connotation of *reports* and the polemical connotation of *empowering*—reveals her dilemma.

Is Care Ultimately an Ethical Theory?

Because the ethic of care has been the subject of debate for only two decades, it is probably premature to speculate on whether it represents an ethical theory, similar in scope to, say, utilitarianism, or whether it represents an aspect of people's ethical nature that is insufficiently addressed by major ethical theories.

Perhaps this duality itself represents a false choice. Discussions of care often suggest a thinly veiled competition, with some commentators arguing that the traditional ethical approaches encompass and address care and others arguing that care is superior to traditional approaches. For instance, Rita Manning (1992) writes that rights and responsibilities represent a moral minimum "below which no one should fall and beyond which behavior is morally condemned" (p. 50). By contrast, Owen Flanagan and Kathryn Jackson (1993) comment that it makes sense to see care as more important than justice: "there is no incoherence in putting care first when it comes to creating the possible conditions for family, wider community, and individual character in the first place" (p. 82).

Brabeck (1993) represents a popular framing of the relationship between justice-oriented ethical approaches and the ethic of care:

When Gilligan's and Kohlberg's theories are taken together, the moral person is seen as one whose moral choices reflect reasoned and deliberate judgments that ensure justice be accorded each person while maintaining a passionate concern for the well-being and care of each individual. Justice and care are then joined; the demands of universal principles and specific moral choices are bridged, and the need for autonomy and for interconnection are united in an enlarged and more adequate conception of morality. (p. 48)

In my view, the most reasonable approach to care is to avoid the competitiveness. Annette Baier (1993), who describes the process of making ethical theories as "good clean intellectual fun" (p. 21), contrasts justice perspectives and the care perspective metaphorically. Justice perspectives are painted with a broad brushstroke; the care perspective is a mosaic, assembled tile by tile. Each approach is incomplete: the broad brushstroke because it misses the fine detail that the real ethical dilemmas of life actually consist of, and the mosaic because it lacks the comprehensiveness and coherence of a systematic theory. There is no need—certainly no need at the present—to sum up, to classify, to evaluate different approaches and choose a winner. The discussion is proceeding; let's let it continue.

Another way to look at this question is to try to see care as a set of questions and concerns that have been addressed several times in the long tradition of Western ethics. Eva Feder Kittay and Diana T. Meyers (1987) see two major antecedents for the ethic of care: Aristotle and Hume. Aristotle's emphasis on making appropriate decisions that reflect the context of persons, actions, and institutions is clearly related to the ethic of care, with its emphasis on particular context. Hume's emphasis on the emotional ties that motivate action—ties beginning in the family and radiating outward—is also clearly related to the care perspective. (See Annette Baier's "Hume, the Women's Moral Theorist?" [1987] for a detailed look at this question.) I see one more antecedent: W. D. Ross (see Chapter 5 in this book). Ross' insistence that a person's actual duty in a particular situation might violate one or more *prima facie* duties is a reasoned defense of the idea that context, including personal and familial relationships, can outweigh abstract principles. Although Ross does not address care using the same terms as modern commentators do, he removes a formidable barrier to a serious consideration of care.

The ethic of care, which emphasizes particular commitments, is clearly related to another popular approach to ethics, virtue ethics, because virtue ethics emphasizes those aspects of character, such as honesty and faithfulness, that make a caring relationship possible.

VIRTUE ETHICS

Virtue ethics is related to the ethic of care in that both are agent-based, as opposed to action-based. That is, both approaches focus primarily on the character of the agent, not on the correctness or incorrectness of the action that the agent might take. The ethic of care emphasizes the connections between specific individuals. Virtue ethics emphasizes those aspects of character that enable a person to make good decisions. The connections between the two approaches are especially strong in the way they value friendship. For the ethic of care, of course, friendship is a fundamentally important relationship. For virtue ethics, particularly as first described by Aristotle, friendship is a necessary condition for living the good life.

Friendship relationships, as well as relationships that extend beyond the personal to include the whole community and the larger society, are important in all varieties of virtue ethics. Business ethicist Robert Solomon, for example, in his widely acclaimed book *Ethics and Excellence* (1992), defines virtue primarily in terms of connections to the greater *polis*. Virtue, he writes, is

an exemplary way of getting along with other people, a way of manifesting in one's own thoughts, feelings, and actions the ideals and aims of the entire community. Thus honesty is a virtue not because it is a skill necessary for any particular endeavor or because it is "the best policy" in most social situations but because it represents the ideal of straight dealing, fair play, common knowledge, and open inquiry. (p. 192)

In this section, I briefly review Aristotle's seminal approach to virtue ethics, then review some modern commentators on the subject. Finally, I will present some of the major criticisms of virtue ethics.

Aristotle's Ethics

The popularity of contemporary accounts of virtue ethics, ranging from the popular trade books by William Bennett to the debates on school boards about whether "character" ought to be taught in public schools, might suggest that virtue ethics is a modern development. In fact, virtue ethics enjoys perhaps the most prestigious pedigree of all the approaches to ethics discussed so far. Aristotle's *Nicomachean Ethics* (trans. 1953), a set of lecture notes, is now seen as the core text in the study of virtue ethics. The *Ethics* is the subject of numerous full-length studies; I will attempt here only to summarize a few main points Aristotle makes in setting out his conception of ethics.

- *Ethics is a branch of politics and is therefore meant to be practical.* The goal of politics is to create a set of institutions and circumstances that enable the population to contribute to the welfare of the state. In the same way, the goal of ethics is to reinforce the characteristics of individuals that enable them to play their roles in contributing to the welfare of the state. To the Greeks, the individual was a microcosmic version of the state. To flourish, the individual, like the state, must be governed according to reason. Related to this principle is the idea that the goal of ethics is not to create an abstract theory of how to act appropriately but rather to be of practical benefit. An abstract theory cannot have practical benefit, for the simple reason that most people are indifferent to theory.

- *Ethics is nonprincipled and imprecise.* For Aristotle, the study of ethics was nonprincipled, unlike Kantian ethics or utilitarianism. Aristotle did not offer a principle or set of principles that would enable a person to determine the correct course of action in any given situation. He believed that the study of ethics, being based on human personality and values, was too imprecise to be rule based. As he wrote, "It is a mark of the educated man and a proof of his culture that in every subject he looks for only so much precision as its nature permits" (pp. 27–28). Mathematics permits precision; ethics does not. In addition, Aristotle believed that it is futile to focus on actions rather than actors. Only a virtuous person would act appropriately; therefore, it makes sense to concentrate on teaching people to be virtuous.

- *Virtue is the means of achieving happiness.* Every human enterprise has a goal. The goal of medicine, for example, is health; of military science, victory. The ultimate goal or end, the intrinsic good toward which we as people aim, is happiness. All other goods are instrumental to our pursuit of happiness. In turn, happiness consists of living a virtuous life, a life characterized by the disposition or settled habit of acting wisely. Two words deserve comment here. First, *habit.* A virtuous person is not a person who sometimes acts wisely. Rather, a virtuous person has been taught to act wisely all the time; it has become a habit. Second, *acting.* A person is virtuous not by abstaining from performing actions. For Aristotle, there is no cloistered virtue. A person is virtuous by making correct decisions in the real world.

- *Acting virtuously is self-reinforcing.* A virtuous person feels pleasure in acting virtuously. This pleasure reinforces the disposition to act virtuously in the future. Although acting virtuously is habitual, it is also conscious and willful. (A child or an adult of diminished mental capacity cannot act virtuously.) For this reason, deriving pleasure from exercising virtue is necessary if a person is to continue to act virtuously.

- *The main virtues are courage, temperance, wisdom, and justice.* Courage is the virtue of acting appropriately in the face of danger or fear. Temperance is the virtue of acting appropriately in pursuing pleasurable experiences. Wisdom—Aristotle's word is *phronesis*, which is often translated as *judgment* or *practical wisdom*—is "a rational faculty exercised for the attainment of truth in things that are humanly good and bad" (p. 177). It is "the power of seeing what is good for themselves and for humanity" (p. 177). Justice, which concerns the fair apportionment of goods between the individual and the greater community, is the perfect virtue "because the man who possesses justice is capable of practicing it towards a second party and not merely in his own case" (pp. 141–142). Justice "is the only virtue which is regarded as benefiting someone other than its possessor" (p. 142).

- *Acting virtuously consists of finding the golden mean.* Virtue consists of having the right feelings "at the right times on the right occasions towards the right people for the right motive and in the right way ..." (p. 65). This idea of appropriateness is at the heart of Aristotle's concept of the golden mean. In most cases, virtue consists of avoiding the extremes of excess and deficiency. The golden mean that defines courage, for example, is the midpoint between foolhardiness and cowardice. However, some feelings and actions, such as adultery, are by definition wrong and therefore have no golden mean. Finding the golden mean is not always easy; there is no algorithm for doing so. Instead, finding the golden mean might be said to require *phronesis*.

- *The highest form of activity is the contemplative life.* The virtuous life is lived according to reason. For most people, a cornerstone of a reasoned life includes friendship, a moderate approach to pleasures, and cultivation of intellectual virtues. The highest form of activity, a life suited to the very few, is the contemplative life, for contemplation is the faculty of our species' most special characteristic: rationality. (Today, of course, we recognize the elitism inherent in this sentiment, for Aristotle was a member of the ruling class, a class that relied on the labors of women, the working classes, and slaves. Aristotle was no democrat.)

Contemporary Approaches to Virtue Ethics

The contemporary thinker who has perhaps done most to foster the discussion of virtue ethics is the American philosopher Alasdair MacIntyre, whose book *After Virtue: A Study in Moral Theory* was first published in 1981.

MacIntyre offers a historical account of the concept of virtue in the Western world, from the Homeric age through the present. His thesis is that virtue is a historically and culturally determined concept. For example, the Homeric ideal of virtue is the warrior. The Athenian ideal is the cultivated gentleman. The Christian ideal is the saint. For MacIntyre, then, there is no single set of virtues. Rather, virtues are

those dispositions which will not only sustain practices and enable us to achieve the goods internal to practices, but which will also sustain us in the relevant kind of quest for the good. . . . The catalogue of the virtues will therefore include the virtues required to sustain the kind of households and the kind of political communities in which men and women can seek for the good together and the virtues necessary for philosophical enquiry about the character of the good. (p. 219)

On the basis of his definition of virtue, MacIntyre (1981) criticizes the ethics of the modern capitalist system. He argues that we have replaced the Aristotelian idea of virtue as excellence with a debased utilitarian idea of virtue as effectiveness. Whereas Mill's utilitarianism emphasized the welfare of society as the essential characteristic of rightness, the modern business person aspires only to superficial success, measured in return on investment. MacIntyre argues that the modern business person, trapped in the pursuit of wealth instead of virtue, is in fact not a utilitarian but an emotivist (one who believes that all statements about ethics are merely expressions of the speaker's personal feelings) or a relativist (one who believes that all statements about ethics are right if they are in accord with the beliefs of the prevailing culture). Only by returning to the Greek ideal of excellence, MacIntyre argues, can the modern citizen resume the quest for virtue.

In *Quandaries and Virtues: Against Reductivism in Ethics* (1986), Edmund Pincoffs argues that foundational approaches to ethics, such as Kantian rights and utilitarianism, are wrongheaded aberrations in the history of Western ethics. He describes the foundational approaches as "quandary ethics," that is, theories that provide step-by-step instructions that tell you what to do when you find yourself in an apparent moral quandary. But quandary ethics

is a newcomer. . . . Plato, Aristotle, the Epicureans, the Stoics, Augustine, Aquinas, Shaftsbury, Hume, and Hegel do not conceive of ethics as the quandarists do. If they are read for their theories—that is, for the grounds that they give for making particular difficult moral decisions—their teachings are inevitably distorted. To give such grounds, such justifications of particular difficult choices, was not their objective. They were, by and large, not so much concerned with problematic situations as with moral enlightenment, education, and the good for man. (pp. 14–15)

Quandarists are reductivist in assuming that there is "an essence of morality" (p. 31). Pincoffs writes, "No more reason exists to believe that there is an essence of morality than that there is an essence of beauty" (p. 31). Why should we believe that there is only one appropriate course of action in a given situation? Rather, ethical action requires "morally defensible arbitrariness" (p. 60).

> Our decisions are not arbitrary in any damaging sense. We must balance justice against justice, against kindness, against honesty, and so forth. And we must then consider what to do. Given overall concern for others, our moral judgment will consist in the sensitivity and care with which we weight these considerations against one another. (p. 60)

In fact, virtues and vices are no more complex than "dispositional properties that provide grounds for preference or for avoidance of persons" (p. 79).

Interestingly, Pincoffs, alone among the commentators on virtue ethics that I am aware of, sees in Kant's second formulation of the Categorical Imperative—that we are to treat ourselves and others as ends and not merely as means—a link to virtue ethics:

> The second formulation . . . comes close to being a virtue consideration. It would be so if it told us to be respectful of other people, to be concerned about them, to have that motive in our dealings with them. Perhaps that is what Kant means. I think that it is. (p. 107)

This is perhaps a less than ringing endorsement of Kant's version of the Golden Rule; still, it is a remarkable statement about the philosopher so often reviled by ethicists.

Problems with Virtue Ethics

Virtue ethics is vulnerable to three major criticisms:

- *Virtue ethics doesn't accommodate change.* A central strength of virtue ethics—that it sees people in the context of their own communities and societies—is also a drawback, for if the community or larger society is fundamentally flawed, the individual who cultivates truly virtuous characteristics, such as courage and the love of justice, might be an alien in his or her own community. By relying on community norms and interconnections, Ewin (1995) argues, virtue ethics does not allow for the possibility of change in a community.
- *Virtue ethics focuses exclusively on individuals.* The focus on the ethics of the individual ignores the large, impersonal institutions such as those that make up the business world. Virtue ethics offers little of practical value on, for example, the question of a company's official position on

offering bribes when negotiating in cultures in which bribery is customary.

- *Virtue ethics offers no clear guidelines for decision making.* One problem that results from this lack of guidelines is that there is no procedure for dealing with the possibility that two virtues might conflict in a particular situation. John Boatright (1995) expresses the dilemma this way: "A close examination of the virtues . . . may resolve some conflicts, but either we land back in the position that, properly understood, the virtues cannot conflict, or we appeal to something other than virtue, that is, to some other ethical foundation" (p. 355). Boatright also comments on the relationship between virtue ethics and foundational theories: "The connection between the virtues and action is, by comparison [with foundational theories], much less direct. It may well be that an honest person does not have to think about whether to tell the truth, but [Robert] Solomon [1992] himself points out that anyone who thinks this shows that telling right from wrong is easy has never had to 'downsize' a staff of good employees" (p. 356). The most derisive phrasing of this problem is that of Lawrence Kohlberg (1981), who refers to the "bag of virtues": a jumble of positive characteristics without a rational approach to acquiring, ranking, or employing them.

Pincoffs (1986) challenges this last criticism: that virtue ethics is merely a bag of virtues. He writes:

For a trait to count as a virtue, there must be reason to think that the person who bears that trait is quite generally preferable to the person who does not. In thinking what the most general grounds of preference are, we assemble a coherent set of assumptions about "the human situation," both individual and communal. (p. 171)

Still, it can be objected that no scholar of virtue ethics has attempted a sufficiently detailed exposition of the theory to illuminate how individual virtues can bring about a systematic change on the communal level.

Of all those writing on virtue ethics, only Aristotle (to my knowledge) implicitly addresses the objections that virtue ethics is not a practical approach to ethics beyond the individual level and that virtue ethics offers no decision-making guidelines. In his argument that we should seek only as much precision as a subject allows, Aristotle suggests that beyond general recommendations about how children are to be educated to acquire virtue, this subject does not allow a great deal of specificity.

A broader question about virtue ethics concerns the relationship between the agent and the action. What is the essential difference between a foundational approach to ethics—one that values acting ethically—and virtue ethics, which values being virtuous so that one habitually acts ethically? Aristotle (trans. 1953) addresses just this question: "The *doer* must be in a certain frame of mind" when he carries out the virtuous action (p. 61). He must do the act with full consciousness of what he is doing, he must "will" the action, and will it for its own sake, and the act must proceed from "a fixed and unchangeable disposition" (p. 61). In other words, the gap between Aristotelian virtue and utilitarianism is clear, for utilitarianism places no such emphasis on the agent. But the gap between Aristotelian virtue and Kantianism is less wide, for Kant places a similar emphasis on the "good will" of the agent.

Still, it might be objected to Aristotle that a person who consistently and consciously acted ethically (according to some coherent foundational ethic) would by definition embody those very virtues that Aristotle and other virtue ethicists advocate. In other words, just as a virtuous person consistently acts virtuously, a person who consistently acts virtuously is a virtuous person.

POSTMODERN ETHICS

To the extent that virtue ethics rests on the Aristotelian idea that we should seek only as much specificity as a subject allows, it is similar to the third approach I want to discuss: postmodern ethics. In another way, too, the two approaches are similar: both argue that ethics is ultimately embedded in the ideals, mores, and practices of local communities. However, the differences between postmodern ethics and virtue ethics are great. I begin the discussion of postmodern ethics by describing postmodernism itself.

What Is Postmodernism?

Postmodern ethics is of course a subset of postmodernism. Unfortunately, postmodernism is more a spirit or an attitude than a theory that lends itself to clear definition or even articulate description. In fact, *postmodern* is in serious danger of losing meaning altogether through overuse, with all manner of artifacts, movements, ideas, media, and notions assigned the label. As pointed out by Hans Bertens (1995), *postmodern* carries different technical meanings in fields as diverse as literature, music, art, dance, photography, sociology, economics, and law. In addition, the word carries another, broader set of connotations when it is used to refer to a new sensibility in society at large. Still, for our purposes here, a good brief description of postmodernism is provided by Lester Faigley in *Fragments of Rationality* (1992). The "key assumption" behind the different threads of postmodernist thought, Faigley writes,

is that there is nothing outside contingent discourses to which a discourse of values can be grounded—no eternal truths, no universal human experience, no universal human rights, no overriding narrative of human progress. This assumption carries many radical implications. The foundational concepts associated with artistic judgment such as "universal value" and "intrinsic merit," with science such as "truth" and "objectivity," and with ethics and law such as "rights" and "freedoms" suddenly have no meaning outside of particular discourse and are deeply involved in the qualities they are alleged to be describing objectively. (p. 8)

The postmodernist who has written most extensively about ethics is Michel Foucault, who for more than a decade analyzed and critiqued Kant. Foucault's critiques are complex and subtle, and over the course of his writings he modified his views considerably, but his major thesis is that Kant's description of an autonomous, willful subject—a person of rationality and free will—is a fiction. In works such as *The Order of Things* (trans. 1970) and *The Archaeology of Knowledge* (trans. 1972), Foucault argued that people have always been "discursive formations," created by their communicative participation in their own societies and cultures, and therefore wholly incapable of exercising the transcendent reason and will that Kant ascribes to them. (For an excellent discussion of the history of Foucault's critiques of Kant, see Christopher Norris's *The Truth about Postmodernism* [1993].)

To explain in a little more detail the concept of postmodern ethics, I focus on the writing of Jean-François Lyotard, another of the principal architects and exponents of postmodern thought. Lyotard defines postmodernism by contrasting it with modernism:

I will use the word *modern* to designate any science that legitimates itself with reference to a metadiscourse . . . making an explicit appeal to some grand narrative, such as the dialectics of Spirit, the hermeneutics of meaning, the emancipation of the rational or working subject, or the creation of wealth. (1991b, p. xxiii)

By contrast, "Simplifying to the extreme, I define *postmodern* as incredulity toward metanarratives" (p. xxiv). These "grand narratives," Lyotard argues, serve

to allocate our lives for the growth of power. In matters of social justice and of scientific truth alike, the legitimation of that power is based on its optimizing the system's performance—efficiency. The application of this criterion to all of our games necessarily entails a certain level of terror, whether soft or hard: be operational (that is, commensurable) or disappear. (p. xxiv)

The privileged people who subscribe to, validate, and profit by a metanarrative, such as those who believe capitalism is the economic system that most fairly distributes wealth to all people, are in fact using terror to subjugate the Other—the unskilled, the handicapped, women, minorities, and so on.

Postmodernism Applied to Ethics

What is the relationship between *postmodernism* as a general cultural term and *postmodern ethics*? First, postmodernism dispenses with all foundational ethical approaches, just as it dispenses with all other grand narratives. In their place, postmodernism offers what Lyotard calls *language games*: local, contingent types and styles of communication practiced within different social institutions. For example, ethicists practice one kind of language game, scientists another. Ethicists cannot create a Truth any more than scientists can.

If Lyotard rejects foundational ethical approaches, how does he propose reaching ethical decisions or resolving ethical dilemmas? He doesn't. He writes that "justice as a value is neither outmoded nor suspect" (1991b, p. 66), but that we must create "a multiplicity of justices," for justice "consists in working at the limits of what the rules permit, in order to invent new moves, perhaps new rules and therefore new games" (1991a, p. 100).

Clearly, then, postmodern ethics is closely related to postmodern rhetoric. For Lyotard and other postmodernists, ethics does not precede rhetoric; rhetoric precedes—and creates—ethics. For this reason, postmodern ethics is becoming a subject of interest to a number of rhetoricians. Even when these rhetoricians avoid Lyotard's overstatement, abstraction, and fondness for neologisms, we can see the postmodern outlines clearly.

James E. Porter (1993), for instance, describes postmodern ethics as "a process of inquiry necessarily tied to the act of composing" (p. 208). He writes that a "postmodern approach to ethics differs from traditional ethics because it is grounded in community or local standards; it does not rely on, nor would it attempt to seek, a universal ground for ethical action" (p. 216). For Porter, postmodern ethics is an approach to negotiating among traditional and cultural values, disciplinary or field values, community values, and individual values. These clusters of values he calls *sites*. "Ethical judgment in this scheme is the process of placing principles from various sites in dialectic. Authority derives not from any particular set of principles—but from their interaction" (p. 222).

Criticisms of Postmodernism and Postmodern Ethics

Because the ideas behind postmodernism—and their expression—are so provocative, the debate about it has been, and continues to be, heated. Opponents write books with titles such as *The Truth about Postmodernism, The Persistence of Modernism,* and *Against Postmodernism.* One analyst, Alex Callinicos (1990), comments that "much of what is written in support of the idea that we live in a postmodern epoch seems to me of small calibre intellectually, usually superficial, often ignorant, sometimes incoherent" (p. 5). Another analyst, Hans Bertens (1995), uses a sharper weapon—precise, understated diction—in offering his view:

It's not the world that is postmodern, here, it is the perspective from which that world is seen that is postmodern. We are dealing here with a set of intellectual propositions that to some people make a lot more sense than they do to others. Although the omnipresence of the postmodern and its advocates would seem to suggest otherwise, not everybody subscribes to the view that language constitutes, rather than represents, reality; that the autonomous and stable subject of modernity has been replaced by a postmodern agent whose identity is largely other-determined and always in process; that meaning has become social and provisional; or that knowledge only counts as such within a given discursive formation, that is, a given power structure—to mention only some of the more familiar postmodern tenets. (pp. 9–10)

Postmodern ethics is vulnerable to three main criticisms:

- *Postmodern ethics is vague and inconsistent.* Both proponents and opponents of postmodernism have noted that it is internally inconsistent. As Faigley (1992) writes, "There is no way of working quickly through the contradictions described in discussions of postmodernity as a cultural condition, nor is there any satisfactory definition of postmodernism. Indeed, the assertion that there is no satisfactory definition of postmodernism is a positive expression of postmodernism" (pp. 3–4). Using a memorable metaphor, Faigley comments that postmodern theory "can resemble a terrorist bomb that demolishes bystanders and even its maker as well as the target" (p. 44). This internal inconsistency characterizes discussions of postmodern ethics. A hallmark of postmodernist thought is that it rejects binary oppositions such as individual/group, body/mind, theory/practice, writing/thinking, classical/romantic, art/science, and male/female. Yet the word *postmodern* exemplifies, in its prefix-root structure, exactly this sort of binary thinking: there is modernism, with one set of beliefs, and then there is postmodernism, which either rejects modernism or offers at least a significantly different set of beliefs. Porter's (1993) article, for instance, contains numerous comparisons between "postmodern ethics" and "traditional ethics." This binary thinking, while perhaps inevitable in argumentative texts, rather than expository ones, particularly those written early in a community's dialogue about a subject, oversimplifies that subject and discourages further exploration of the devalued item. Why bother looking, for instance, at the ethical theories of Aristotle, Kant, or Mill if they are all "traditional ethics"?
- *Postmodernism is descriptive rather than prescriptive.* Postmodernism's proponents do not feel intellectually obliged to validate that description. As Linda Flower (1993) remarks, people like herself who work within the modernist tradition always feel obliged to provide evidence for their assertions. Postmodernist theorists, on the other hand, "prefer boldly to assert their arbitrary, interpretive, or politically interested stance as an

unavoidable act but in that happy gesture also avoid responsibility for testing the fit between claims and external evidence" (p. 173). Postmodernism can offer no foundational values, no principles, no rules. It cannot even offer any advice more specific than that we must try to remain open to other people's views and work together constructively. Porter (1993) writes, for example, that ethics "certainly involves principles—but it always involves mediating between competing principles and judging those principles in light of particular circumstances" (p. 218). True, but what are those principles? Are they all equally valid? Should we use different principles at different times? In different circumstances? How do we mediate between different principles? If we are not to seek consensus, what should we do when we reach dissensus? On these and many other fundamental questions, Porter, like other proponents of postmodern ethics, is silent. Patricia Bizzell (1990) has written cogently about the need to find nonfoundational theories that nevertheless offer constructive proposals for creating rational dialogues about values, but this need has not yet been satisfied.

- *Postmodernism is relativistic.* If there is no coherent normative theory against which our ideas and actions can be measured, the scope of our discussions is narrow—only the ideas expressed by those in our community—a troubling prospect. The advice that we negotiate among competing viewpoints presumes that all those viewpoints are reasonable, a dangerous presumption in this (or any other) age. Carolyn Miller (1993, p. 85) has written about the "vicious circularity" of a postmodern rhetoric that disdains foundationalism in favor of a "constant praising of Athenians among Athenians," a rhetoric that values communalism at the expense of critical, abstract reasoning. Perhaps the most devastating critique of relativism in rhetoric and ethics is Stephen Katz's (1992) description of what might be called the worst-case scenario: the ethic of expediency demonstrated by Nazi technical communicators. (For a detailed discussion of the problem of relativism in postmodern thought, see Freadman and Miller [1992]).

In short, postmodernism in general and postmodern ethics in particular are vulnerable to charges of internal inconsistency, ineffectualism, and relativism. Carolyn Miller (1993) suggests that "postmodernism may leave us with a community that is so fragmented, perforated, intermittent, and attenuated that it no longer performs any rhetorical work" (p. 91). When postmodernist thought is applied to ethics for technical communicators, it can forestall the discussion of other approaches: traditional and nontraditional ethics alike. The result can be that we overlook a rich body of ethical thought that might be of significant value.

CONCLUSION

Of the three ethics discussed in this chapter, the ethic of care offers the greatest promise to redress the imbalance of foundational ethical approaches, which place too little value on personal and familial relationships. Whether care will achieve an autonomous status rivaling or even supplanting Kantianism or utilitarianism cannot be foreseen. More likely, the concerns that are central to an ethic of care will become another value, like justice, rights, and utility, in a flexible set of values.

Virtue ethics will likely remain another lens, similar to foundational approaches, through which we view ethical obligations. But only a fundamental rethinking of the role of public education, the kind of plan recommended by Aristotle at the end of his *Ethics*, would lead to a significant change in the way ethics is viewed by the typical citizen.

Postmodern ethics, being by definition descriptive rather than prescriptive, will probably remain for some time a fashionable way to describe ethics (as well as many other aspects of life) rather than a constructive attempt to advance our understanding of ethics.

In the next chapter, I present a rough outline of an approach to ethics for technical communicators, an approach that synthesizes the best elements of foundational approaches (rights, justice, and utility) and the ethic of care. My idea, which derives from the thinking of John Rawls and Jürgen Habermas, is based on the premise that the most effective decision-making model for disputes about values and ethics is one that permits all stakeholders access to free, uncoerced participation in open dialogue.

7

Toward an Approach to Ethical Decision-Making

In this chapter, which concludes the first part of the book, I summarize the discussion of foundational approaches, then describe an approach to decision-making that exploits the strengths of the foundational approaches while avoiding their central limitations. The foundational approaches endure because they tap into our most essential human qualities; however, each of the approaches is fundamentally flawed as a procedural guide.

Before presenting my own approach, I briefly review two contemporary approaches—John Rawls's theory of justice and Jürgen Habermas's discourse ethics—that I believe are fundamentally important to a defensible modern account of rights and justice. I also discuss a promising development in business ethics: the link between ethics and the quality movement.

Next, I present my own approach, which combines discourse ethics with the values of traditional foundational ethics approaches and the ethic of care. I follow this discussion with a look at two well-known ethics cases to show how my approach offers insights that can prove useful in thinking about the ethical dilemmas they present. I conclude the chapter with a note about the teaching of ethics and technical communication.

THE STRENGTHS AND WEAKNESSES OF
FOUNDATIONAL APPROACHES TO ETHICS

Helping people learn how to live active and honorable lives has long been the goal of foundational ethical systems. From Socrates through roughly the first half of the 20th century, ethical theory in the Western world was largely foundational. That is, it consisted of attempts to answer the question "What is good, and how ought we to behave to achieve it?" The two best-known foundational theories are the Golden Rule and utilitarianism, but implicit in all foundational theories is the premise that if you can determine the relevant facts in the case, you can apply the theory to determine an appropriate course of action. Foundational theories are therefore deductive, top-down approaches to ethics. You begin with a theory of value underlying proper conduct, then examine the alternative actions to determine the extent to which they are in accord with that theory. On the basis of this examination, you determine which action is correct. For example, if you believe that the correct action is the one that maximizes benefits and minimizes costs, and you have determined that action A produces more benefits and fewer costs than action B or action C, it follows that action A is the correct action to take.

Of course, this oversimplification is so extreme that it risks portraying some of the greatest thinkers of our tradition as almost simpleminded. With the exception of Kant, who clearly was not simpleminded but whose categorical imperative tolerated no exceptions, all the major ethicists admitted exceptions to their foundational theories. Still, foundational theories share the premises that the questions about goodness and appropriate behavior are important, that rationally articulated principles can help people answer them, and that people are essentially rational or at least capable of rationality.

Earl R. Winkler (1993) explains the ultimate goal of foundational philosophers:

The holy grail . . . is a single, comprehensive, and coherent theory that is based in universal, basic principles, which, in their turn, yield more particular principles and rules that are capable of deciding concrete issues of practice. . . . One justifies a particular judgment by showing that it falls under a rule, and the rule by showing that it is a specification of a principle, and the principle by showing that it is grounded in the most abstract levels of normative theory. (p. 350)

As suggested by the holy-grail metaphor, this coherent foundational theory has remained elusive, but certainly not for lack of effort. Indeed, one of the greatest challenges for the student of foundational theories is that there are too many of them. Over the past two and a half millennia, Western ethicists have articulated a dizzying variety. James Rachels (1993) assembles this abbreviated list of some of the "higher order considerations" in the most influential approaches:

- that pain, frustration, and ignorance are bad
- that friendship, knowledge, and self-esteem are good
- that human life has a special value and importance
- that human interests have a fundamental importance that the interest of other animals do not have
- that people should always be treated as ends-in-themselves, and never as mere means
- that personal autonomy—the freedom of each individual to control and direct his or her own life—is especially important
- that each of us has special obligations and responsibilities to our own family and friends
- that there is an important moral difference between causing harm, and merely allowing it to happen
- that there is a difference in stringency between our strict duties and other duties which are matters of "mere" charity or generosity
- that a person's intention, in performing a given action, is relevant to determining whether the action is right. (pp. 117–18)

Kevin Possin (1991) spins out a similar list, limited to varieties of utilitarianism, concluding that "ethical rules are all too plentiful" (p. 66). Although the number of approaches can be disconcerting and even intimidating, especially for the nonspecialist, the fact that there are so many carefully articulated and subtle foundational theories indicates, at the least, that for a number of centuries, very bright people have thought the enterprise of creating foundational ethical theories worthwhile.

But if the quest for a single coherent foundational approach has long fascinated philosophers, the enormous numbers of differences among the approaches suggests that many or most or all of them are seriously flawed. In previous chapters, I have tried to explain some of the more obvious problems with the major approaches. For example, an Athenian gentleman had the leisure to contemplate the Good because women, slaves, and other nonelites were doing all the work. Kant's examples intended to support his first formulation of the categorical imperative—"I am never to act otherwise than so that I could also will that my maxim should become a universal law"—are riddled with elementary logical flaws. Mill's defense of utilitarianism confuses *desired* with *desirable*: he declares that the only way to determine what is desirable is to look at what people actually desire. In short, there are significant cracks in some of the foundations.

Perhaps more significant than these technical problems is the criticism that foundational approaches do not *work*, that they fail to provide sufficient practical guidance in real-world situations. Even if we agree, for instance, that our actions should demonstrate a respect for the rights of others, we still do not know what to do when we confront complex problems. The most serious critiques of foundationalism have focused on problems in medical ethics. For example, Winkler and Coombs (1993) describe the dilemma this way:

> What, for example, could it mean to respect properly the personhood of a potential anencephalic organ donor? In the experience of many philosophers actually working in medical ethics, most of the real work of resolving moral problems occurred at the level of interpretation and comparison of cases. Recourse to abstract normative principles seemed never to override case-driven considered judgment. (p. 3)

Attempts to apply the principle to the case often provide clear insights into the lack of precision or coherence of the principle, rather than step-by-step procedures for resolving the case.

RECENT RESPONSES TO FOUNDATIONALISM

Recognizing these shortcomings of foundational approaches, early 20th-century ethicists began calling for a radical revision of foundationalism, which I treat in Chapter 5. Dewey argued that we should consider ethics as a way of thinking about values, not as received truth, and that we should therefore test our ethical models and refine them according to scientific principles of experimentation. If an ethical principle proves useful, it is good. But Dewey never provided anything more specific than this critique. G. E. Moore severed hedonism from utilitarianism, depriving the popular normative theory of its underlying theory of value. W. D. Ross underscored the limitations of utilitarianism, arguing persuasively for the primacy of duties and obligations in a coherent approach to ethics. However, while his flexible decision-making model avoids Kant's excesses, it offers little beyond the commonsense idea that we have to determine whether the details of the particular situation justify breaking any of our traditional obligations.

Today, many ethicists are working to formulate and refine an ethic of care, but their efforts are hindered by a split between those who wish to incorporate care into an existing approach to ethics and those who wish to substitute care for existing approaches. At this point, care is an important value rather than a coherent approach to ethics. Another popular contemporary approach, virtue ethics, is decidedly nonfoundational in that it is based on the premise that the real world is too complex to ever support any approach that focuses on acts; only by educating people in the virtues can we hope to equip them with the insights necessary to make wise decisions.

And, finally, postmodern ethics is not merely nonfoundational but actually anti-foundational. In its current formulations, the various versions of postmodern ethics remain descriptive, not prescriptive, and therefore offer little to those who wish to advance our thinking about ethics.

In the centuries since people in the Western tradition have been thinking and writing seriously about ethics, we seem to have done a much better job explaining why the different approaches to ethics are inadequate than in sketching a coherent approach that seems even potentially useful. While this state of affairs might seem discouraging for those who believe that it should be possible to systematize clear thinking, we should not despair. The ethicist and rhetorician Stephen Toulmin (1985), discussing his service on the National Commission for the Protection of Human Subjects, notes that, in ethics,

the best we can achieve in practice is for good-hearted, clear-headed people to triangulate their way across the complex terrain of moral life and problems. So, starting from the paradigmatic cases that we do understand—what in the simplest situations harm is, and fairness, and cruelty, and generosity—we must simply work our way, one step at a time, to the more complex and perplexing cases in which extremely delicate balances may have to be struck. (p. 149)

Toulmin is right, of course: there is no user's manual for resolving ethical dilemmas wisely. But to ignore the approaches of the greatest students of ethics, incomplete and inadequate as they sometimes are, surely will not make the task faster or safer or surer. There is probably considerable wisdom in the commonplaces of moral thinking—such ideas as treating people as we would like to be treated, caring for the needy, considering the effects our actions are likely to have on others—ideas that have stood the test of time. Such ideas seem to value instincts and states of mind that all people, ancient and modern, educated and illiterate, have agreed reflect the best that our species can offer on the subject of ethics. If these commonplace ideas seem unwilling to be shaped into a system of ethics, they surely must figure prominently in our thinking about what kind of people we wish to be and how we wish to treat others.

Before discussing an approach to ethical decision making that I think incorporates the best of what we have thought about morality, I want to discuss briefly two ideas about rights and justice articulated by contemporary thinkers that I believe provide the background necessary for my approach.

TWO CONTEMPORARY THEORIES OF JUSTICE AND RIGHTS

Two enormously influential contemporary philosophers—John Rawls and Jürgen Habermas—offer different but related theories of justice and rights. Neither thinker would consider himself a traditional ethicist whose goal is to present a theory of value and of normative ethics; both paint on a much larger canvas. Rawls describes a theory of justice that depends on a rational structuring of the public institutions of a society. Habermas is a critical theorist who presents a theory, discourse ethics, intended to ensure that individuals test and evaluate moral norms through the process of free, uncoerced public discussion.

Neither Rawls nor Habermas offers a practical agenda. Neither thinker strolls his country's corridors of power. Yet both philosophers are fundamentally important for one simple reason: each presents a rational defense of fundamental human rights and justice against the forces of unfettered utilitarianism. In describing a set of institutions and processes that gives voice to the needs of the full citizenry, from the elite to the displaced, Rawls and Habermas describe a core set of values that must be protected in a modern meritocratic social system that values power and money.

John Rawls's Theory of Justice

Just as Kant offered a reasoned alternative to utilitarianism, the contemporary American John Rawls, perhaps this century's most influential philosopher on the subject of individual rights, offers an alternative to the popular ethical theory called emotivism. Articulated by such philosophers as A. J. Ayer and Charles Stevenson in the first half of our century, emotivism held that any discussion of ethics is merely an expressive act; it reveals the speaker's personal feelings but has nothing to do with reason. We cannot enlist reason in our own thinking about ethics, and we cannot use reason to bring others to our own point of view. Rawls's book *A Theory of Justice* (1971) is an attempt to reestablish the link between ethics and reason that Kant had described two centuries before.

In his book, Rawls describes the principles of fairness that would undergird the political, legal, economic, and social institutions of an ideal society. The most influential part of his theory is the statement of two principles that would permeate the fair society:

1. Each person is to have an equal right to the most extensive total system of basic liberties compatible with a similar system of liberty for all.
2. Social and economic inequalities are to be arranged so that they are both:

    a) to the greatest benefit of the least advantaged, and
    b) attached to offices and positions open to all under conditions of fair equality of opportunity. (p. 302)

The details of Rawls's concept of a fair society are beyond the scope of this book; in fact, a 1982 bibliography of secondary sources (Wellbank, Snook, & Mason) annotates some 2,500 books and articles.

However, the philosophical basis of *A Theory of Justice*, which derives clearly from Kantian ethics, relates directly to the present discussion. Like other philosophers such as Hobbes or Rousseau, who examine a state of nature that precedes civilization, Rawls describes what he calls the *original position*. This original position is not meant as a description of a literal time or place, but rather a logical premise that makes possible the process of creating a fair society. In the original position, the people who come together to create a society each want the society to work to their particular advantage. That is, their first priority is to prosper, not to do good for their fellow citizens.

But there is one distinctive feature of these people in the original condition: they are ignorant of their own personal characteristics. They don't know how they will fare in what philosophers call the natural lottery. That is, they don't know their age, gender, race, or physical or mental attributes. They are operating, Rawls says, from behind *a veil of ignorance*. Rawls argues that in such a situation they will use the *maximin principle*, a feature of games theory that holds that a rational person will choose a situation that maximizes his or her minimal opportunities. That is, a person will choose the best worst-case scenario. A person who does not know whether he or she is male or female presumably will not choose to create a society that permits sex discrimination. A person who does not know whether he or she is healthy or disabled presumably will not choose a society in which those who cannot work are allowed to starve.

As philosopher Stephen L. Darwall (1980) argues, Rawls's ideas derive from and extend and apply Kant's. In its general outlines, Rawls's ideal society, based on the principles of equality and affirmative action to raise the social and economic fortunes of the least advantaged, is Kantian in that people are to be treated as ends, not merely as means. Specific features of Rawls's society are also Kantian. His concept of the original position derives from Kant in that ethical principles can be and should be derived by rational thought. His specification that society be defined by persons acting from behind a veil of ignorance follows from Kant's concept of people as autonomous beings who act on the basis of reason, not on contingent factors such as self-interest or desire. And Rawls's idea that individuals legislate not only for themselves but for all others derives from Kant's universalizability principle.

Rawls's concept of the ideal society thus offers a simple way to illustrate Kant's complex ideas about free will: it is difficult to imagine a person in the original position—not knowing whether he or she would be the technical communicator or the purchaser of a product—approving the idea of lying in product advertising.

Despite his enormous acclaim and influence in the philosophical community, Rawls is modest about his contributions. As he describes his thesis, it "is highly Kantian in nature. Indeed, I must disclaim any originality for the views I put forward. The leading ideas are classical and well known" (1971, p. viii).

Discourse Ethics: An Alternative Framework

Foundational ethical approaches seek to answer the question "What should I think about ethics?" *Discourse ethics* is an approach that seeks to answer the question "How should I think about ethics?"

Discourse ethics, also called *communicative ethics,* is an approach most closely associated with Jürgen Habermas and his colleague at the University of Frankfurt, Karl-Otto Apel (see Benhabib and Dallmayr [1990] for an introduction to discourse ethics). Although Habermas and Apel differ in some of the details of their theories, they both see discourse ethics as a variation of Kant's categorical imperative. Kant argued that an ethical act is one that an individual could, without contradiction, will to be universally applicable law. Discourse ethics changes the focus from the individual's thought processes to the process of open and free discourse among all interested parties. In this way, discourse ethics holds that an ethical norm or action is one that has been, or could have been, agreed to by all affected parties. Instead of a person's formulating his or her views in private, discourse ethics calls for the person to express those views in a public forum, testing their validity as universal norms. Whereas Kant thought of universalizability in terms of noncontradiction, Habermas and Apel think of it in terms of a test of communicative agreement.

Discourse ethics derives from a number of thinkers other than Kant. Habermas refers often to the American pragmatist G. H. Mead (1863–1931), who described the concept of "universal discourse" or "ideal role taking," by which people in a group discussion would imagine the perspectives of others and try to reach consensus with them. Habermas also refers frequently to speech-act theory, most closely associated with J. L. Austin (1911–1960), in which utterances are classified as constantives (statements that are either true or false) and performatives (statements that are neither true nor false but that make something happen). Common examples of performatives include the utterances involved in getting married, making a promise or a bet, or christening a ship. Provided that the performative utterances are expressed correctly, in the proper context, they are equivalent to action. For Habermas, discourse ethics depends on speech-act theory, for discourse ethics is the means of realizing action—creating and testing norms—through the medium of discussion. Just as speech-act theory includes the idea that performative utterances are measured against existing cultural norms, discourse ethics holds that arguments are offered within the context of existing ethical norms.

A third thinker to whom Habermas refers often is Lawrence Kohlberg, whose theory of moral development is discussed in Chapters 2 and 6.

Habermas sees Kohlberg's theory of moral development as charting "a principled morality in which we can recognize the main force of discourse ethics" (1990, p. 117). Just as Kohlberg argued that all people in all cultures progress through a preconventional morality to a conventional morality and (perhaps) to a postconventional morality, Habermas argued that the procedural rules of discourse ethics provide a universal norm for discussion, even though the content of the discussion will vary from culture to culture.

Finally, Habermas acknowledged a debt to John Rawls. Although Habermas sees a number of links to Rawls, he argues that his approach is logically prior to Rawls's. Rawls starts with the ethical perspective of the original position, then goes on to describe the institutions that derive from it; Habermas believes that discourse ethics is the proper means of deriving the ethical perspective in the first place.

Discourse ethics makes no claims about the correctness or incorrectness of particular actions or ideas; rather, it comments only on the nature of the discourse itself. What are the principles of proper discourse? Matthias Kettner (1993) explains that proper discourse is characterized by five "morally relevant constraints":

- *Generality constraint.* The dialogue is open to every stakeholder, or at least every stakeholder's views are represented.

- *Autonomous evaluation constraint.* Every participant has the right to offer his or her views and challenge those of others.

- *Role-taking constraint.* Everyone must try to view his or her own ideas as objectively as possible, making them open to reconsideration in light of the evolving discussion.

- *Power-neutrality constraint.* All views are to be listened to without prejudice based on the power relations among the participants. A view expressed by a powerful person will not be considered persuasive simply because of the speaker's status.

- *Transparency constraint.* All participants have to be open in describing their own values and plans. Participants may not overtly or covertly pressure other participants into articulating (or not articulating) a view by threatening to harm their interests socially, politically, or economically. (pp. 34–36)

For Habermas, these procedural rules foster the ideas of "equality of respect, solidarity, and the common good" (1990, p. 201), which are common to all cultures. As Habermas wrote in 1973, "Discursively redeemable norms and generalizable interests have a non-conventional core; they are neither empirically found already to exist nor simply posited; rather they are, in a non-contingent way, both *formed* and *discovered*" (p. 177).

The best way to understand discourse ethics, Habermas argued (1990), is as an extension of the normal discourse we carry on every day.

> There is only one reason why discourse ethics, which presumes to derive the substance of a universalistic morality from the general presuppositions of argumentation, is a promising strategy: discourse or argumentation is a more exacting type of communication, going beyond any particular form of life. Discourse generalizes, abstracts, and stretches the presuppositions of context-bound communicative actions by extending their range to include competent subjects beyond the provincial limits of their own particular form of life. (p. 202)

Admitting that there is no logical justification for the validity of discourse ethics, Habermas writes (1990) that its strongest rationale is quite simple: "there is no identifiable alternative to our kind of argumentation" (p. 116).

Although the idea of a procedure for rational, free, uncoerced discussion that will safeguard rights and promote justice is attractive, discourse ethics has been criticized on four main grounds:

- *Discourse ethics is vague.* Nobody, not even Apel or Habermas, has described in detail how to achieve ideal discourse in a real world.

- *Discourse ethics is relativistic.* The results of any dialogue depend on the cultural backgrounds, the moral stances, and the reasoning powers of the participants in the dialogue. Why should we assume that an orderly discussion will produce enlightened results?

- *Discourse ethics is unworkable in pluralistic societies.* As J. Donald Moon argues (1995), moral community "may not be possible in societies characterized by value pluralism—and these are the very societies in which discourse ethics is most applicable" (p. 114). Discourse ethics will result in argumentative stalemate unless the participants share a number of core cultural and ethical values. Discourse ethics is based on the premise that people share the belief that formal argumentation enables us to propose, refine, and test values and norms, that we are intelligent, principled people of good will, or that at least the majority are, and that the rest are capable of changing their views—and willing to do so—when presented with strong arguments. This premise itself might be invalid in modern pluralistic societies.

- *Discourse ethics is unworkable in hierarchical communities.* Discourse ethics is intended as a set of procedures to guide whole societies as they create and refine moral norms and derive social policies from them. But the society in which most people actually work out moral norms is the work world, not the larger social and political world. In a work environment, which is usually hierarchically structured, there is little chance that Habermas's uncoerced environment of argumentation can be achieved.

In the next section, I discuss modern efforts to involve workers more actively in workplace decision-making.

Although Rawls's theory of justice and Habermas's discourse ethics are limited, they articulate the important value expressed by Kant in his second formulation of the categorical imperative: the need to treat people with respect, as ends and not merely as means. The theories of Rawls and Habermas are certainly vulnerable to the charge of impracticality; yet they can have important educational value in improving the tenor and outcomes of the decision-making processes in which we all participate. Together, they are a Robert's Rules for ethical discussion.

QUALITY AND ETHICS IN THE WORKPLACE

In the previous section, I mentioned that a serious problem in thinking about discourse ethics is that the arena in which most people actually engage in significant discourse about public issues is not the broad *polis* but the more local environment of their workplace, which is likely to be hierarchically organized. In this environment, I suggested, the uncoerced participation advocated by Habermas and other discourse-ethics proponents is unlikely to flourish.

There is, however, an important development in business management theory, both in the U.S. and internationally, that holds significant promise of realizing at least some of the characteristics of discourse ethics. I am referring to what is broadly called the *quality movement*.

One aspect of the quality movement is the setting of standards. As Robert J. Craig (1994) explains, businesses seek to meet different sets of standards, such as Military Standards, ISO 9000 standards, the Malcolm Baldridge Award Criteria, and the Deming Prize. Because ISO 9000 is an important set of international standards, I will discuss it briefly here.

ISO 9000, a set of standards published by the International Organization for Standardization, based in Geneva, Switzerland, and mirrored in the United States by the ANSI/ASQC Q 9000, was originally published in 1987 to provide an international set of processes to be used by companies large and small to implement a quality system. A company that wishes to be certified as meeting one of the ISO 9000 standards follows the procedures outlined in the ISO documentation, then applies to a relevant certifying board, such as Underwriter's Laboratory in the United States, to inspect the company for conformity to the standards. That certifying board then rules that the company does or does not comply with the relevant ISO 9000 standard.

The reason that many thousands of companies in the U.S. and abroad are applying for ISO certification is that countries in the European Community now require that manufacturers of certain types of products and services—mostly those related to health, safety, and the environment, such as automobiles, chemicals, medical devices, and food—be ISO-certified.

Although there are many elements to ISO 9000, two are central:

- *Management responsibility* refers to a set of obligations undertaken by managers: to publish a policy statement about the company's commitment to quality, to clearly define quality-related responsibilities, to oversee the continuous improvement of the company's operations, and to routinely review the company's operations, assessing compliance and identifying opportunities to improve them.

- *Quality system* refers to a "quality manual" that a company must write to document all its policies and operations. This quality manual describes, in general and in detail, all the quality-control procedures of the company (Craig, 1994).

As Weiss (1993) describes the process of registering for ISO compliance, a company first elicits management's commitment, then trains employees in the best quality procedures, implements the procedures, conducts an internal audit of its performance, arranges for certification by a certifying board, and finally responds to any stipulations presented by the certifying board.

Obviously, making a commitment to ISO certification is a major undertaking by a company, an undertaking that usually involves the technical communicators in the company. As Weiss (1993) suggests, ISO certification is essentially a massive documentation process based on the premise that the best way to ensure high quality is to specify every process carried out by the company.

Although the International Organization for Standardization website (1999) contains numerous testimonials from corporate executives about the value of implementing ISO standards, there is no way to determine the extent to which the process leads to improved product quality, performance standards, or reduced costs. It makes sense, however, to assume that when senior managers make a sincere, comprehensive effort to examine, improve, and document the company's operations, there will be a positive effect on both the performance and the ethical climate in the organization. For a useful discussion of the technical communicator's role in documenting an ISO quality system, see Fisher (1995).

ISO standards overlap to a large extent with many of the core principles of *total quality management* (TQM). There are many varieties of TQM described and analyzed in the management literature. Perhaps the most prominent advocate of TQM is W. Edwards Deming, but other proponents include Philip Crosby, Joseph M. Juran, and Kaoru Ishikawa. (See Flood [1993] for an introduction to TQM.) A broad range of management principles intended to increase the effectiveness of an organization's operations,

TQM was a response to the declining quality of manufacturing and business organizations following World War II. Flood argues that the Industrial Revolution and, later, the "scientific" principles of Frederick Taylor led to an overemphasis on efficiency at the expense of quality and effectiveness. Manufacturers and businesses alienated workers by treating them like machines. Workers responded by acting appropriately, and quality suffered.

Although different varieties of TQM offer different lists of core principles, the following five ideas appear in most:

- TQM is a program of continuous improvement of business and management practices. TQM is a business climate rather than a finite initiative.
- TQM requires the full support of upper management.
- TQM requires focusing on the needs of customers. Customers include not only external buyers but the organization's own employees.
- TQM requires active participation of all workers. Employees need to be able to communicate with other workers and management and have a formal role in determining policies.
- TQM focuses on preventing problems rather than merely responding to them. Rather than ensuring quality through inspection (removing defective products before they are sent to customers), TQM focuses on efforts to fix those practices that allow the problem to occur in the first place.

To those skeptics who feel that TQM seems awfully like common sense, TQM advocates happily agree. Yes, it does seem fairly obvious that treating people like people, instead of like things, is likely to make them feel more a part of the·organization and encourage them to work harder, smarter, and more honestly. Involving workers more centrally in the operations of the organization is smart because no one in the organization knows better than they do how to do the job effectively. Yet, TQM advocates point out, most modern organizations have not involved workers in significant ways. Therefore, TQM is news.

Recently, a number of management scholars and business ethicists have pointed out the link between the principles of the quality movement and ethics. Raiborn and Payne (1996), for instance, comment that the focus on worker empowerment in TQM is consistent with Kantian rights, Rawlsian justice, and utilitarianism. Steeples (1994), an examiner for the Malcolm Baldridge National Quality Award, argues that there is a strong correlation between the quality movement and improved ethics. She writes that in every case in which quality improved, ethics also improved, as measured by tangential factors such as decreased absenteeism and employee theft and core issues such as improved product quality and customer satisfaction. These benefits "occurred merely as a latent benefit of quality improvement" (p. 74). Improving ethics was rarely the goal of TQM. Roth (1993) argues that by improving communication, broadening decision-making, and rewarding work groups rather than individuals—aspects of many quality programs—"ethical behavior is automatically encouraged" (p.6).

The title of Roth's article—"Is It Quality Improves Ethics or Ethics Improves Quality?"(1993)—suggests, however, a major problem with most of the current research on the link between the quality movement and ethics. The subject simply does not lend itself to rigorous empirical research. In a comprehensive and devastating critique of modern business-ethics research, Randall and Gibson (1990) conclude that most of it is flawed in significant ways. The most obvious problem is that it relies on survey research that asks respondents to state how they would respond to certain hypothetical situations. Obviously, this methodology is subject to bias: many respondents tell the researchers what they want to hear (this is called the *social desirability bias*) rather than what they really think. In addition, responding to a hypothetical scenario is not the same as making decisions and acting on them in real life. The fact is that there is no valid and reliable empirical way to study the relationship between the quality movement and ethics. Life is too messy to support valid experimental studies, and people are not genetically identical lab rats. Case studies can provide useful insights about the experience of a particular organization, but case studies do not necessarily provide reliable, generalizable results.

There is probably a lot of truth in Robert Solomon's (1993) statement that "scientific studies" that attempt to draw causal links between business practices and ethical behavior are nonsense. Still, from a theoretical perspective, management practices that empower workers are consistent with the goals of discourse ethics and the Kantian notion of treating people as ends. Steeples (1994) describes the relationship this way:

TQM offers a systematic way for organizations to link values and value. Experience shows that total quality companies are successful because they translate what customers value into quality requirements and practices. In that context, ethics can be viewed simply as a primary set of customer values. (p. 75)

That high-pitched whirring sound you hear is Kant spinning in his grave as he learns that ethical behavior is a subset of utilitarian concern for customer values. Nevertheless, most of us would agree, if reluctantly, that treating people with dignity because it will improve the bottom line is better than not treating them with dignity at all.

A TWO-PART APPROACH TO ETHICAL DECISION-MAKING

I would like now to describe a simple two-step process that can be used to help people at all levels—students and professionals alike—think through ethical dilemmas they will confront as technical communicators. You will notice immediately that there is no "Figure 1. Ethical Decision-Making Flowchart." In this context, I am uncomfortable with words such as *flowchart* or *method*, which have connotations that are inappropriate here. Both words suggest a systems approach that is more appropriate to computer programming than to thinking about difficult ethical problems. What I am offering here is merely an approach, a set of questions that can help people organize their thinking about the ethical problem. I do not at all mean to suggest that it is a *system*, a way to manage input to lead to a desired output; ethical problems of any complexity cannot be resolved neatly.

In addition, I want to be clear that there is nothing strikingly original in the ideas I present. I draw on the work of philosophers and social critics from the time of Aristotle through the present day, as well as various business-ethics scholars. However, given that these sources are discussed so rarely by scholars in technical communication, I feel justified in presenting my approach.

First, let me offer a rationale for this approach. Then, I will describe the approach in a little more detail.

A Rationale for the Approach

My approach is an attempt to combine the strengths of discourse ethics and foundational approaches. The principal strengths of discourse ethics are two.

First, the procedural guidelines of discourse ethics increase the chances that important values of rights and justice are protected. A person thinking alone about an ethical dilemma is likely to overlook the perspectives of one or more other stakeholders. An environmentalist who believes that wetlands should never be developed might overlook the perspective of the owner of a wetland property. Getting these two people in a room, along with other stakeholders, increases the chances that all perspectives are voiced and thereby decreases the chances that anyone's rights are violated. The resulting decision is likely to be more just than it would otherwise be.

Second, discourse ethics increase the chances that the discussion is rational. In a free and uncoerced forum, people have a right to ask "Why do you say that?" This question—the "Why?" question—is of course the fundamental technique used in the dialectic method. The "Why?" question is Socrates's best tool in Plato's dialogues; by forcing his opponent to justify what the opponent has just said, Socrates leads him to logical contradiction. The "Why?" question is still the most direct and effective technique for encouraging people to examine the premises and logical development of their arguments. We carry out this technique (silently) when we read letters to the editor in our local newspaper and (out loud or in the margins) when we ask our students to examine their reasoning in an essay.

A rational discussion carried out according to the principles of discourse ethics inevitably uncovers the core values of the discussants. Regardless of the topic being debated, within a few seconds or, at most, a few minutes, each participant reveals his or her core values. For example, a local governance committee is discussing a proposal that would permit the public to learn the identity and addresses of people who have been convicted of sex crimes. Proponents say they want to protect their children from sexual predators. Opponents say that the sex offender has already paid his debt to society and ought to be able to live in peace. What they are arguing is, of course, the relative merits of utilitarianism and rights-based ethics. The proponent is saying that the greatest good for the greatest number can be achieved by enabling people to know that the person living at 116 Maple Street served a sentence for rape, and the opponent is saying that the rights of the person at that address would be violated if his conviction became public knowledge.

Naturally, the discussion can get complex when a proponent of the proposal asserts, as a matter of fact, that most sex offenders are never rehabilitated. Opponents dispute this assertion, and the discussion takes an empirical tack, with people offering their views on whether convicted sex offenders in reality are likely to pose a continuing threat. At this point, an exasperated proponent of the legislation might say, "I don't care if the chances are only one in a hundred that he is still a threat; I have three kids to protect. I don't give a damn about his rights. He gave up all his rights when he raped that school girl." A comment such as this, although rhetorically messy, is about as clear a statement of core values as a person can make. The discussion can go in a number of directions at this point: it can reach an impasse, it can be resolved by a decisive vote, or it can return to questions of value.

But the important point is that an unfettered discussion will, sooner or later but probably sooner, involve the discussants in frank debate about the values at the heart of foundational ethical approaches: rights, utility, care, and justice. Although it is true that no philosopher has created a coherent algorithm for resolving ethical dilemmas, it is also true that any serious discussion of an ethical dilemma is an examination of the competing claims based on the values debated by the foundational ethicists.

Ultimately, the justification for studying Kant or Mill or any of the other serious ethicists is that the issues they address are inescapable. We should study foundational ethicists not because their systems answer all our questions but because they don't. If we have thought seriously about utility, for example, whenever we make utilitarian arguments we are likely to be especially sensitive to the fact that utility does a poor job in addressing issues of justice. In understanding the limitations of utilitarianism or any of the other foundational approaches, we force ourselves to see the complementarity of the core values and the complexity of their interrelationships. We approach all ethical dilemmas with less certainty but more subtlety.

The process I want to sketch is flexible, fluid, and recursive. The questions you pose for yourself will usually yield tentative, incomplete, and inadequate answers. You will abandon one line of inquiry and start another. You will return to a line of inquiry that seemed a dead end, and all of a sudden it will yield a new insight. You will resolve the problem, then realize significant shortcomings in your solution. The process is anything but linear and conclusive.

With those caveats, let me explain the approach. The approach has two parts: (1) trying to determine the most ethical course of action and (2) trying to determine the most ethical *available* course of action.

Determining the Most Ethical Course of Action

Determining the most ethical course of action involves using a discourse-ethics framework in which to consider how alternative courses of action address important values.

Let me explain, first, what I mean by carrying out the process of ethical inquiry in a discourse-ethics framework. Obviously, you should seek the views of as many people as you can, using one-to-one dialogues, focus groups, formal meetings, or whatever other means are possible and appropriate. The important point is that you should not try to think through a complex problem by yourself. Just as collaboration in writing is likely to improve a document's quality because the authors will have more information and more insights to work with, collaboration in thinking through an ethics problem will help you see shortcomings in your reasoning and ensure that you are giving voice to as many different stakeholders as possible. You will thereby increase the likelihood that you reach a conclusion that is just and respects people's rights.

Beyond this rather obvious point about the need to include different stakeholders, it is useful to try to impose the other main procedural strictures of discourse ethics: free, open, and uncoerced communication. Certainly, these strictures are unattainable in most cases. Yet it is important to try to impose them because they set the tone for the deliberative process; they create an atmosphere in which people treat one another—and, by extension, their views—respectfully.

The most comprehensive and accessible explanation of the important values to consider is that of Cavanaugh, Moberg, and Velasquez (1995). These three business-ethics scholars focus on four values: utility, rights, justice, and care. This model, which the authors call URJC (to indicate the four values), calls for addressing four key questions, as shown in Figure 7.1.

Figure 7.1
The Utility-Justice-Rights-Care Model

Utility: Does the course of action optimize the satisfaction of all relevant constituencies? This question encapsulates, obviously, the central insight of utilitarianism. Notice, too, that it hints at discourse ethics with its phrase "all relevant constituencies."

Rights and duties: Does it respect the rights and duties of the individuals involved? This question summarizes Kant's central insight in his second formulation of the categorical imperative.

Justice: Is it consistent with the canons of justice? This question draws most directly on the work of John Rawls. A course of action is not right if it leads to an unfair distribution of costs and benefits.

Care: Does it arise from an impulse to care? This question incorporates the insights of Carol Gilligan and other scholars. Cavanaugh, Moberg, and Velasquez (1995) describe the central tenets of the care perspectives as including relations between unequals, private encounters, and an emphasis on context and connection. The values of care, which include personal relationships, effective communication, teamwork, and trust, are "often at the core of solutions to contemporary business issues" (p. 403).

The four questions posed in Figure 7.1 are not presented as a heuristic. It's a bulleted-items list, not a numbered-items list. There is nothing to be gained by suggesting, for example, that rights and duties are "more important" than utility, or that you should think first about utility, then justice. The important point is that, in your discussions with others and in your own thinking, you should consider all four sets of values.

At this point, it is necessary to keep in mind two points about the difficulties involved in applying these values:

- *Each set of values can be applied in different ways.* For instance, consider the following situation, which is sketched in the Cavanaugh, Moberg, and Velasquez (1995) article. As a manager in a company, you are responsible for appointing someone to fill a vacant position. Should you appoint a friend of yours in the company, someone you know will do a competent job, or should you follow company policies and conduct an open search? In this situation, the care ethic can be applied in several different ways. Obviously, you want your friend to prosper. Maybe you know that the friend is going through a rough period and really wants the position and needs the extra income. So the care ethic, applied in this way, seems to suggest that it is right to appoint your friend to the position. From a different perspective, however, the same care perspective can be used to justify carrying out an open search, for you have a responsibility to care for and protect the interests of other groups—the owners of the company and other employees with whom the new person will work—and an open search is the most effective way to identify the best person for the job. (That person, of course, might be your friend.) In other words, considering the four values requires careful thought and consultation with as many stakeholders as possible. It is not a simple, mechanical process.

- *Each set of values is likely to lead to a different conclusion about the correctness of a course of action.* If it is possible that thinking about any one of the four values can lead to conflicting conclusions, it is obvious that considering all four of the values is likely to lead to conflicting conclusions. For example, a course of action might seem right in addressing people's rights but wrong in addressing the interests of utility.

Let me be clear about what I think the URJC model can do and cannot do. It can increase the chances that your thinking process is as clear and logical as it can be, that it relies on the best available facts, and that it addresses the perspectives of as many stakeholders as possible. What it cannot do is provide a step-by-step method for arriving at the "right" decision about the best course of action.

Determining the Most Ethical Available Course of Action

It is difficult to determine the best solution to an ethical dilemma, but doing so is only half the job, for in an organizational context, people rarely have the luxury of reaching their own conclusions about the best course of action and simply proceeding to implement it. Most of the time, people have to receive approval from management or persuade management that their course of action is best.

But what should you do after failing to secure that approval or persuade management that a particular course of action is best? At this point, you face a new set of alternative courses of action, which can include the following:

- going along with the manager
- trying once again to persuade the manager to approve
- going over the manager's head
- consulting the company's ombudsperson or ethics officer (if there is one)
- blowing the whistle

The appropriate step to take next is to return to the URJC model, analyzing each of the reasonable alternative courses of action. This time, however, you have autonomy: if you decide that the correct action at this point is to try once again to persuade the manager to approve the desired course of action, you do just that. If you succeed, the problem is solved. If you fail, you then face a new set of alternative courses of action. Eventually, final actions are taken, and the situation is resolved. (Naturally, the resolution will seem more satisfactory to some stakeholders than to others.)

A LOOK AT TWO CASES

To help clarify the points I have been making in this chapter, I would like to look briefly at two cases: the *Challenger* disaster and the Intel Pentium chip case. I choose the *Challenger* case because it is important and well-known, and because it shows the crucial link between ethics and rhetoric in the fateful discussions that preceded the launch decision. I choose the Pentium case because it, too, is quite well known, especially among people who work with computers. In discussing these two cases, I hope to show that, of the available approaches to ethics, the URJC model applied in a discourse-ethics framework offers the clearest and most useful insights for practical decision making.

The *Challenger* Case

The *Challenger* case is useful in clarifying the different ethical approaches discussed in this book because it highlights the importance of ethics in technical communication and because the facts of the case have been so well documented in the government investigation and in a number of articles in the rhetoric and technical-communication literature. In my view, the most insightful analysis of the case is Walzer and Gross' "Positivists, Postmodernists, Aristotelians, and the *Challenger* Disaster" (1994).

Walzer and Gross (1994) describe three ways of looking at the *Challenger* disaster: positivist, postmodernist, and Aristotelian. A positivist perspective would hold that the question of whether the O-rings would function properly in abnormally low temperatures is a factual question—either they would or they wouldn't—that can be resolved by empirical investigation. Therefore, the discussions between the engineers (who favored delaying the launch) and the managers (who favored approving the launch) could be described as either poor communication (the engineers expressed their ideas ineffectively) or poor ethics (the managers understood the risk but wanted to maintain the launch schedule). By contrast, a postmodernist would study the discussions between the engineers and the managers as they reflect differing discourse communities: each group had a different organizational role that made it impossible to understand what the other group was saying. Finally, an Aristotelian would analyze the discussions between the engineers and the managers from the perspective of a search for the best available means of persuasion.

Walzer and Gross argue convincingly that the engineers made the better case by explaining the importance of O-ring integrity and clarifying why past flights were successful despite the fact that the O-rings did not function properly. By contrast, the managers, arguing essentially that the flight would not explode because previous flights did not explode, were less convincing. The disaster can be attributed to the failure of the discussants to follow their own procedures: to make the burden of proof lie with those who favor the launch. Whereas the managers should have had to make the case that the launch would be safe, the engineers found themselves in the role of making the case that the launch would not be safe. Given the overwhelming pressure to launch, they were unsuccessful.

Walzer and Gross' analysis suggests clearly that an ethical approach based on foundational values, such as the URJC model, would have illuminated the discussion and facilitated the decision-making process that night in 1986. From a rights or utilitarian perspective, the launch should have been delayed. The Kantian doctrine of treating other people as ends and not merely as means also would have supported a decision to delay, for if the engineers were correct, the lives of seven astronauts would be in danger; there could be no greater violation of rights, obviously, than placing their lives at risk. No other stakeholders had a right nearly as compelling. The utilitarian perspective also would have justified a decision to delay, for the risk to the astronauts, the shuttle program, and those hundreds of thousands of people whose economic fortunes were linked to the shuttle program outweighed the benefits of meeting the launch schedule. The care perspective, too, would have argued for a delay, because the engineers and managers had a clear responsibility to place the welfare of the astronauts above the more abstract value of meeting a launch schedule.

By contrast, postmodernism offers little useful in analyzing the *Challenger* disaster. Walzer and Gross point out the inadequacies of a postmodern analysis of the case that is based on the gulf between the different discourse communities, for there were people present in the discussion—engineer/managers—who in fact were able to understand and relate to both of the sides. In addition, Walzer and Gross clearly show that the disaster was not caused by an ability of one side to make a more convincing case than the other side. A postmodern ethicist such as Lyotard probably would say that the case is already overdetermined, for the NASA procedures—stipulating that the burden of proof be assumed by those favoring a launch—are hopelessly mired in several discredited grand narratives: the grand narrative of scientific objectivity, which falsely claims that science offers the best warrants for decision-making; the grand narrative of rational discourse, which falsely claims that people can speak objectively, transcending their social and cultural perspectives and biases; and the grand narrative of Kantian ethics, which calls for treating people as autonomous, rational beings. A less radical postmodernist, such as Dorothy Winsor (1988), sees the case as an example of the strength of the divisions between different discourse communities and our resulting inability to reach clear conclusions about the relative validity of different knowledge claims. Postmodern ethics would provide no direction on how to prevent such disasters in the future.

Interestingly, the *Challenger* case shows that the procedural rules of discourse ethics do not necessarily ensure good outcomes. From the perspective of discourse ethics, the various stakeholders were in fact represented in the launch discussions. It could be argued that an ideal communicative situation would include the astronauts themselves, but for practical reasons the astronauts themselves were not represented; they could not simultaneously prepare for the next morning's mission and participate in the launch discussion. Rather, the system is structured to make their interests primary: the burden of proof is to be borne by those favoring the launch. In short, although the communicative situation was not obviously flawed, it was unsuccessful even though the participants officially reached consensus to launch. Walzer and Gross show that the process by which the burden of proof shifted from the managers to the engineers was not overt and conscious. Perhaps because the engineers raised their concerns very late in the decision-making process, in response to the unusually cold temperatures at the launch site, they might have felt unconsciously that they, rather than the managers, had to bear the burden of proof.

Indeed, given the complexity, urgency, and importance of the launch discussion, we can conclude that its failure to prevent the launch is certainly understandable. If we accept the premise that all parties to the discussion acted in good faith and to the best of their abilities—a premise that has not been disputed, to my knowledge—the *Challenger* disaster highlights an important limitation of discourse ethics: the outcome of the discussion will reflect the quality of the discussion on that particular occasion.

The Intel Pentium Processor Case

The Intel case involves the company's mishandling of a defective product (see Williams [1997] for a discussion and analysis of the case). In late 1994, a mathematics professor discovered that the Intel chip in his personal computer produced inaccurate results when he performed a particular kind of complex calculation. Responding that the average user would encounter an error only once every 27,000 years of use, Intel offered to replace the defective chip only for those customers who could demonstrate that they were doing calculations that might cause the chip to fail. Two weeks after Intel announced this replacement policy, IBM conducted its own tests and, concluding that the flaw would occur not every 27,000 years but every 24 days, halted shipment of its computers containing the Pentium chip. Shortly thereafter, Intel instituted a no-questions-asked replacement policy.

From the perspective of rights, the Pentium case is quite straightforward: the question is whether Intel was treating its customers with respect, as people who are entering into a relationship with Intel and who deserve to be treated honestly and fairly, or merely as dollar signs. Intel's duty was clear: to admit the problem with the chip, explain that most users probably will not have a problem with it, and let customers choose from a set of options: refund, replacement, or rebate. No other stakeholder has a comparable claim to a countervailing right.

From a utilitarian perspective, the Intel case is similarly clear. Intel's failure was to look only at its own short-term interests, rather than consider the customer's viewpoint or the company's long-term interest. If the company had considered the problem from the customer's perspective, it would have concluded that customers deserved to get what they paid for (a good chip) or some other arrangement selected by the customer. Alternatively, Intel might have asked itself what course of action would lead to its own long-term best interests. With the question posed this way, the company would have realized that its most valuable asset is a reputation for honesty, fair practices, and quality, and that the most ethical course of action (and, incidentally, the smartest action) therefore would be to suffer the short-term financial consequences of fixing the problem. This approach, exemplified by Johnson & Johnson after the Tylenol poisonings in 1982, has been widely praised from the perspectives of business practice and ethics.

The justice perspective would also have supported an enlightened returns policy, for it is obviously unfair that some users receive a good chip and others receive a flawed chip, if both groups are paying the same price. The care perspective, as well, would have supported an enlightened returns policy, for Intel should have considered it a primary responsibility to care for its customers.

This case also offers interesting insights into the strengths and limitations of discourse ethics. Intel's actions obviously violated the central tenet of fairness in that the company failed to solicit the views of its customers as it considered its options, as well as failed to consider the numerous angry phone calls and e-mail. Ironically, the Intel executives *were* thinking according to the principles of discourse ethics, for they proposed an ethical returns policy from the beginning but were overruled by their CEO.

Discourse ethics would, in fact, have proved an effective tool in helping the Intel CEO consider his options. Yet discourse ethics alone is useful here in a less direct and less compelling way than the URJC model, because discourse ethics doesn't consider the Intel action directly; it doesn't say that the Intel action is unethical because it treats its customers unfairly or does more harm to the interests of the various stakeholders than another action would. Rather, discourse ethics critiques the decision-making process itself, a critique that, in this fairly simple case, is enough to highlight the flaw in Intel's thinking.

But what if the situation had been that all the Intel executives and a representative group of users agreed with the CEO? In such a case, discourse ethics would prove to be considerably less powerful than the URJC model, for a central flaw of discourse ethics is that while it advocates procedures for fair and open debate, it doesn't comment on the fairness, reasonableness, or wisdom of the people in the discussion.

Finally, a postmodern approach to the Intel case would be inconclusive, for a postmodernist would say that the case demonstrates that different parties see the situation from their own perspectives. Postmodernism offers no tools for either understanding the ethics of the case or resolving it.

I am not arguing here that only foundational values can provide an effective guide to the ethics of this case. Nor am I arguing that all ethics cases are as easy to approach as this one. However, this brief look at different approaches to the Intel case suggests that the value theories of foundational theories address the ethics of the case directly, whereas discourse ethics applied in isolation address the case indirectly, by focusing on the process of discussing the situation. The best approach, in my view, is to examine the core values or rights, justice, utility and care in the open sunlight of a discourse-ethics model.

CONCLUSION: A NOTE ON TEACHING ETHICS IN A TECHNICAL COMMUNICATION CURRICULUM

I have tried to sketch an approach to thinking about ethics that avoids the extremes of radical foundational theories, which know everything, and radical postmodern theories, which know nothing. My approach is an attempt to address the most compelling human values within a procedural context that increases the chances that all stakeholders are represented and that the discussion is conducted fairly.

A question that arises concerns our responsibilities to our students regarding ethics. Are we obliged to teach ethics? Are we competent to do so? Do we have the time to do so? If so, how should we go about it?

The answer to the question of whether we feel obliged to teach ethics appears to be yes. As I suggested in Chapter 1, all the current textbooks in technical communication address ethics, although they do so in very different ways and with varying degrees of success. And the trade books on ethics and technical communication published for practitioners in the last few years suggest, as well, that we think ethics is an important topic for the technical communicator to consider. The ethics cases published in *Intercom*, the STC magazine, also attest to the perceived importance of ethics.

Are we competent to teach ethics? This is a somewhat more difficult question. In part, I agree with Kant's statement that thoughtful adults know as much about ethics as do trained, professional philosophers. As I have tried to point out in this book, however, the technical details of ethics are extremely complex and subtle; understanding Kant, for instance, like understanding Shakespeare, is a lifelong task. What I have tried to present in Part I of this book is a general introduction to ethics. From my perspective, the material covered in a general introduction such as this is necessary for a teacher of technical communication, not because a sophomore is likely to ask the teacher to explain the major limitations of Bentham's utilitarianism, for example. Rather, studying the major writers discussed here, including Aristotle, Kant, Mill, Rawls, and Gilligan, is the best way to think clearly about what we mean when we use such terms as *rights, utility, justice,* or *care.* These words are more than just code words for the different threads of Western ethics; they are the values that make us civilized.

And let me state just once, for the record, a point that is probably fairly obvious. When I recommend that we study the thinkers described in this book, I am not suggesting that you read this book. I am recommending that you read the primary sources that I refer to. If the quotations I have presented throughout Part I of this book suggest that these thinkers rarely display the clarity and precision achieved routinely by the best technical communicators, I hope the quotations also show that these thinkers often demonstrate a wit and sometimes even a beauty of expression that technical communicators rarely have the opportunity to display on the job.

Do we have time to teach ethics? Certainly, every instructor of the basic service course in technical communication is under considerable pressure to fit more and more into the course, especially as new technologies proliferate and the kinds of communication our students do increase. But as Hall and Nelson (1987) argue, if we as instructors wish to resist the charge that we are unwittingly indoctrinating students into the corporate ethic of expediency, we had better find the time to address ethics. As Hall and Nelson state, our job "is not to abandon the study of useful rhetorical principles but to teach the responsible, ethical use of the tools and to increase our students' understanding of their responsibilities to serve the public interests" (p. 75).

On the question of how to teach ethics, there appears to be no consensus on such curricular questions as whether to require a course in ethics, integrate ethics into all courses, or do some combination of the two. Local needs and resources should dictate how to teach ethics. A standard model for an undergraduate technical communication curriculum calls for a basic ethics course (offered by every philosophy department), plus attention to ethics throughout the technical-communication courses themselves. One week of ethics instruction in the basic technical-communication course, plus references throughout the courses when the need arises, such as when discussing proposals or graphics, is common. For graduate students, a fuller treatment of ethics is appropriate; the program in which I teach requires a seminar in the ethics of technical communication. This seminar addresses general ethical theories, business ethics, and technical communication ethics. Needs vary from program to program, of course, but one point on which we all can agree, I think, is that ethics is complex and important, and that doing justice to it in our courses requires some preparation by the instructor as well as some class time.

In Part II of this book, I address some of the major ethical questions routinely faced by technical communicators. In each chapter, I discuss the ethical question, then present and critique the relevant scholarship on the question. Finally, I present a case that demonstrates the ethical question, then respond to the case.

Chapter 8 deals with the question of truthtelling in product information.

II

Issues and Cases

II

Issues and Uses

8

Truthtelling in Product Information

In his essay "Down the Slippery Slope: Ethics and the Technical Writer as Marketer," John Bryan (1992) recounts a dilemma he faced when, as a technical communicator for an architectural and engineering firm, he became the company's marketing director. Sitting down to write promotional copy for his company, Bryan noted that, for the first time in 15 years, his company was not included in the *Engineering News-Record* list of top 500 design firms. He considered three options in planning the promotional copy:

- Drop all reference to the *Engineering News-Record* list. This option was undesirable for rhetorical reasons: the list was prestigious.

- Explain that his company was dropped from the list because of economic factors that had nothing to do with its quality and ability to complete projects successfully. This option was also undesirable rhetorically because it called attention to the company's being dropped from the list.

- Write something such as, "For 14 of the last 15 years, *Engineering News-Record* has ranked us among the top 500 design firms in the nation." This option was most desirable rhetorically, but it seemed misleading because it suggested that the one year that the company did not appear on the list was in the more distant past.

In this chapter, I discuss the ethics of truthtelling in advertising and product information. At first glance, it would seem that there is little to discuss: you should tell the truth because of the Golden Rule. However, the question of truthtelling is considerably more complex than that.

One question that arises immediately is whether truthtelling in the business world is related to ethics. Some people believe that business is a game that is played according to its own rules. Sellers exaggerate about how much the product is worth, and buyers lie about how much they are willing to pay for it. At some point in the middle, the buyer and seller reach an agreement about the actual value of the product. In other words, business today is a highly automated rug bazaar.

Other people believe that although it might be desirable to bring private standards of truthtelling into the world of business, doing so would be too dangerous. If you cannot tell whether the person with whom you are dealing is honest, for your own survival you have to assume not and act accordingly.

Still others feel ethical misgivings about some of the choices they make in the workplace but, because of economic necessity, see no alternatives. If you need the job to support yourself and your dependents, sometimes you need to compromise your ethical standards. Fulfilling your other obligations is a more important value than being scrupulously honest on the job.

Even those who believe it necessary to be honest all the time when they write about their company's products probably would acknowledge that there are some valid exceptions. For instance, you are preparing to write the user documentation for your company's latest version of its spreadsheet. As you study your competitors' products, you conclude that all of them are simply better than your company's. They are easier to install and use, more powerful, less buggy, and less expensive. Does this mean that instead of beginning the manual with the company's traditional "congratulations" boilerplate you should express your regrets?

I begin with a brief explanation of why advertising ought to be considered along with other product information in this discussion of truthtelling. Next, I address—and reject—the contention that advertising is, by definition, an unethical enterprise. Then I examine a popular framework for discussing manipulation in product information, concluding that manipulation is less a matter of the truthfulness of a message than of the writer's rhetorical intent. I consider the role of audience in discussing the ethical problems inherent in a *caveat emptor* approach to product information. I argue for a limited paternalistic approach to truthtelling in product information: the writer is ethically obliged to avoid deception by providing accurate technical information that the reader could not be expected to discover. However, the writer is not obliged to provide accurate nontechnical information that the reader could be expected to discover. Finally, I present a case that dramatizes some of the issues discussed in the chapter.

RELATING ADVERTISING TO OTHER PRODUCT INFORMATION

Before I begin the discussion of the ethics of truthtelling in product information, I want to address two possible objections to including advertising in this survey:

- Ads are written by advertising copywriters, not by technical communicators.

- Ads are generically different from other product information because they are persuasive, not informative.

The first statement—that different people write the different kinds of information—is sometimes true but sometimes false. As suggested by my reference to John Bryan's article (1992) about ethical dilemmas facing the technical communicator who also writes advertising and other marketing materials, many technical communicators are what Bryan calls *boundary spanners:* people who perform more than one function in an organization. In small companies, in particular, the technical communicator is responsible for a number of communication functions that fall outside the narrow definition of technical communication. The technical communicator writes not only the standard product information—manuals and other materials published on the Web, loaded on a CD, or included in the box—but also press releases, advertising copy, and even copy that appears *on* the box.

The second statement—that ads are generically different from other product information—is more complex. A simple dichotomy between the two is that ads are argumentative (that is, meant to persuade people to buy a product or service), whereas other product information, such as manuals, is expository (supposed to be straightforward advice or instruction on how to use the product safely and effectively). After all, everyone knows that ads, by their very nature, are likely to contain exaggerated claims, misleading assertions, and even outright lies. By contrast, other sorts of product information, such as user's manuals, imperfect as they usually are, are at least honest.

This idea is, I think, false. Ultimately, it is impossible to separate advertising from other forms of product information. Although a user's manual is not an advertisement, the technical communicator is expected to make the case, however subtly, that the reader will find it easy and pleasant to use the product, and that the product will help the reader perform the intended task effectively. Often, the technical communicator is also expected to advance the idea that the manufacturer's other products are also the best on the market.

Sometimes, this mingling of advertising and instruction is easy to spot. When a flashlight manufacturer states in its instructions sheet that the user should buy the company's own brand of batteries, most users know that any brand will also work. (I'm not defending the decision to include this sort of misleading comment; I'm merely suggesting that most people disregard it because they understand that you don't need to use Eveready batteries in an Eveready flashlight.)

With more complex products, however, this sort of covert advertising can be much harder to spot. For instance, the manual that comes with Microsoft FrontPage 98 (Microsoft Corporation, 1997) instructs the user to install Microsoft's browser, Internet Explorer, also included on the FrontPage 98 CD-ROM, because it is "the recommended browser for use with FrontPage" (p. 6). This use of the word *recommended* is ethically suspect in two ways. First, Internet Explorer is not recommended; it is required. FrontPage will not install properly without it. The manufacturer does not want to state explicitly that its browser is required for its Web editor to install, but that is the case. Second, *recommended* is suspect because it suggests that, once FrontPage is installed, the Web developer should rely on Internet Explorer for testing the site. This suggestion is obviously self-serving: the Web developer should of course test the site using not only Internet Explorer, but also Netscape Navigator and any other available browsers. Microsoft's decision to describe Internet Explorer as "recommended" is a function of a corporate decision to make the FrontPage manual an advertisement for another of the manufacturer's products, a decision that, in this case at least, sacrificed clear and honest communication for the marketing function.

Because technical communicators often do write advertising copy, and because product information and advertising often intermingle, I think it is appropriate to include advertising along with other kinds of product information in this discussion of truthtelling.

IS ALL ADVERTISING UNETHICAL?

A discussion of truthtelling in advertising and other product information is based on the premise that some practices in these kinds of communication are ethical and some are not. Otherwise, there would be no point in examining the question in the first place.

However, this premise is not universally shared. Throughout our century, numerous commentators have argued that all advertising is, by nature, unethical. The common criticisms of advertising are these seven:

- *Advertising encourages monopolistic conditions by stifling competition.* Big companies can afford to buy more ads than small companies can; the rich get richer and the poor get poorer. The result is that consumers have fewer options when they want to purchase a product.

- *Advertising is a wasteful industry.* Manufacturers spend hundreds of billions of dollars a year—which we as consumers pay for—trying to get us to buy one brand rather than another. Without the ads, we would still buy all those different brands anyway.

- *Advertising promotes mindless consumerism.* John Kenneth Galbraith, in *The Affluent Society* (1958), argued that ads do not merely respond to people's desires for products. Ads actually create the desires in the first place. Consumers are therefore being manipulated by large ad companies and manufacturers.

- *Advertising encourages the use of dangerous products such as tobacco and alcohol.* Some of the biggest advertisers are makers of products that are known to cause terrible health problems.

- *Advertising glorifies sex, violence, and stereotypes, manipulating people by playing on their fears and insecurities.* It is wrong to suggest that people who buy a particular toothpaste or a particular beer thereby become attractive and popular.

- *Advertising often includes misleading or false statements.* By definition, such advertising is unethical.

- *Advertising degrades the use of the language.* Although some ads use language cleverly, it is not only the pedantic English teacher who finds "Just do it" to be intellectually unsatisfying. Ads not only coarsen and degrade the language; they also erode our ability to think clearly and deeply by filling our minds with illogical nonsense.

Although the typical person instinctively agrees with at least several of these ideas, every one of them is controversial. Defenders of advertising respond that ads are an integral component of the free-market system, enabling people to learn about new products and make informed choices. A company can make a terrific product, but if the public doesn't hear about it, it will fail, thus depriving people of its benefits. Certainly, people pay the cost of the ads, but obviously it is a cost they are willing to pay; otherwise, advertised products would not sell, and manufacturers would stop advertising. If ads encourage the use of dangerous products and appeal to people's desire for social acceptance and status, people must want those products and crave social acceptance and status. To argue that advertising money would be better spent on solving some of our nation's "important" problems misses the point: people have a right to spend their money as they desire, even on beer, cigarettes, and bright red sports cars. To try to prevent people from doing as they wish is unethical because it violates their autonomy.

On the question of ads that mislead and lie, government agencies such as the Federal Trade Commission and the Food and Drug Administration are charged with the responsibility of weeding out dishonest claims in ads. The question of whether advertising degrades our language is complex in two ways. First, many people would argue that the question concerns aesthetics, not ethics. No adult is misled by the puffery ("Nothing rides like a Buick") and the meaningless blather ("Coke is it") anyway. Second, it is not possible to determine causality in the relationship between coarse ads and coarse use of language. In some cases, ads create and popularize dumb catch phrases; in other cases, the advertising copywriter merely picked up dumb phrases that people were already using.

Obviously, I am not attempting a thorough discussion of the question of whether advertising is essentially unethical. The economic questions that need to be addressed in such a discussion are the subject of book-length studies, and there appears to be no clear consensus even on the facts relating advertising expenditures and sales figures. And the questions about language use are not the kind that empirical research can answer easily.

For these reasons, I agree with the consensus of the major business ethicists (see, for example, Beauchamp & Bowie [1993], Boatright [2000], and Velasquez [1998]) that there is no compelling reason to conclude that advertising is inherently unethical. Rather, advertising, like any other form of communication, is subject to abuses. The most constructive approach to discussing the ethics of advertising and other forms of product information is to identify and address the abuses rather than the enterprise itself.

PERSUASION, MANIPULATION, AND COERCION

One way to clarify the discussion of the ethics of advertising and other product information is to look at the effect of the information on the reader's ability to make informed, autonomous decisions. Business ethicist Tom L. Beauchamp (1993) has described a continuum for measuring the extent of the influence of information. At one end of the continuum, the reader has complete control over his or her decision-making powers. At the other end, the reader has no control. Beauchamp plots three points on his continuum: *persuasion, manipulation,* and *coercion.*

The most desirable form of influence is persuasion, which Beauchamp defines as "a deliberate and successful attempt by one person to encourage another to freely accept beliefs, attitudes, and values, or actions through appeals to reason" (1993, p. 476). An honest, clear business proposal would be an example of effective persuasive writing because it presents good reasons for its readers to accept the writer's view of reality and proposed plan of action. After reading the proposal, readers believe that the writer has gathered the appropriate information, analyzed it logically, and presented a plan of action that would have a good chance of proving useful for the reader.

Along with the obvious objection that the proposal can *seem* to be clear and honest and therefore in fact be persuasive even though it is unclear and dishonest, there is another complication in discussing persuasion. In my view, Beauchamp's discussion of good reasons confuses logic and epistemology. In terms of logic, *good reasons* refers to the validity of the argument. Certainly, most people would agree that a good reason to buy a particular basketball shoe, for example, would be that it incorporates a new design that reduces the chance of injury and improves athletic performance. If an independent authority—a reputable association of foot doctors, for instance—reported these benefits of the shoe, that would be powerful evidence that the shoe is in fact better than others.

But is it a good reason to buy that shoe if the only feature that distinguishes it from other similar shoes is that a famous basketball player endorses it? Most parents would say no, but many teenagers would say yes, even though they are fully aware of how product endorsements work. Even if the star athlete made no contribution at all to the design or style of the shoe, the teenager is steadfast in asserting that the parent doesn't have to understand; the parent merely has to accept that it's a good reason (or a *good enough* reason) to the teenager. (The clever teenager then expands the discussion of good reasons by asking how many times the parent has taken the $40,000 sport utility vehicle off road.)

My point is that the idea that persuasion is based on *good reasons*, in the sense of valid argumentation, is itself complex, because, in the real world, the best definition of *good reasons* is "those reasons that I agree with."

The essential characteristic of persuasion as a means of influence is not that the argument is logically valid but that the reader or listener has full access to honest, clear information. In other words, the key concept is epistemology, not logic. You might think your child is crazy for wanting you to give the basketball star $10 (which he surely needs less than you do) when you buy the shoes, but if you decide to make the purchase you are in fact responding to persuasion. Even though you are unhappy about making the purchase, you are not being manipulated by the information from the shoe company. (Rather, you are being manipulated the way all parents are: by their children.)

At the other end of Beauchamp's continuum of influence is coercion, which he defines as the process of "deliberately using force or a credible threat of unwanted, avoidable, and serious harm in order to compel a particular response from another person" (1993, p. 476). In coercion, the reader has lost all decision-making control, and the presence or absence of information is actually irrelevant. Coercion is extremely rare in product information; Beauchamp offers the example of a company that was prosecuted for advertising to a starving population that it would offer food and medical care in exchange for blood.

Far more prevalent than coercion is the middle category on the continuum: manipulation. Beauchamp defines manipulation as "an attempt to induce one to believe what is not correct, unsound, or not backed by good reasons" (1993, p. 478). Product information and ads can manipulate by misrepresenting a product, such as by claiming that it can perform tasks that in fact it cannot, by failing to mention its limitations, by suggesting that it is being offered at a reduced price when it isn't, and by using numerous other tactics that we are all familiar with as consumers.

One complication in discussing manipulation is that it is tempting to equate deception with making false statements. Although it is true that the two often do go together, they are not the same. To say that a statement is true or false is to make a claim about the world. The statement "Tire X is rated for 40,000 miles" may be true or false, depending on whether the tire has met federal guidelines for mileage. To say that a statement is deceptive, however, is to describe the speaker's intent. If an ad from a tire store says that Tire X is rated for 40,000 miles, but it is in fact rated for only 20,000 miles, the statement in the ad is false, but it is not deceptive unless the person who wrote the statement knew that it was false and was intending to make the tire seem like a better value than it actually is.

Product information is full of false statements that are not deceptive and true statements that are. The puffery in ads—the figures of speech meant to create impressions of power, sexuality, and luxury—are usually false; that is, they are not empirically verifiable statements about the world. (See Ivan L. Preston's *The Great American Blow-Up: Puffery in Advertising and Selling* [1975], the classic study of advertising and language.) For instance, to say that Budweiser is the "king of beers" is literally a false statement; there was no coronation ceremony. Yet the statement is not deceptive, for it is not intended to fool readers into thinking that Budweiser literally won some sort of contest among all beers and was awarded the title "king of beers."

By contrast, the Federal Trade Commission ruled in 1973 that Anacin's claim that it has "a unique pain-killing formula that is superior to all other nonprescription analgesics" was true but deceptive. The claim was true in that Anacin contains aspirin, which is a unique pain-killing formula that is superior to all other nonprescription analgesics. However, it is deceptive in that it strongly implies that only Anacin contains this unique formula, whereas in fact many other products contain exactly the same ingredients. (See Boatright [2000] for a discussion of the Anacin case.)

Beauchamp's continuum of influence has been criticized for oversimplifying the subject. Ethicist R. M. Hare (1984), for instance, argues that the use of the continuum wrongly suggests that a statement is ethical to the extent that it approaches the persuasion side and unethical to the extent that it approaches the coercion side. Hare writes that Beauchamp's continuum distracts us from the real point.

We want to know when, and for what purposes, and by what means, advertisers are justified in trying to get us to do things; and the important point here is not going to be where their acts of control lie on the continuum of influence, but whether they are doing it on wrong occasions, or for wrong purposes, or by wrong means. (p. 24)

In other words, communication in product information is rhetorical. It involves a writer, a message, an audience, and a complex set of surrounding circumstances. Information is deceptive if the message is intentionally crafted in such a way that it tends to encourage the audience in those circumstances to reach false conclusions about the subject.

In discussing persuasion and manipulation, I have focused on the writer's intent and on the message itself. However, a rhetorical approach to an ethical analysis of product information requires that audience also be considered. Legally, audience characteristics are important. For instance, federal government agencies established to protect consumers pay particular attention to the profile of the intended audience of any product information. If that audience consists largely of children or of others who might be assumed to be less skilled than the average adult in understanding product information, the standards of clarity and accuracy to which the writer is held are made more rigorous. For example, when messages intended for children (such as television commercials for toys) are brought before the Federal Trade Commission, the commission tends to rule conservatively. This principle is in accord with common sense and with basic ethical thinking, which sees children as less autonomous than adults. (I discuss this concept in more detail in Chapter 9.)

CAVEAT EMPTOR

In discussing the ethics of product information, ethicists have always considered the role of audience. The question is posed this way: What is the proper relationship between the writer (or speaker) of product information and the reader or listener? How much vigilance should the reader or listener be expected to exercise? In all rhetorical acts, the roles of the writer and the reader are intertwined, but in the case of product information, the relationship between the writer and the reader is especially sensitive. The writer feels an implicit (or perhaps even explicit) pressure to make the product seem to be an excellent value by emphasizing its strengths and deemphasizing (or hiding) its weaknesses; the reader, who is considering purchasing the product or who has already bought it, wants to know exactly what the product can and cannot do. The last thing the reader wants is a sales pitch or a covert ad for other products sold by the company.

Traditionally, the proper writer–reader dynamic was thought to be *caveat emptor:* let the buyer beware. The writer was under no responsibility to provide clear and honest information to the reader. It was the reader's responsibility to examine the product and its accompanying information and determine the true value of the product. A model of *caveat emptor* is horse trading. The seller is expected to exaggerate and lie about how good the horse is; the buyer is expected to look the horse over carefully and figure out for himself whether the horse is a good value.

The most widely known defense of *caveat emptor* is Albert Z. Carr's essay, "Is Business Bluffing Ethical?" (1993), originally published in 1968 in the *Harvard Business Review*. Carr argued that business is like a poker game. It has a fixed set of rules, established by the government, which the businessperson is obliged to follow. But the businessperson is not obliged to tell the truth at all times in dealing with suppliers, competitors, and customers. As Carr explains,

To be a winner, a man must play to win. This does not mean that he must be ruthless, cruel, harsh, or treacherous. On the contrary, the better his reputation for integrity, honesty, and decency, the better his chances of victory will be in the long run. But from time to time every businessman, like every poker player, is offered a choice between certain loss or bluffing within the legal rules of the game. If he is not resigned to losing, if he wants to rise in his company and industry, then in such a crisis he will bluff—and bluff hard. (p. 454)

The answer to the question Carr posed in the title of his essay—Is business bluffing ethical?—was an emphatic, Machiavellian yes.

In the last three decades, however, *caveat emptor* has come under attack. The consumer movement was born in the 1960s in response to widely discussed books such as Ralph Nader's *Unsafe at Any Speed* (1965) and Rachel Carson's *Silent Spring* (1962). Nader argued that the American automobile manufacturers in general, and General Motors in particular, knowingly sold unsafe cars. Carson argued that the pesticide industry was polluting the environment, thereby harming the ecosystem and endangering people. In 1962, President Kennedy proclaimed a "consumer's bill of rights," which included the idea that the public has a right to safety and to be informed. The federal government subsequently enacted a number of laws to protect these rights: the Fair Packaging and Labeling Act (1966), the Truth-in-Lending Act (1968), the Child Protection and Toy Safety Act (1969), the Consumer Product Safety Act (1972), and the Magnuson-Moss Warranty Act (1975). (See Boatright [2000] for a discussion of the consumer movement.)

The consumer movement is based on the premise that *caveat emptor* no longer makes sense. A consumer cannot be expected to be the knowledgeable buyer who can see through the exaggerations or lies of the seller. Whereas a prospective buyer of a horse might indeed be able to study the horse and learn much about its condition, the typical consumer who wishes to buy a computer or an automobile is much less qualified to see the truth beneath the claims; the products are simply too complex.

Defenders of *caveat emptor* assert that the marketplace solves this problem: if you want accurate information, buy it. Read magazines published by independent organizations, such as Consumers Union; study trade magazines, such as *PC Week* or *Car and Driver*, which report on benchmark tests. The recent growth in popularity of third-party software manuals suggests that, regardless of whether we approve of *caveat emptor*, we are resigned to living with it in some aspects of our lives; most of us have learned that if we want high-quality information about a complicated piece of software we have just bought, a third-party reference manual will likely be more satisfactory than the manufacturer's own documentation.

Still, the fact that some consumers can protect themselves from being victimized does not justify *caveat emptor*. For one thing, less capable or less vigilant people continue to be victimized. For another, vigilance is expensive. *Caveat emptor* introduces into the exchange what economists call *disutility*. That is, the careful consumer has to spend time and money to avoid being taken advantage of, time and money that could have been spent more productively.

THE ETHICAL OBLIGATION TO PROVIDE CLEAR, ACCURATE INFORMATION

If unlimited *caveat emptor* describes an unsatisfactory relationship between the writer and the reader, precisely what relationship would be more satisfactory? The opposite pole, paternalism, is similarly unsatisfactory. Paternalism occurs, according to Ebejer and Morden,

when an individual, presumably in a position of superior knowledge, makes a decision for another person to protect this other from some type of harm. Paternalism implies that the first person deprives the second of liberty of autonomy. This infraction on liberty is thought justified because, in the mind of the first person, it is "for his own good." (1993, p. 473)

The model of paternalism used to be the doctor–patient relationship. The patient expected the doctor to know what is best for the patient. If the doctor recommended that the patient undergo a certain procedure, the patient usually did so. Even in medicine, however, this unlimited paternalism is out of favor. The physician is a service provider, not a father figure. Patients get second and third opinions, then decide how to proceed.

In some situations, paternalism survives. Medical ethicists, for example, still debate whether it is always, sometimes, or never appropriate to give a terminally ill patient an accurate prognosis. As Sissela Bok (1978) points out, however, arguments in favor of well-meant lies "are made by the liar but never by those lied to" (p. 13).

More appropriate as a principle is a kind of limited paternalism. In explaining this concept, Ebejer and Morden (1993) use an example of a driver who thinks her car needs a new exhaust system. She goes to a muffler shop and tells the technician that she is willing to spend the money to have the system replaced. The muffler technician examines the car and concludes that the problem is minor: the tailpipe has a hole in it and needs to be replaced, but the rest of the exhaust system is fine. The technician has three choices:

- The *caveat emptor* response. Replace the whole system, an expensive job.
- The paternalistic response. Refuse to replace the whole system, offering instead to replace only the damaged tailpipe.
- The limited paternalistic response. Explain the situation honestly and let the driver decide whether to replace the whole system or just the tail-pipe.

Ebejer and Morden argue that the limited paternalistic response is ethically best, because it gives the driver the most autonomy. She can decide to do the inexpensive repair, which is all that is necessary, or replace the whole exhaust system, if for some reason she wishes to. In addition, if she doesn't trust the technician's diagnosis, she can go to another muffler shop.

For any sort of exchange to be ethical, the two participants must understand what they are giving and what they are getting. But that does not mean that the seller is obliged to communicate all information to the buyer. Rather, it is the seller's responsibility to analyze the buyer and determine what information he or she would want to know and is entitled to know. Obviously, this is not a robust theoretical principle but rather a rough guideline.

A few examples from Holley (1993) clarify this viewpoint. A car dealer buys a dozen inexpensive cars that were in a flood in another part of the country. Is he ethically obliged to inform the prospective buyer that the cars were in a flood (and, implicitly, to price them accordingly)? Of course, for the buyer would want to know the history of the car and is entitled to know.

A real-estate agent is showing a house to a buyer. The reason the seller wants to move is that the neighbors have loud parties, and there has been some minor vandalism by local children. Is the agent ethically obliged to inform the buyers? Holley says no, even though most buyers would indeed want to know these facts. Holley explains that "in most cases failing to know these facts would not be of crucial importance" (1993, p. 467). The facts are "borderline information," for although buy-ers want everything about their new homes to be perfect, they can pursue remedies to decrease the problems of the loud neighbors and the minor vandalism. However, Holley points out, if the buyer had earlier told the agent that it is very important to him that the neighborhood be quiet and peaceful, then the facts would be "more central" to the buyer's decision. The agent would be ethically obliged to inform the buyer truthfully about the neighborhood problems.

Ebejer and Morden (1993) add another perspective on the ethical obligation to provide information by retaining an important feature of *caveat emptor*. They argue that the seller is obliged only to provide accurate technical information that the buyer cannot be expected to know. The seller is not obliged to provide negative information that the typical buyer can be expected to determine or figure out. For instance, a buyer in a stereo store wants to purchase a system that costs $500. The salesperson has answered all the buyer's technical questions accurately and has determined that the system will in fact meet the buyer's needs. The buyer asks the salesperson if there is anything else he should know about the product. Is the salesperson ethically obliged to mention that the exact same stereo system is on sale at a store across the street for $400? No, that knowledge is freely available to the careful shopper.

Even though Ebejer and Morden's argument seems reasonable, something seems wrong. Ethicist William Shaw (1993) writes,

Most advertisers would be shocked at the suggestion that honesty requires an objective presentation of the pros and cons of their products, and in fact consumers don't expect advertisers or salespersons to be impartial. Nevertheless, it is not clear why this moral value should not be relevant to assessing advertising. (p. 363)

Shaw's idea, more wistful than practical, brings us back to an important point: a purely ethical analysis of the responsibility to provide honest and accurate product information would call for a thorough rethinking of how humans carry out all exchanges (and perhaps considerable tinkering with our DNA). Were we to treat ourselves and others as ends and not merely as means, as Kant dictates, or were we to act in such a way that maximizes the benefits to all affected parties, as Mill recommends, we would eliminate all deceptiveness from our product information, and we would stop concealing negative information. Shaw (1993) points out that many sellers do indeed come very close to meeting this ethical ideal, "at least when they are fortunate enough to sell a genuinely good and competitive product or when they do not work on commission" (p. 363).

CASE AND ANALYSIS

The following fictional case is intended to dramatize some of the major issues discussed in this chapter. Following the case is my analysis of it.

Case

Rhonda Winters is the manager of the Technical Publications department at Millennium Visions, Inc., a manufacturer of communications software. One of Millennium's major products is Electron, a sophisticated e-mail program that retails for about $50. In the Technical Publications department are two other writers and a graphics specialist.

One of the writers, Ed Reed, forwards to Rhonda Winters an e-mail from Customer Support. In the last couple of days, Customer Support reports, the company has received over 20 phone calls from customers who are worried about a new virus, called Achilles, that is said to be circulating by e-mail on the Internet. Achilles is rumored to be a kind of time bomb: twenty days after it is received and opened, it will erase all the files on any disk on which it is stored. Customer Support wants to know whether the department has heard of it, whether the rumors about it are true, whether Electron is vulnerable to Achilles, and what Customer Support should say to customers who call.

In the past, the Technical Publications department has not responded to reports about viruses, and there have in fact been no reports of any virus that affects Electron or that are circulated through Electron.

Rhonda Winters calls a meeting with Ed Reed and the other writer, Alicia Martinez, to discuss the problem. At the meeting, the department reaches a consensus that the appropriate first step is to try to learn as much as possible about the virus. Since Electron is an important product with more than 10,000 current customers, Rhonda authorizes Ed and Alicia to drop what they are doing and work with her to learn the facts about the virus. The department is about a week away from finishing the documentation for the new version of Electron, which will ship in less than a month. Rhonda agrees to meet later that day to pool the department's information and try to decide how to respond to the problem. Rhonda sends an e-mail to the Customer Support person who alerted her to the potential problem, advising him of her plans and promising to get back to him as soon as she can.

When Rhonda meets with her group later that day, she learns the following:

- Several reputable sites on the Internet that monitor viruses indicate that there have been a number of reports that Achilles does indeed exist and that it does erase disks. However, two of these virus-watch sites caution that such reports can be fraudulent, publicized by the person who made up the rumor in the first place. Every month there is a report about a virus that is spread by e-mail. There are no confirmed reports about Achilles from respected sources, and none of the other manufacturers of e-mail software report anything about the virus on their sites.

- None of the company's software engineers have heard of Achilles. It is technically possible, they say, that such a virus could exist, and there is no way to tell whether Electron would stop it. "My guess," one of the software engineers said, "is that it would infect Electron, just as it would any e-mail software."

- The Legal department reports that the disclaimer that accompanies Electron protects the company from liability even if the rumors turn out to be true.

Rhonda starts to talk over their options with her writers.

Alicia argues for doing nothing. "Look, there are reports of hundreds of new viruses every month, and most of them turn out to be hoaxes. Besides, if Legal says we're okay with liability, we don't have to do anything now. Let's just wait and see if we get some confirmed reports. In the meantime, tell Customer Support to tell anyone who calls that we're investigating it."

"I don't know, Alicia," Ed responds. "If we do nothing and this virus turns out to be real, we're going to look pretty bad if it hits a lot of our customers. Especially if we could have done something to help them out. And it could happen just when we're rolling out the new version."

Alicia replies, "But if you publicize it now and it turns out to be another hoax, we look like fools, and that could hurt our sales of the new version."

Rhonda wants to talk a little bit about how they could publicize it. "What are our options for getting the word out?" she asks.

"Well," Ed responds, "we could put it on Millennium's site. That wouldn't cost anything. Or we could contact customers individually."

"That would cost over fifty cents each, for a service bulletin mailing. A lot cheaper than that for e-mail. Just the cost of compiling the mailing list from the database, maybe a few hundred dollars."

"Yeah, but how thorough is that going to be?" Alicia asks.

"What is the return rate on the registration cards for Electron?" Ed adds.

"It's pretty low," Rhonda responds. "A little less than 20 percent, I think."

"And what do we say, anyway?" Alicia asks. "You might want to back up your hard disk? Or you might want to save your e-mail on a floppy? How effective is that going to be? Most people don't back up anyway, unless it's automatic. I say, let's just keep our eye on the virus-watch sites on the Net and if this Electron turns out to be real, then we do something."

What should Rhonda do?

Analysis

This is going to be a difficult decision to make. Rhonda does not now have—and she might never get—accurate information about whether the virus exists and, if it does, whether it would affect her customers. In addition, she couldn't alert all her customers; most customers have no reason to visit the company site, and she lacks contact information for most of them.

It is of little comfort that the company might not be liable for incidental damages if the virus is real. Rhonda wants to treat them as well as she can, because it's the right thing to do and because she wants to keep them as satisfied customers. The question is whether the best course of action is to do something now or wait until she understands the problem better.

The advantage of taking action now is that if the virus is real, Rhonda could prevent serious problems for at least some of her customers. However, if she sounds the alarm now and the virus is a hoax or wouldn't affect her customers, she will have wasted money and encouraged customers to waste time planning for a nonexistent threat.

If Rhonda waits until the situation becomes more clear, she will probably avoid the expense and embarrassment of having sounded a false alarm. But if the threat is real, the alarm might be too late.

From my perspective, the most ethical course of action is for Rhonda to make a reasonable attempt to tell her customers what she knows about the problem. First, she should craft a clear, honest message for the Web site, summarizing what she knows about the virus and what she recommends: being sure you back up your disk frequently or reconfigure your e-mail so that it is saved on a floppy disk and not on your hard drive. She should end the message by stating that she will update it as soon as she learns anything new.

In addition, she should e-mail those customers for whom she has contact information, including the same message she put on the company's Web site and recommending that they visit the site frequently for updates. The e-mail would be inexpensive to send, and it could go out in less than a day. Finally, she should post messages to the electronic discussion groups that her customers are likely to subscribe to or visit.

On the question of looking foolish for sounding a false alarm, in my view honesty is the best course of action, from both an ethical and business perspective.

If Rhonda tells the truth about the threat, she is enabling customers to make up their own minds about how, or whether, to respond. She is treating them as people, not merely as customers whom she doesn't want to anger. And she lets them determine the utility of taking action. If they wish to go to the trouble of preparing for the threat, they will do so; if they don't, they won't. They will carry out their own utilitarian analysis of costs and benefits. This course of action is also in accord with the care perspective: she is caring for her customers by giving them the information they need on which to base their own decisions on how to proceed.

From a business perspective, if I were a customer I would appreciate any efforts the company has made to keep me informed. I would consider its vigilance to be a sign of respect for me, not a sign of irresponsible panic.

9

Liability and the Duty to Instruct and Warn

In 1998, 92,200 people died of fatal injuries, and 19.4 million people received disabling injuries. Medical expenses, property damages, and other costs related to these injuries totaled $480.5 billion (National Safety Council, 1999). Every year in the United States, some 35,000 legal opinions are written (Strate & Swerdlow, 1987), and manufacturers pay more than $100 billion to plaintiffs and their attorneys (Huber & Litan, 1991).

How do these statistics relate to the technical communicator? The relationship is clear and important. In the past three decades, legal precedent has established that manufacturers are liable for injuries suffered by customers when a product is found to be defective. And courts routinely rule that one of the main causes for considering a product defective is that the information that accompanies the product—instruction sheets and manuals, as well as warnings and other safety information affixed to the product—is missing, incomplete, misleading, or difficult to read or understand. Courts today see technical communication as a crucial link between the manufacturer and the consumer; the communicator is the agent responsible for ensuring that the consumer can acquire a full and accurate understanding of the dangers involved in using a product.

Providing this full and accurate understanding is a legal obligation of the manufacturer. In addition, it is clearly an ethical obligation, whether the question is approached from a perspective of rights, utility, justice, or care.

However, this is not to say that the question of the manufacturer's duty to warn the customer is simple. Modern trends in liability law are highly controversial. Whereas at first glance it might seem obvious that companies should be held responsible for injuries caused by use of their products, critics have raised serious questions about the effectiveness and fairness of modern approaches to liability. And these questions are not likely to be resolved soon.

In this chapter, I review the evolving law of product liability, focusing on the role of the technical communicator in preventing injury. Then, I present practical guidelines for the technical communicator to follow to reduce both the incidence and severity of injuries and the manufacturer's vulnerability to product-liability suits. Finally, I offer a case that dramatizes some of the issues discussed in the chapter.

THE EVOLVING LEGAL ATTITUDE TOWARD LIABILITY

Traditionally, three forces work to improve the safety of the hundreds of thousands of products manufactured and used in our culture.

First is the market system itself. Manufacturers react to market forces by including as much safety as the public seems to want. If an automobile manufacturer believes that customers are willing to pay more for safety features such as side air bags, it will offer them, and it will advertise the feature.

Second is the system of governmental regulatory agencies. The Consumer Product Safety Commission, for example, created by federal legislation in 1972, is a five-person organization charged with evaluating product safety, drafting standards, collecting data, performing research, and coordinating local, state, and federal product-safety regulations concerning more than 10,000 consumer products. The commission is empowered to issue product recalls, issue public warnings, and require manufacturers to issue refunds. (See Shaw [1993] for a discussion of the role and effectiveness of regulatory agencies.)

Third is the legal system. Although there is some statutory law (laws created by legislatures) that affects liability law, most of the relevant rulings derive from case law (decisions handed down in court cases). The realm of civil law that most concerns the technical communicator is *tort liability,* the field of law that governs injuries and damages between two parties who are not contractually bound to each other. For instance, tort liability covers cases in which two cars collide or a person is hurt while using a woodworking tool. Tort liability cases can involve individuals, companies, and government agencies. Although most tort cases are settled before they go to trial, case law sets the precedents that influence how plaintiffs and defendants settle their grievances.

Because tort law is primarily case law rather than statutory law, it is especially vulnerable to shifting trends in judicial ruling. In the 20th century, United States courts have taken three fairly distinct approaches in handling liability cases: the contract approach, the due-care approach, and the strict-liability approach. In the sections that follow, I discuss each approach, focusing on the ethical principles underlying them and the practical implications for technical communicators.

In general, my presentation follows the chronology of prevailing legal opinion; the contract approach held sway until early in the 20th century, the due-care approach in the first half of the century, and strict liability today. However, in different municipalities and states, elements of all three approaches still intermingle. Therefore, technical communicators need a basic understanding of all three approaches.

The Contract Approach

Traditionally, the obligation of the seller to the buyer was thought to be defined by the contract that accompanied the sale. The contract stipulated the rights and responsibilities of both parties.

Any claims or warranties about product performance made in the language of the contract are said to be *express* claims or warranties. If, for instance, the product instructions say that the product is warranted to be free of manufacturing defects for five years, that warranty is legally binding, and a person who buys a product that does not live up to that express warranty can seek legal redress. In addition, the seller is legally obliged to fulfill any *implied* claims or warranties. An implied claim or warranty can be an oral statement made to the buyer by the seller that the product will perform a specified task or will have certain characteristics. A claim can also be implied in the language or visuals of product information. If, for example, a photograph in an instruction manual for a weedwacker shows a child operating the device, the manufacturer is implying (knowingly or unknowingly) that the device can be operated safely by children.

Velasquez (1998) summarizes the four main principles inherent in the contract approach to the relationship between the buyer and the seller:

- *The seller must comply with the terms of the sales contract.* The Uniform Commercial Code, which governs business transactions, defines express and implied claims and warranties and stipulates that, for legal purposes, they are part of the sales contract. The product must be effective; that is, the buyer must be able to carry out the tasks for which the product was manufactured. The product must have at least the service life stated or implied in the contract; that is, it must last at least as long as the warranty stipulates. The product must be able to be maintained for that service life, a requirement that means that the manufacturer must continue to make parts and materials available for that period. And the product must be safe to operate. What is *safe?* Safety is a question of *acceptable, reasonable risk.* As explained, for example, by the National Commission on Product Safety in 1976, "Risk of bodily harm to users are [*sic*] not unreasonable when consumers understand that risks exist, can appraise their probability and severity, know how to cope with them, and voluntarily accept them to get benefits they could not obtain in less risky ways" (qtd. in Velasquez, 1998, p. 329). Safety is also measured according to the concept called *state of the art,* which refers to the level of engineering and scientific expertise and common practice in effect when the product was made. For instance, a gas-powered lawnmower produced in 1965 does not have a kill switch, a device that stops the blade from turning when the operator lets go of the handle. That technology was not used in lawnmowers at that time. But after it was introduced in the 1980s, it became state of the art. After that time, a lawnmower sold without it would not be considered state of the art.

- *The seller must disclose the nature of the product.* The seller is more knowledgeable than the buyer about the strengths and weaknesses of the product. Therefore, the seller is obliged to explain, orally and in writing, the functions the product can and cannot do, as well as the dangers of using it.

- *The seller must avoid misrepresenting the product.* As discussed in Chapter 8, a fundamental principle of free transactions is that the seller must not misrepresent the product. If a software program has a bug that makes it incapable of performing a function that the consumer might reasonably assume (on the basis of the product information) it can perform, the seller must state this fact clearly.

- *The seller must avoid the use of duress and undue influence.* In describing the product, the seller must refrain from inappropriately appealing to the buyer's fears, immaturity, ignorance, or any other characteristics that would hinder the buyer's ability to decide freely whether to purchase the product. The classic example of coercion is the unscrupulous funeral director who plays on the buyer's grief. Another example would be an unscrupulous car dealer who persuades a young driver to buy a powerful sports car by playing on his insecurities.

Notice two points about these principles.

First, all of them are based on a simple ethical principle: a business transaction is fair only if the buyer is provided honest, comprehensive information about the product. From a Kantian rights perspective, this principle derives from the obligation to treat people not merely as things but as autonomous beings. From a utilitarian perspective, this principle derives from the idea that everyone benefits from an honest system of free enterprise, a system that specifies the buyer's rights.

Second, these principles are all about technical communication. Most of the focus is on the sales contract itself, but the seller is obliged as well to fulfill any oral claims or warranties made to the buyer.

The contract approach to the relationship between the buyer and the seller is appealing because it appears to ensure a fair transaction. If the seller provides accurate, comprehensive, clear information about the product—warts and all—the buyer has an opportunity to make a free, informed decision about whether to purchase the product and (if he or she decides to) how to use it effectively and safely. The contract approach appears to fulfill the goals stipulated by ethicists—and by writers of technical-communication texts. If the seller violates any express or implied claims or warranties and the buyer is injured or suffers a loss, the buyer can bring a charge of negligence. If the buyer is injured as a result of violating any of the terms of the contract, the seller is protected legally because the buyer is negligent. What could be fairer?

In fact, the contract approach has been criticized on three major bases:

- *Buyers can rarely achieve a comprehensive understanding of the product.* Despite the best efforts of a seller, a buyer rarely has the expertise or the time to examine the product thoroughly. In addition, we are perhaps asking more than human nature affords when we assume that the seller will do a perfect job explaining the deficiencies of the product.

- *Sellers can disclaim any responsibilities.* The Uniform Commercial Code explicitly permits the seller to disclaim responsibility for all implied claims or warranties. The "As Is" printed on the window sticker of a used car is an example of this tactic. In most industries, disclaimers are printed in small type. Few people who rent an apartment or buy a house wade through all the small print in the contracts. In the software industry, many products contain explicit statements that the manufacturer does not warrant that the product will perform as specified in the product information, and that the manufacturer disclaims responsibility for any incidental damages caused by the use of the software. Although such disclaimers do not necessarily hold up in court (as discussed in Chapter 11), they can severely limit the buyer's legal options.

- *A contract is too simple an instrument for modern transactions.* A traditional contract operates according to a legal principle known as *privity,* which states that the contract applies only to the two parties that signed the contract. Therefore, if you buy a Ford from Midtown Ford and the car is defective, you can seek redress only from that dealership, not from Ford Motor Company. Today, of course, there might be five or six companies that "own" the product as it makes its way to the buyer from the manufacturer through different wholesalers and retailers.

These problems led the courts to turn away from the contract approach to liability. In the 1916 case *MacPherson v. Buick Motor Car,* a driver was injured when a wheel fell off his Buick. The carmaker held that it bore no responsibility for the injury because the plaintiff had a contractual relationship only with the car dealership, not with Buick itself. The New York Court of Appeals found for the plaintiff, arguing that MacPherson had every right to expect that the Buick would be safe to drive under normal conditions, that he would have no way of inspecting the car and discovering that a wheel would fall off, and, therefore, even though MacPherson had no contractual relationship with Buick, the carmaker was legally liable for the defect in its product. As explained by Shaw (1993), the MacPherson case marked a turning point in legal thinking, beginning the era of the due-care approach to product liability.

The Due-Care Approach

The due-care approach to liability acknowledges that the party that writes the contract usually gets the better deal. Whereas the contract approach suggested that the buyer can protect his or her interests by reading the contract carefully and refusing to sign until it is satisfactory, the due-care approach is based on the idea that reality is not usually that simple. Often, the buyer does not have the time and the technical and legal expertise to negotiate a fair contract with the seller. The due-care approach offers more protection to the buyer by requiring the seller not only to live up to the express and implied claims in the contract but also to exercise due care in preventing injuries—even if the seller has disclaimed responsibility and the buyer has agreed to the contract. For this reason, Manuel Velasquez (1998, p. 334) calls due care a weak version of *caveat vendor:* "let the seller beware."

The manufacturer, however, is not responsible for every injury. The word *due* in the phrase *due care* means "appropriate." The manufacturer is responsible for making every reasonable effort to ensure the safety of the person using its products. But the manufacturer is not responsible, either ethically or legally, for injuries that result from careless use or use that explicitly violates warnings in the product information.

The ethical warrant for the due-care approach is clear: the ethic of care (see Chapter 6). The ethic of care emphasizes special responsibilities that apply in unequal relationships. For instance, police officers have special relationships with the public; teachers, with their students; and parents, with their children. In all these instances, the power relationship between the two parties is unequal, and the more powerful party is responsible both for providing special assistance and protection and for refraining from harmful acts that exploit the power difference. In the due-care approach to product liability, the manufacturer is the more powerful party for the simple reason that a manufacturer knows its products much better than the buyer does. Therefore, the manufacturer has a special responsibility to exercise appropriate care in its relationship with the buyer.

In the due-care approach, the manufacturer's responsibilities extend to three areas:

- *Design*. The product must incorporate safe design; that is, it must be designed according to engineering state of the art. It must use appropriate materials and be able to withstand normal wear and tear. The manufacturer must be ready to prove that it performed appropriate usability testing.
- *Manufacture*. The manufacturer must be prepared to show that the manufacturing process incorporates rigorous quality-control procedures to prevent defects to individual products that come off the assembly line.
- *Information*. Under the due-care approach, product information—from advertising to instruction manuals, online help, and warning stickers affixed to products—is seen as a separate product, not merely an adjunct to the main product. (The typical instruction sheet today bears its own product number.) Seeing the information as a product is important: a manual, for instance, can be viewed by the courts as a defective product. Courts have found that manufacturers have not exercised due care in designing and testing the product information. (I will discuss this point in more detail later in this chapter.)

Under the due-care approach, product information is subjected to much more scrutiny than it was under the contract approach. The manufacturer must consider the capabilities of the audience, including age and general reading ability, ability to understand the concepts expressed, and ability to read and understand English. For instance, if a product is sold in an area in which many people do not speak English, the manufacturer can be held responsible for providing warnings in English and the other popular languages. In addition, the manufacturer's responsibility to the buyer extends beyond the time of purchase; the manufacturer must notify buyers about any safety information that is discovered after the manufacture and sale of the product.

Under the due-care approach, courts have sometimes been quite expansive in attributing importance to product information. For instance, Boatright (2000) describes a case in which the owner of a Pontiac Trans Am sued the carmaker after he was injured in an accident while driving more than 100 miles per hour. Referring to a principle called *invited misuse*, the court decided in the driver's favor. The court cited the facts that Pontiac entered modified versions of the Trans Am in races, supplied them for high-speed chase scenes in action movies, and provided dealers with a videotape showing scenes from the races and the movies.

Although the due-care approach is generally viewed as more satisfactory than the contract approach to liability, legal scholars and ethicists have pointed out four problems that have led many courts to reject it as an appropriate basis for settling liability cases:

- *Due care cannot be measured.* A plaintiff argues that the manufacturer did not exercise due care; the manufacturer argues that it did. Nothing in the concept of due care offers criteria by which to examine the competing claims. In a 1947 ruling, Judge Learned Hand argued that three factors are relevant in determining due care: the chance that an injury will occur, the severity of the injury, and the cost of preventing the injury (Boatright, 2000). The manufacturer's responsibility for preventing the injury increases as the chance or severity of injury increases or the cost of preventing it decreases. As sensible as this principle is, it does not make the due-care approach less vague.

- *Due care focuses on the manufacturer's actions, not on the product in question.* A consumer is at a distinct disadvantage in trying to prove that the manufacturer was negligent, because the manufacturer typically controls access to its own internal records. For instance, it took some decades to publish the internal documents showing that tobacco companies have known for decades that smoking cigarettes is inherently dangerous.

- *Due care cannot logically be fulfilled.* Even if a manufacturer provides compelling evidence that it designed, manufactured, and described its product according to the highest professional standards, the presence of an injured consumer in a courtroom is visible proof that the manufacturer apparently did not foresee and prevent every conceivable problem.

- *Due care is paternalistic.* The special protection afforded the buyer comes with a price: the buyer is treated as a person not fully responsible for acting prudently. (See the discussion of paternalism in Chapter 8.) Although it is impossible to say what Kant would think about due care, it is reasonable to guess that he would have concluded that it overcorrects the problems of the contract approach. In protecting the buyer from the potential abuses in the inherently unequal relationship with the manufacturer, due care can be seen to impose unjust burdens on the manufacturer. You should be held responsible for knowing that you could get hurt driving your Trans Am at more than 100 miles per hour.

The dominance of due care in American legal thinking ended in the early 1960s, when courts found in favor of plaintiffs despite the fact that the plaintiffs did not prove that the manufacturers failed to exercise due care. The courts held that the buyer's right to expect that products are safe is more important than the manufacturer's right to require that the plaintiff prove the manufacturer was negligent. These opinions led to the introduction of the approach called strict liability.

The Strict-Liability Approach

Section 402A of the second *Restatement of Torts,* written by the American Law Institute in 1964 and adopted by all 50 states and the District of Columbia, is the most direct statement of *strict liability:*

1. One who sells any product in a defective condition unreasonably dangerous to the user or consumer or to his property is subject to liability for physical harm thereby caused to the ultimate user or consumer, or to his property, if (a) the seller is engaged in the business of selling such a product, and (b) it is expected to and does reach the user or consumer without substantial change in the condition in which it is sold.
2. The rule stated in Subsection (1) applies although (a) the seller has exercised all possible care in the preparation and sales of his products, and (b) the user or consumer has not bought the product from or entered into any contractual relation with the seller. (qtd. in Boatright, 2000, p. 296)

In a footnoted comment on Section 402A, the writers define "unreasonably dangerous" as "dangerous to an extent beyond which would be contemplated by the ordinary consumer who purchases it, with the ordinary knowledge common to the community as to its characteristics" (Boatright, 2000, p. 298). In short, a product is defective only if it is more dangerous than the ordinary consumer would expect it to be on the basis of the product information. A gun, therefore, is not defective merely because it is a dangerous item. People know that you can shoot yourself or someone else accidentally if you are not careful. That is, a gun is "reasonably dangerous," or, to be more precise, "very dangerous but not unreasonably dangerous." However, a gun that blows up when it is fired, injuring the user, would obviously be considered defective.

Although some of the 50 states incorporate elements of the contract approach and the due-care approach in their own laws, Section 402A has had widespread influence in our legal system. Clause 2a effectively strikes due care, and Clause 2b dispenses with the contract approach (and the related idea of privity). Strict liability, then, is what Velasquez (1998) calls the strong version of *caveat vendor.*

It is important at this point to distinguish strict liability from the concept of absolute liability. In strict liability, the plaintiff has to prove that the product is defective, in terms of design, manufacture, or product information. (Whether the plaintiff was also at fault in leading to the accident is not relevant.) In absolute liability, a manufacturer is liable, regardless of whether the product is defective. Absolute liability as a theory has no legal power; it is merely a concept expressed to highlight the central characteristic of strict liability: that the product must be shown to be defective in some way.

The ethical arguments offered to defend strict liability focus on utility. By placing a greater burden on the manufacturer in case of injury, strict liability motivates the manufacturer to make every possible effort to make the product safe. In this way, strict liability goes further than the due-care approach, which primarily motivates the manufacturer to *demonstrate* that it is making the effort.

A related argument based on utility is the deep-pockets theory: only the manufacturer is financially able to compensate the injured user, who rarely carries sufficient private insurance to cover the long-term effects of a serious injury. From this perspective, strict liability is an efficient way to internalize the costs of producing the product. Without strict liability, the costs are externalized; that is, the injured consumer has to bear all the costs. Strict liability is the theory that enables a society to manufacture and use dangerous products.

George G. Brenkert (1993) offers an additional argument that combines a justice-based perspective and a utilitarian view. Brenkert argues that a person injured by a defective product is thereafter restricted as a producer and, consequently, as a consumer. He or she cannot compete fairly in the employment market and therefore cannot participate fully as a consumer. For this reason, Brenkert argues, the injured party should be compensated. For the injured party, strict liability is a matter of compensatory justice. For the society as a whole, it's a matter of utility.

The obvious ethical criticism of the strict-liability approach is also based on justice. It simply is not fair, critics contend, to penalize the manufacturer that has done everything possible to make the product safe. A basic principle of ethics, as discussed in Chapter 2, is that a party is blameworthy for an action only if he or she acted with both freedom and the knowledge of the harm that would result. Of course, to penalize a manufacturer 10 years after the product was manufactured for failing to include safety features that did not exist when the product was made violates a basic sense of fairness.

If the ethical arguments are reasonably direct and clear the pragmatic arguments—about whether strict liability in fact improves safety—are considerably more complex.

Consumer advocates such as Ralph Nader argue that strict liability is the most effective way to help millions of consumers who have no other way to protect themselves from unsafe products. These advocates furnish lists of products that were either withdrawn or improved as a result of strict-liability legal cases: the Ford Pinto, the Dalkon Shield IUD, flammable baby clothing made from Flanelette, defective respirators that killed firefighters, and so forth. (See Drivon [1990] for the consumer-advocate argument.)

Opponents of strict liability offer three main arguments:

- *The main group helped by strict liability is attorneys.* Estimates of the proportion of the $100 billion annually that goes to attorneys rather than their plaintiffs range from half (Huber & Litan, 1991) to two thirds (Settle & Spigelmyer, 1984).

- *Strict liability actually has a negative effect on safety.* Huber and Litan (1991) argue, for instance, that manufacturers hesitate to introduce new products with safety improvements because an improvement can be held up as evidence that the older product was unsafe. Strict liability makes it difficult or, sometimes, impossible for manufacturers to buy liability insurance. Strict liability is often described as a regressive tax, discouraging product innovation and making it impossible for poor people, for instance, to afford modern medicine that is prohibitively expensive because of the extra cost of liability insurance built into its price. (See Committee for Economic Development [1989] for a full discussion of the business perspective on strict liability.)

- *The extra warnings that result from strict liability are ineffective in reducing injury.* Priest (1988) points out, for instance, the irony that many accidents are due to bizarre behavior that likely would not have been prevented by explicit warnings. Huber (1988) comments that the new concern for safety in product information assumes that the buyer is "a sort of idiot genius of a most peculiar kind, now incapable of reading the manufacturer's disclaimers and warnings when they were given, but absolutely fluent and competent with them when they were not" (p.60).

Incontrovertible facts about the effectiveness of strict liability as a deterrent are hard to find, for it is impossible to record the number of accidents that do not occur. As Huber and Litan (1991) point out, "The larger social impact of the law is found far downstream from the case report or the legal treatise, precisely where the effects of the law are most difficult to measure" (p. 1). The Conference Board, a business organization, issued a report in 1988 (McGuire, 1988) concluding that strict liability has indeed improved product safety. The next year, it issued another report (Weber, 1989), in which executives reported that liability expenses indeed retard safety by discouraging innovation.

Velasquez (1998) effectively summarizes the dilemma of strict liability when he writes that the approach is "essentially an attempt to come to grips with the problem of allocating the costs of injuries between two morally innocent parties: The manufacturer who could not foresee or prevent a product-related injury, and the consumer who could not guard himself or herself against the injury because the hazard was unknown" (p. 341).

Figure 9.1 summarizes the basics of the three legal approaches to liability.

Figure 9.1
Three Legal Approaches to Liability

The contract approach. The buyer and the seller have entered into a contact. The contract is subject to express and implied warranties and disclaimers.

The due-care approach. The seller is responsible for living up to the warranties but also for exercising due care in preventing injuries.

The strict-liability approach. The seller is responsible for any injury to the buyer due to a defective product, even if the buyer was also at fault, the seller exercised due care, and the buyer did not have a contract with the seller.

THE TECHNICAL COMMUNICATOR'S DUTY TO INSTRUCT AND WARN

Regardless of the ethical and legal uncertainties resulting from evolving approaches to liability, one point is clear: the technical communicator will play an increasingly important role in manufacturers' efforts to produce products that are safer to use.

The manufacturer's responsibility is to instruct and to warn. "To instruct" means to provide information, usually in some sort of instruction sheet, manual, or online file, on how to use a product properly and safely. "To warn" means to provide warning labels on the product to help the reader use it safely. As Camm, Ross, and Scott (1993) point out, however, the distinction is more a matter of U.S. legal terminology than of practical import. United States courts expect manufacturers to include warnings in the product information that are coordinated with the same warnings on the product itself.

Camm, Ross, and Scott (1993) also caution that every country in the world has its own laws and legal procedures governing product liability. Therefore, manufacturers that sell their products outside the United States need to consider local practices regarding liability along with all the other aspects involved in localizing the product.

In an excellent article, attorney Pamela S. Helyar (1992) presents a set of recommendations for technical communicators, based on recent cases in which U.S. courts have ruled that product information is inadequate and has therefore contributed to plaintiffs' injuries. Figure 9.2 lists Helyar's recommendations for technical communicators.

Figure 9.2
Helyar's Recommendations for Technical Communicators

Recommendation	Commentary
Understand the product and its likely users.	Courts assume that the manufacturer is the expert on the product. The courts also assume that the manufacturer has carried out appropriate research to determine the buyer's demographics and capabilities, and written the information to accommodate that profile.
Define the product's functions.	The information should provide the reader an understanding of what the product is expected to do.
Define the product's limitations.	The information should explain the product's shortcomings, such as that a hard-wired smoke detector will not function if the circuit to which it is wired fails.
Explain how to assemble, install, use, store, and dispose of the product safely.	The information should be clear and complete, addressing such issues as how to use tools properly, what safety clothing or equipment the person should use, how to perform each step, how to anticipate and prevent hazards, and how to store or dispose of leftover materials.
Explain how to test and maintain equipment.	If the product is the kind that the user can safely test and maintain, the information should explain clearly how and when to carry out the procedures, warning of dangers.
Explain how to perform first aid and to respond to emergencies.	The information should provide clear instructions on how a user (or an onlooker) should respond when dangerous substances are touched or ingested.
Write clearly, meeting the needs of the audience.	The information should use common words, simple and grammatical sentences, brief paragraphs, and logical sequences. The writing should be clear and easy to understand for the intended readers.
Use clear, simple graphics that meet the needs of the audience.	The information should include graphics that are clear, simple, and accurate, with fully labeled components. Readers should be able to use the graphic quickly and easily in the intended environment. Information for products to be used by children or by adults who do not speak English should use graphics liberally, especially to warn of hazards.

Warn the audience about the risks of using the products.	The information should explain the nature of the risk (electrical shock, poisoning, etc.), the practices that can lead to the risk, the extent of the harm that can be caused, and the practices the reader should use to reduce or prevent the risk. The information should use mandatory language (words such as *must* instead of *should*) to reduce or prevent the risk. The information should avoid warning of every possible danger; overwarning dilutes the potency of the most important warnings.
Provide warnings that are large and legible and placed in the appropriate location.	The information should contain warnings that are large enough to be read easily and that stand out from their background. Warnings should employ whatever means are necessary—color, type size, text attributes such as boldface or italics—to make the warning emphatic. Warnings should be placed in the appropriate location on the product itself and in the product informaton. Warnings should precede, not follow, the dangerous steps. Warnings should be durable enough to remain on the product for the life of the product. Camm, Ross, and Scott (1993) recommend that a safety page be placed near the beginning of the product manual.
Follow government standards and regulations.	The information should adhere to standards and regulations published by appropriate regulatory agencies, such as the Occupational Safety and Health Administration or the Department of Transportation. These standards address issues such as the kind of signal word to use. The American National Standards Institute, the International Organization for Standardization, and other standards organizations have their own definitions of individual signal words. In general, the signal words have the following meanings:

- *Danger* alerts readers of an imminently hazardous situation that will result in death or serious injury.

- *Warning* alerts readers about a potentially hazardous situation that will result in death or serious injury.

- *Caution* alerts readers about a potentially hazardous situation that might result in minor or moderate injury.

	(See the American National Standards Institute site [www.ansi.org] for links to many standards organizations.)
Follow company standards.	The information should follow the company's own standards and procedures for quality control and testing.
Usability test the product, its information, and materials or information provided by suppliers.	The information should be usability tested. Courts look for documentation proving that the manufacturer carried out comprehensive usability tests not only on the finished product and its information but also on any components supplied by subcontractors. The greater the risk of injury, the more thoroughly the manufacturer must test.
Publish information using the most appropriate media.	The information should be published using the best means, including in advertising, on the box, on the product, in the information, and in recall letters. The manufacturer should try to ensure that users (not merely retailers) learn of safety risks. The manufacturer's responsibility does not end at the time of sale; all relevant information gained from users and from research and development must be disseminated to users throughout the lifetime of the product.
Maintain complete records of efforts to improve safety.	The manufacturer should maintain complete records so that it can prove that it has acted in good faith in making the product and its accompanying information as safe as possible. These records should include complete information about the personnel—usability experts and attorneys—who carried out the analyses.

Helyar's list reads like a lecture on the principles of effective technical communication: from audience analysis through usability testing, from invention through delivery. No other article that I am aware of in technical communication scholarship shows more dramatically the strong link between technical communication and ethics. Without fanfare and without resort to abstruse theory, Helyar shows, clearly and directly, that technical communicators who do their jobs professionally play a critically important role in making it safe for people to use the artifacts of a high-tech culture.

Smith and Shirk (1996) add to Helyar's article by recommending that someone in the organization keep abreast of current rulings in product liability. If the organization does not have a legal department, that task can fall to the technical communicator. Strate and Swerdlow (1987) provide a useful summary of how to research legal matters, focusing on the resources that describe cases according to subject area and according to the geographical area in which they are heard. Smith (1989) also reviews the basic resources for researching legal cases.

CASE AND ANALYSIS

The following fictional case is intended to dramatize some of the issues described in this chapter. Following the case is my analysis of it.

Case

Karen Brightman is the owner of Lake Adventures, a small company located in Rawlings, Montana. Lake Adventures is the only company that rents motorboats, sailboats, and jet skis on Lake Rawlings, a popular resort destination.

The state of Montana regulates the rental of jet skis because they can be dangerous to operate. They travel very fast (more than 40 miles per hour), and they often capsize because they are narrow. The state requires that a rental company read a one-page statement about safety to anyone wishing to rent a jet ski, and that the renter view a 12-minute video about safety. Upon completing these two requirements, any person age 14 years or older may rent a jet ski. The renter is required to carry a card signed by the renter, stating that he or she has listened to the safety information read by the rental agent and viewed the safety video.

It is Sunday morning on Labor Day weekend. Yesterday the weather was perfect, and all Brightman's equipment was rented. Today and tomorrow look like they will also be excellent days. A good Labor Day weekend can account for a third of the company's summer revenues. The most popular items in the company's inventory this year are their 15 jet skis.

A family comes into the store, wishing to rent a jet ski for two days, at a price of $150. Brightman has just one jet ski not already reserved for pickup later that day. She reads the required safety information to the man and his 18-year-old daughter, the two people who will be operating the jet ski. Brightman inserts the videotape into the VCR. The tape starts to play, then stops. The VCR automatically shuts off. She pushes the eject button. The cassette comes out, trailing a stream of videotape. The tape is broken.

The renter tells Brightman it's okay, because he viewed the same videotape when he rented a jet ski at another resort in the state a few months ago. He assures her that he is quite experienced with jet skis.

Brightman explains to him that he is required to sign a card stating that he has viewed the videotape. He responds that he is perfectly willing to sign the card. Brightman asks if he still has the card he signed when he rented the jet ski at the other resort. He does not.

She states that she is not permitted to rent him the jet ski unless he and his daughter view the video. He becomes angry, pointing out that he and his family have spent quite a bit of money on this weekend's activities. He offers to sign anything she wants, including a statement that he will not hold her or her company liable for any injuries he or his family incur resulting from their use of the jet ski.

Brightman asks him to hold on a minute while she tries to find out if it is possible to secure another copy of the videotape. She fails: no government offices are open, and she knows of no other nearby rental company that has a copy of the video that she can borrow or copy. She realizes that, if she doesn't figure something out, she will lose thousands of dollars of revenues because she probably will not be able to rent any of her 15 jet skis.

She has liability insurance, with a one-million dollar limit. She tries to reach her agent to ask him if it is permissible to do as the renter requests by having him sign a disclaimer statement. The agent is out of town for the holiday weekend. She cannot reach the company headquarters, either.

Should she do as the renter requests, by having him fill out a disclaimer statement or letting him sign the card stating that he has viewed the safety video?

Analysis

Karen Brightman is in a difficult situation. She stands to lose a lot of money if she cannot rent her jet skis. She wants to figure out some way to rent a jet ski to this family and to the other renters who will be coming in later in the morning. She has no reason to believe that this renter is lying about his experience with jets skis, no reason to doubt that he has in fact viewed the video and filled out the card, and no reason to doubt that he would operate the jet ski safely.

But Brightman must not rent a jet ski to him. Nor should she rent one to anyone who has not already met Montana's regulations on the use of jet skis.

This case can be approached from two perspectives: the law and ethics.

First, the legal issues. If Brightman is not an attorney authorized to practice in Montana, she has no way of knowing how to write a disclaimer that would protect her from liability and ensure that the renters operate the jet ski safely. The Montana regulations make no provision for writing your own disclaimer statement. And she should not count on her insurance in case of an accident, either, for the policy surely would not protect her if she violates any state regulations.

Even if the renter is a person of good faith, he could certainly sue her for providing a defective product—the incomplete instructions—in case of an accident. Brightman has no choice but to secure another copy of the video, or get her broken copy fixed, fast.

From the perspective of ethics, Brightman must not rent the jet ski to this family—or to anyone else—until she has fully complied with the state regulation calling for a renter to watch the videotape. Even though Brightman has no reason to doubt that the man has in fact viewed the videotape and would operate the jet ski safely, Brightman has to consider the ethics behind the regulation.

It is possible, however unlikely, that the man is lying in order to rent the jet ski, or that he or someone else in his family might operate the jet ski unsafely. In this case, viewing the videotape might have reduced the chances of an accident. (The quality of the videotape is irrelevant here, so long as the instruction it contains is not actually counterproductive.) And because an accident could injure or kill someone other than the man or one of his family members, it would be inadequate simply for Brightman to protect herself legally against liability, even if such protection were available. The perspective of care dictates that she do all that she can to protect not only her customers but also the other people on the lake. Certainly, complying with the state regulation calling for renters to watch this videotape is reasonable.

Viewing the problem from other ethical viewpoints leads to the same conclusion. The operator of the jet skis and the other people on the lake have a right to be protected from unreasonably dangerous activities. By granting Brightman the license to rent the equipment, the state is entrusting her to obey the relevant regulations, and she has a duty to do so.

From the utilitarian perspective, Brightman herself and the people who wanted to rent the jet skis are going to experience negative utility. She will lose money by not renting the equipment, and the vacationers will not have the opportunity to enjoy the activities that they planned to pursue. However, the would-be renters will be spared the chance (however small) of a much greater negative utility because they will not be injured by her equipment. The other people on the lake will experience positive utility in that they will be exposed to less risk.

The justice perspective, although not particularly relevant in this case, also calls for the same conclusion. It would not be just if some would-be renters—or entrepreneurs such as Brightman—were required to abide by the state regulation but others weren't.

In this case, the issue of liability is clear. Renting the jet skis in violation of the state regulation would be very risky for Karen Brightman. The issue of ethics, though perhaps less obvious, is similarly clear. It would be wrong for Brightman to rent the jet skis. Like a manufacturer selling a product that is defective because of inadequate documentation, Brightman would be selling a service that is defective because of inadequate documentation.

10

Ethical Relativism and Multicultural Communication

Stories of how multicultural misunderstandings can sour a business relationship are common. McDonald's offended many Islamic customers when it introduced disposable paper bags adorned with flags of the world. The company didn't realize that the Saudi flag contains verse from the *Koran*, and that it is a sacrilege to desecrate that holy book. American carmakers are still perplexed about their dismal sales in Japan, even though the dealers there must realize that, in Japan, the steering wheel is on the right side, not the left. One more: an American manufacturer of deodorant created an advertising campaign in Japan in which a cute octopus applies the deodorant under each of its eight arms. The campaign failed: in Japan, an octopus has eight legs, not eight arms (Bathon, 1999).

These kinds of misunderstandings can have serious effects on the economy of the United States, for we are the largest player in the global economy. In 1997, the United States exported almost one trillion dollars' worth of goods and services (U.S. Bureau of the Census, 1998). Direct investment abroad by U.S. companies in 1997 totaled $860 billion (U.S. Bureau of the Census, 1998). For many of the 30,000 U.S. companies that export products and services, exports make up from a quarter to a half of the company's revenues (Thrush, 1997). Exports are responsible for four of five new jobs created in the United States (Lustig & Koester, 1999). Clearly, the United States depends on the global economy.

In addition, the population of the United States itself is truly multicultural. Each year, the U.S. admits almost one million immigrants; this year, one in ten U.S. residents is foreign born (U.S. Bureau of the Census, 1998).

Technical communicators, more than almost any other professionals, are connected to this global economy. For one thing, most technical communicators work in high-technology industries, which are a mainstay of the global economy. For another, technical communicators are in the business of communicating information, a process that almost immediately leads to numerous ethical dilemmas. Working in a multicultural context, technical communicators must confront serious challenges that go far beyond the obvious fact that most people on Earth do not read or speak English.

To communicate information effectively with a person from another culture, the technical communicator needs to understand that the reader's response to the communication—even the reader's ability to understand it in the most basic sense—is shaped by a number of cultural factors, some obvious and some quite subtle. What are the laws in the reader's culture? What economic system is used? What is the degree of nationalism? What is the nation's history and geography? What are its religious beliefs? Its dominant philosophical traditions? Its attitudes toward issues of race and gender?

For example, laws and practices around the world differ substantially on such issues as product safety, truthtelling, puffery, and children's advertising. In some countries, product safety and labeling laws and regulations are more rigorous than those in the United States; in other countries, they are nonexistent. In some cultures, dangerous pesticides and other chemicals imported from the United States are used routinely, even though virtually all the workers who handle them are not literate in English and would have no way of knowing how to use them safely. In some cultures, young mothers are encouraged to switch from breast feeding to infant formula, even though polluted water can make formula deadly for children.

The many serious and complex questions related to the ethics of multinational business are beyond the scope of this book. I do not discuss, for example, Union Carbide's ethical responsibility for the Bhopal chemical tragedy, which killed some 2,000 people and injured over 200,000. Nor do I discuss the Lockheed bribery scandal, which led to the downfall of a Japanese government and to the passage of the Foreign Corrupt Practices Act in this country. There are numerous issues involving the ethics of multinational business—including bribery and corruption practices and the effects of trade on the economy, culture, and environment of the host country—that are beyond the scope of this book. (For an excellent treatment of these issues, see Thomas Donaldson's *The Ethics of International Business* [1989].)

What I concentrate on in this chapter is the role of the technical communicator addressing an audience from another culture (whether that audience lives in the communicator's own country or another country). I begin by surveying the technical-communication literature on the ethics of multicultural communication. Next, I turn to the concept of cultural relativism, explaining why the fact that people around the world have different cultural practices does not mean that every culture's ethical positions are equally valid. Then, I survey the literature on the ethics of multinational corporations, applying selected guidelines to our question about the ethics of multicultural communication. Finally, I present a case that addresses the subject of this chapter.

CULTURAL RELATIVISM AND ETHICS

To discuss ethics in a multinational context, I need to distinguish ethics from a related but separate issue: cultural relativism.

As I discussed in Chapter 2, *cultural relativism* is a descriptive term; it refers to the fact that different cultures have different values, customs, and practices. Much of the recent scholarship in technical communication concerns our need to be aware of cultural relativism as we communicate with people from other cultures.

Limaye and Victor (1991), for example, discuss a number of issues—issues of cognitive frames, concepts of time and space, objectivity and subjectivity, business practices, and approaches to writing—that technical communicators need to understand. William Horton's article "The Almost Universal Language: Graphics for International Documents" (1993) is a detailed examination of the ways graphics conventions differ around the world. Horton includes a set of recommendations on how to avoid confusing or offending international readers by using inappropriate graphics.

Nancy L. Hoft's book for practitioners, *International Technical Communication: How to Export Information About High Technology* (1995), is our field's most comprehensive discussion of the many aspects of culture that technical communicators need to be aware of when they create multicultural communication products. She recommends performing an international-user analysis, planning a management strategy, and considering issues of design for both print and online documents. Deborah Andrews's recent textbook, *Technical Communication in the Global Community* (1998), includes a chapter, "Writing for Audiences Across Cultures," that focuses on the fact that frames of reference differ from one culture to another.

The goal of the many studies of multicultural communication is to help people from the United States understand the extent to which people's ways of looking at the world differ, to suggest ways that writers from the United States can develop a greater awareness of cultural differences, and to propose strategies for accommodating these differences in their technical communication. These studies, in short, are aimed at reducing the "ugly American" factor.

Although these studies are valuable, it is important to note the goal of these writings. They seek to provide practical advice to help technical communicators avoid making blunders that might make the communication unclear or offensive. Behind this purpose is a clear message: if we are to communicate effectively, we must avoid cultural imperialism. If we do not, the products that our communications support will fail in the marketplace. In other words, the scholarship and textbooks on multicultural issues for technical communicators are instrumental in purpose.

There is nothing wrong with an instrumental purpose, of course. A greater awareness of cultural issues is, in fact, necessary for our continued economic success, and indirectly helps broaden our understanding of human diversity. Like all professionals, technical communicators benefit from a more comprehensive understanding of the rich variety of human life.

The problem arises, however, when the scholars make the transition—usually without realizing it—from cultural relativism to ethical relativism. *Ethical relativism,* as I discussed in Chapter 2, is a normative idea: that the ethical beliefs and values of a culture are correct in that culture. The way that people in France see things and do things is the right way—for the French. The values of the South Koreans are the right values, if you are in South Korea. There are no beliefs or values that transcend a particular culture.

Technical-communication research on the ethics of multicultural communication does not explicitly espouse ethical relativism. A more accurate claim would be that this research does not clearly discuss the relationship between cultural relativism and ethics. This omission enables the reader to infer that we need not think about the ethical positions that our writing reflects and projects. I think that this inference is wrong; we do need to think about the relationship between our words and our ethics. Although the instrumental advice offered by technical-communication scholars is not unethical, it is not fully satisfactory. It fails to provide a clear picture of the ethical issues at the heart of multicultural communications, and it fails to provide clear advice for the technical communicator who wishes to think through the ethical implications of different communication choices.

Before addressing the question of ethical relativism in more detail, I want to give a few examples of how the technical-communication literature addresses the question of the ethics of multicultural communication.

In *International Technical Communication*, Nancy L. Hoft (1995) describes the issue of ethical differences between cultures in terms of the danger of offending our readers.

Discrimination and prejudice exist in every country in the world. In some countries they are more pronounced. To use an American expression, "Don't pour salt on an open wound." What is perceived as unacceptable in one country may be expected in another. Knowing this information ahead of time can help you avoid embarrassing mistakes.

In the U.S., for example, it is best to be sensitive to portrayals and discussions of women or African-Americans, which, if handled insensitively, can suggest discrimination and prejudice. Portraying and discussing women and African-Americans in graphics or written examples without considering the significance of these subjects in the U.S. is taking the serious risk of greatly offending many people. Obviously this is detrimental to your goal of creating effective international technical communication.

Do your homework and know what forms of prejudice and discrimination exist in the target country. (p. 71)

Hoft is saying that if a practice is prejudicial or discriminatory in your target country, avoid it; if not, presumably there's no problem.

In their book *Ethics in Technical Communication: Shades of Gray*, Allen and Voss (1997) state that there are three universal principles:

- Human sacrifice, torture, and political repression are bad in any society.
- It is wrong to be indifferent toward the suffering of others.
- People have a right to a reasonable level of material existence.

Then, Allen and Voss write,

Once we wander outside the parameters of the humanistic principle, however, cultural relativism kicks in. Thus, matters such as religion, diet, etiquette, sexual mores, and the like are areas where we should not judge nor meddle with the values and practices of other cultures. (p. 239)

To argue that except for these three universal ethical principles we should be mute is inadequate. Certainly, diet and etiquette should not concern us. But if our audience's religious views include the tenet that men are superior to women, and that women therefore should not receive formal education or be permitted to work outside the home, is it appropriate to let ethical relativism "kick in"?

In discussing the fact that sex roles in the workplace differ widely, William Horton (1993) comments as follows:

This raises an ethical dilemma. By modifying your graphical strategy, are you pandering to the forces of oppression? Resolving this conflict will test your judgment and your courage. You can, of course, design graphics that prominently illustrate your values or those of your culture and "if the savages don't like it, let 'em use somebody else's products." This extreme fails on two counts. First, if your graphics draw attention—of the censors or the users—to the social relations depicted, those graphics become ineffective in communicating about the product. Second, there is no clear consensus about what are correct values or how to show them. What is politically correct in Northern California may be considered too liberal for rural Kansas, stilted and forced in France, and blasphemous in Saudi Arabia. (p. 688)

In other words, ethical imperialism is inappropriate because it will hurt sales and because ethical relativism is correct. Ethical questions, Horton suggests, are really questions of aesthetics and political correctness. Horton is right when he comments that this sort of ethical dilemma will "test your judgment and courage," but he does not offer any suggestions on how to act responsibly.

Deborah Andrews (1998) comments on the fact that business practices differ from one country to another:

You may need to redefine your notion of "bribery" to exclude the under-the-counter payments that are common in some countries to get cargo off a ship or to secure licenses from a bureaucrat. . . . You need to follow your ethical compass even if you are in a one-person office 5,000 miles from corporate headquarters and you're not being watched. Countries differ widely in their tolerance of corruption. (p. 59)

Certainly, bribery takes many forms, some of which might be ethically defensible, but how are technical-communication students to know when they "may need to redefine" their notions of bribery? Is the important factor the dollar amount of the bribe? The authority or status of the person receiving the bribe? Other, external economic factors? Supply and demand? Without an ethical framework, Andrews's advice is of little value.

In short, the scholarship on how to deal with the ethical dilemmas involved in multicultural communication is inadequate in two ways. First, it presents a muddled account of the ethical issues involved. And second, it offers no framework for thinking about how to resolve a dilemma. In the next section I try to present a clear account of the issues involved in thinking about cultural relativism and ethical relativism.

CULTURAL RELATIVISM AND ETHICAL RELATIVISM

As the technical-communication scholarship makes clear, cultural imperialism—"ugly American" behavior—is bad business. If we fail to acknowledge the implications of cultural relativism on our business practices, we will indeed jeopardize our economic well-being.

But I want to argue that the ethical relativism that is implicit in technical-communication research is wrongheaded. In Chapter 2, I explained that cultural relativism in no way logically entails ethical relativism. If Culture A believes that bribery is wrong, for example, and Culture B believes that it is right, it is not necessarily the case that both of the cultures are right. There are in fact two other possibilities: that only one culture is right (either Culture A or Culture B), and that neither culture is right (that is, that the situation is complex, with bribery right in some circumstances and wrong in others).

I also mentioned four other problems with ethical relativism:

- *Ethical relativism assumes a homogeneous culture, but most modern cultures are in fact quite heterogeneous.* What is the view, for example, of Canadians on the subject of national identity? It depends on whether you ask the typical English-speaking Canadian or the typical French-speaking Canadian.

- *Ethical relativism breaks down as soon as someone presents a normative statement about people from another culture.* If the people from Culture A say that people from Culture B may not practice Act X, but people in Culture B say that people from Culture B may practice Act X, ethical relativism entails a logical contradiction because people from Culture B simultaneously may and may not practice Act X.

- *Ethical relativism entails that the same practice can be right at one time but wrong at another.* For example, slavery was right in Mississippi in 1850 but wrong in Mississippi in 1950, even though there are no relevant differences between slavery at one time and at the other that would justify the difference in belief.

- *Ethical relativism forestalls the possibility that people's ethical thinking can evolve.* It would be wrong to try to change a person's mind about an ethical matter because what the person presently believes is by definition right. Therefore, there could be no evolution in a culture's ethical thinking.

Norman Bowie offers another argument against ethical relativism: there does seem to be a range of human behavior that everyone in fact agrees is wrong. Torture, murder of the innocent, stealing, breaking promises—these and many other practices are universally rejected. As Bowie (1996) writes, "A nation-state accused of torture does not respond by saying that a condemnation of torture is just a matter of cultural choice. . . . Rather, the standard response is to deny that any torture took place" (p. 92). We universally condemn the atrocities of Nazi Germany, Pol Pot's Cambodian genocide, or the Rwandan genocide. As Bowie also points out, there is considerable agreement among the universal codes of ethical principles, including the United Nations Universal Declaration of Human Rights, the European Convention on Human Rights, and the Helsinki Final Act.

Norman Parfit (1986) offers one additional argument against ethical relativism. Parfit presents a continuum, at one end of which is ethical universalism, the idea that there are values that transcend cultural groups. At the other end is individual relativism, the idea that if a person believes that some action is wrong, it is wrong for that person. In the center of the continuum is ethical relativism. Parfit argues that if ethical relativism is plausible, then so is individual relativism. If the ethical relativist argues against the individual relativist that individual relativism makes a stable society impossible—an idea based on the social-contract theories of Hobbes or Locke—the ethical relativist is vulnerable to the same argument from the universalist. That is, in a multinational world, the ethical relativist is a threat to a stable world order, just as the individual relativist is a threat to the stability sought by the ethical relativist.

My argument, to this point, is that the technical-communication litera-ture on cultural relativism—the diversity of cultural practices and val-ues—implicitly endorses ethical relativism, the idea that values are necessarily correct in the culture in which they are held. Further, I argue that ethical relativism is a flawed doctrine; numerous reasons suggest that it simply is not true that a value is necessarily correct in a culture that es-pouses it.

The fact that a group considers a practice to be right or wrong does not make it so. What is needed is a principle that can assist a person in thinking through whether a practice or value is defensible. In the next section, I dis-cuss several such principles.

PRINCIPLES FOR EXAMINING MULTICULTURAL COMMUNICATION

To my knowledge, no scholar has presented an approach for thinking about the dilemmas that confront a technical communicator who is decid-ing whether and how to modify a message when addressing an audience that holds significantly different values. However, a number of ethicists have presented principles pertaining to moral norms that should govern the actions of multinational corporations when they do business in host countries. These principles can be applied fruitfully to the subject of com-municating in a multicultural context.

First, let me introduce this literature on multinational business. Over the past three decades, as the global economy has grown so rapidly, busi-ness-ethics scholars have taken an intense interest in the complex ethical di-lemmas presented when a corporation sets up operations in a host country. One obvious example of the type of dilemma presented by multinational business is the question of wages and working conditions in the host coun-try. (The host country is the country in which the corporation has set up op-erations.)

Although the corporation might set up a facility in a host country for a number of reasons, including nearness to raw materials or to the market, or because of less-stringent environmental policies in the host country, proba-bly the most common reason is access to inexpensive labor. The challenge faced by the multinational corporation is to determine what wages to offer in the host country.

Some ethicists argue that the corporation is ethically obliged to offer the same wages in the host country that it offers in the home country. They con-tend that to offer lower wages exploits the workers in the host country. But other ethicists counter that offering home-country wages is counterproductive, first because doing so removes the principal reason to locate in the host country in the first place and second because doing so attracts the best workers in the host country, making it impossible for the host country to develop its economic infrastructure.

Yet this argument can be used to justify subsistence wages. If the host country has massive unemployment, such as fifty percent, it is relatively easy for the multinational to attract competent workers by paying below-poverty wages. What ethical principles should the multinational use to determine appropriate wages that enable workers to live a dignified life, without paying so much as to put the local businesses at a disadvantage in attracting labor?

This problem is considerably more complex than my brief sketch indicates, but the important point is that multinational business presents numerous ethical dilemmas that derive from the differences in economic development and cultural practices and values between two nations. Several approaches to thinking through these kinds of dilemmas can help us think through the problem of multicultural communication. In the following sections, I describe several of these approaches.

Guidelines for Multinationals Operating in Developing Countries

Ethicist Richard De George (1986) outlines a number of moral norms that multinational corporations (often abbreviated as MNCs) should respect when doing business with developing nations. Among these norms are the following four:

- *MNCs should do no direct intentional harm.* They should not sell unsafe products that are forbidden in the home country, and they should not grossly pollute the host country. This principle is what De George calls the *moral minimum.*

- *MNCs should contribute by their activities to the host country's development.* They should pay their fair share of taxes and work to develop the host country's "background institutions," such as labor unions and financial infrastructure.

- *MNCs should respect the human rights of their employees.* Regardless of the standards of other employers in the host country, MNCs should respect the human dignity of their workers by setting humane standards for pay and for health and safety measures.

- *To the extent that local culture does not violate moral norms, MNCs should respect the local culture and work with it, not against it.* MNCs are obliged to respect the local customs and values in the host country; however, if a host country's business practices sanction exploitation of a particular ethnic group, for example, the MNC should not take advantage of these practices, even if they are legal.

De George's last point is especially relevant for our subject of multicultural communication, for the typical dilemma faced by the communicator is to decide whether to slant the communication to reflect the values of the audience, when those values seem unethical. For example, if the audience discriminates against women, should the communicator remove women from the product documentation?

Unfortunately, De George's (1986) principle, sensible as it is, offers little explanatory power. He does not elaborate on how we might define whether an action violates moral norms. Presumably, we are to evaluate the practice as we would any practice: according to whatever techniques we ordinarily use, such as the utility-rights-justice-care model discussed in Chapter 7.

Social-Contract Approaches

A number of business ethicists approach the questions of an MNC's obligations from the perspective of social-contract theory. There are a number of social-contract theories, all of which differ in details, but the essential point about social-contract theory is that it sees ethics as a set of rights and duties derived from a voluntary arrangement in which people live together in a society. Dunfee (1993) explains that the social contract in international ethics

is an informal, unwritten, malleable understanding that reflects a basic consensus of the members of the community. In becoming a member of the community one thereby incurs a duty to abide by the basic terms of the implied social contract. The contract changes with time as the community changes, and there are always likely to be free riders who accept the benefits of the community but who refuse to undertake the fundamental duties recognized in the social contract. Social contracts will reflect common behaviors in the relevant community. But they also include aspirational goals, representing higher forms of behavior which would lead to greatly enhanced quality of life in the community if all members were to practice them. Ethical obligations are intertwined throughout such social contracts. (p. 66)

The most famous social-contract theorist was Thomas Hobbes, who argued that it is necessary for people to surrender some of their liberty in order to create a society that preserves the individual's security. Unless individuals cede some power to the state, people's lives would be "nasty, brutish, and short." We would live in constant fear of physical violence at the hands of a stranger.

Immanuel Kant is often described as a social-contract ethicist, for his ideas on ethics are based on the first formulation of the categorical imperative: "Act only according to that maxim by which you can at the same time will that it should become a universal law." This universalizability principle, which I discuss in Chapter 3, is at the heart of social-contract theory, for it establishes the importance of voluntary agreements between people. Kant's interest in promise-keeping is an obvious outgrowth of his social-contract approach.

According to Norman Bowie (1993), the Kantian agreement extends from individual promise-keeping to a society-wide agreement to honor contracts. This willingness to conduct business according to contract is the moral minimum that MNCs are obliged to honor. The implications of this social-contract approach are clear. If bribery is outlawed, a person who offers bribes in the conduct of business is acting unethically by violating the universalizability principle; it is not fair that some people live according to rules while others do not. Similarly, if bribery is a well-known fact of business life in a society, the practice is not necessarily unethical, although it would be if it were practiced inconsistently.

The most detailed social-contract approach to MNCs has been presented by Thomas Donaldson (1989). Donaldson begins by explaining the two reasons that people customarily offer to justify an amoral attitude toward multinational business. The first is ethical relativism, which he counters using the arguments I presented in the previous section. The second reason is, ironically, a reference to the Hobbesian social contract. Hobbes argued that only a strong monarchy could provide the security that would prevent people from killing each other to acquire wealth. The Hobbesian argument against the need to act ethically in international trade, therefore, is that there is no Hobbesian umpire, no international body that has the power to enforce fair economic practices.

Donaldson rejects this argument on the grounds that it is a *non sequitur*: the fact that there is no umpire does not invalidate the moral norms of fair dealing. In fact, Donaldson returns to the social-contract model to defend his own viewpoint. The rationale for any corporation is that the cooperative work of different people working together is more productive than the individual labors of the same people working separately. An MNC should honor rights because the terms of the contract demand that it honor rights as a condition of its justified existence. Why should an MNC resist the temptation to pay its workers in a host country slave wages? Donaldson's answer is clear: "It should resist because in doing so it is honoring a right, and honoring valid rights is something it is required to do under the terms of the social contract" (1989, p. 56).

Against the backdrop of this social contract, Donaldson (1989) spells out 10 minimal rights that MNCs are obliged to provide their workers in host countries:

1. the right to freedom of physical movement
2. the right to ownership of property
3. the right to freedom from torture
4. the right to a fair trial
5. the right to nondiscriminatory treatment (freedom from discrimination on the basis of such characteristics as race or sex)
6. the right to physical security
7. the right to freedom of speech and association
8. the right to minimal education
9. the right to political participation
10. the right to subsistence

MNCs should avoid *depriving* people of these 10 fundamental rights. In addition, MNCs should also feel a "correlative duty" of helping protect people from deprivation of rights 5–10 above. However, MNCs are not ethically obliged to go one step further by aiding deprived workers. Doing so would be praiseworthy, of course, but beyond the MNC's minimal duty.

Finally, Donaldson presents what he calls an ethical algorithm for thinking through ethical dilemmas in multinational business (see Figure 10.1). In these dilemmas, the home country's values appear to conflict with the host country's.

Figure 10.1
Donaldson's Ethical Algorithm

In this type of dilemma . . .	**This formula is appropriate**
Type 1. The moral reasons underlying the host country's view that the practice is permissible refer to the host country's relative level of economic development.	The practice is permissible if and only if the members of the home country would, under conditions of economic development relevantly similar to those of the host country, regard the practice as permissible.
Type 2. The moral reasons underlying the host country's view that the practice is permissible are independent of the host country's relative level of economic development.	The practice is permissible only if the answer to both of the following questions is "no": • Is it possible to conduct business successfully in the host country without undertaking the practice? • Is the practice a clear violation of a fundamental international right?

According to this algorithm, in a Type 1 conflict, a home country would probably willingly accept increased thermal pollution as a price for economic development. However, it probably would not accept increased asbestos pollution, which would be a violation of citizens' fundamental rights. In a Type 2 conflict, minor bribery of an official in a host country would be permitted because it would be impossible to carry out business successfully without it and because the bribery would not constitute a violation of a fundamental right. However, if cultural practices in the host country call for systematic discrimination of persons of a certain sex, race, or ethnicity, the practice would not be permissible (according to fundamental right number 5 above), even though it might be impossible to carry out business in the host country.

Donaldson's social-contract approach has been criticized on a number of counts. Perhaps the most direct criticism is presented by Sorell and Hendry (1994), who argue that Donaldson's Type 1 conflict masks an ethical imperialism. Who is to say, they ask, "Which of the world's cultures is the 'most' developed? Only in economic terms can any kind of objective answer be given, and it is far from obvious why economic development should provide a touchstone for morality: 'rich' is not necessarily right" (p. 213). In addition, Sorell and Hendry argue that Donaldson's Type 2 conflict, with its provision about conducting business "successfully," is insufficiently precise. Under Donaldson's algorithm, they argue, it is permissible to offer a large bribe to an official in a host country, because doing so does not violate any international right and is probably necessary to conduct business successfully. Presumably, an MNC could argue that almost any sort of practice that does not violate an international right and that improves the MNC's chances of conducting business successfully is permissible.

Sorell and Hendry thus conclude (1994) that "there are unlikely to be any simple rules or algorithms that can determine what is ethically acceptable practice across cultures" (p. 221). I agree with that statement completely, yet come to a very different conclusion about the value of Donaldson's approach.

Let me offer three comments about Sorell and Hendry's conclusion. First, Donaldson was ill advised to call his approach an algorithm, which suggests a level of precision that is unattainable. Donaldson has not created an algorithm any more than Kant or Aristotle or Mill did. Second, Sorell and Hendry are right when they say that there are no *simple* rules for determining the ethics of multicultural practices. There are no simple rules for determining an appropriate response to any ethical dilemma; there are only guidelines. And third, rules and algorithms cannot determine anything; only people can determine things.

In this third comment, I am not going out of my way to sound like an English teacher. I believe that there is a real difference between saying that a rule can determine something and saying that a person can use a rule to determine something. By adding a person to the statement, I am suggesting that Donaldson's approach is not a system that will yield the same answer no matter who carries out the analysis. On the contrary, the person carrying out the analysis has everything to do with how it is carried out and what conclusions it reaches. The person carrying out the analysis has to think about whether the practice in question violates any international right, and whether it would be possible to do business successfully without the practice. What Sorell and Hendry criticize as lack of precision I interpret as the necessary subjectivity of any approach to a complex scenario.

Certainly, Sorell and Hendry are correct that the word *successfully* seems almost infinitely elastic when used to modify "conducting business." What does it mean to conduct business successfully? Does it mean that an MNC that wishes to keep bribery to a minimum may bribe only as much as necessary to break even or eke out the slightest profit? Or does it mean that the MNC may offer more bribes, and more lucrative bribes, than any of its competitors, thereby making a serious effort to reap the biggest profit? Or does it mean something in between? Obviously, it can mean any of these three.

Does the imprecision of *successfully* make the algorithm useless? I don't think so. The imprecision of the word is in keeping with all language used in formulating general principles. It is impossible to speak in the abstract about any human phenomenon without using imprecise adjectives and adverbs. The history of ethics, in fact, is the very long and continuing story of the attempt to define the word *good*. Unless the topic is an actual case for which we have full and uncontested data, imprecise language is necessary. (Even in discussing actual cases, precise language often remains elusive.)

What exactly is the value of creating general principles such as Donaldson's? What is to be gained if the managers of an MNC ask themselves these two imprecise questions: Does a practice violate one of the ten international rights, and can our company conduct business successfully if we choose not to implement the practice? Although neither question yields a precise answer, they are the right questions anyway. The questions not only force the MNC to examine its short-term business tactics but also encourage the MNC to define itself. I think it would be extremely useful for MNCs to ask themselves the hard question lurking behind the "successful" question: What exactly does it mean to be a successful MNC? What are the essential characteristics of a successful MNC? How do we measure them? How do we know if we have achieved them? These are, of course, the big questions that all organizations (including universities and their individual departments) need to ask.

Donaldson does not provide an algorithm for determining whether a practice is ethical. What he does provide, however, is a set of questions that can prompt an MNC to examine its business practices as it decides how to debate the ethics of a particular practice.

Process Approaches

A number of business ethicists have turned away from foundational approaches to dilemmas faced by MNCs. Rather than proposing frameworks such as Donaldson's, these commentators focus on the process by which the dilemmas are addressed and resolved.

For example, Nash (1992) sees two types of problems. Type A problems are *acute dilemmas*, where two or more values are in conflict, and upper management has not decided the appropriate course of action. In this case, the process for resolving the dilemma is most important, for some stakeholders will always be unsatisfied by the resolution. Type B problems are cases of *acute denial*, where the MNC knows the right thing to do even though it is not doing the right thing. These cases are usually problems of compliance or implementation: a middle manager, for one reason or another, is not succeeding in carrying out company policy. According to Nash, only the acute dilemmas are actually dilemmas; the cases of acute denial are merely operational matters that do not involve ethical dilemmas at all.

Other business ethicists see futility in the search for universal norms that are both valid and practical. Instead, MNCs should view communication as a way to achieve mutually acceptable norms for the specific situation, even though those norms might be of no value in other situations.

The difference between the views of these process business-ethicists and ethicists such as Donaldson mirrors the difference between discourse ethicists and such foundational ethicists as Mill or Kant or Rawls. The process business-ethicists who study MNCs argue that actual cases are so complex and contextual that any abstract, principled approach melts away under the heat of the facts. Rather, they argue, the appropriate course of action is to try to establish a process of inquiry that includes all the stakeholders and ensures unbiased and uncoerced discussion. As I argued in Chapter 7, I think it is best to combine the perspectives of these two groups by using a principled model, such as the utility-rights-justice-care model, in a discourse-ethics context.

APPLYING THE PRINCIPLES TO MULTICULTURAL COMMUNICATION

Despite its limitations, then, a principle-based approach such as Donaldson's can at least suggest the right questions to ask, questions that can prompt an MNC to think clearly about what actions are entailed by its responsibilities to its various stakeholders.

I would like now to focus the discussion a little more on the two multicultural-communication problems that technical communicators often face: communication problems related to product dumping and information tailoring, and communication problems related to discrimination.

Product Dumping and Information Tailoring

Product dumping is the practice of selling a product in another country that is not sold in the home country. Sometimes the practice carries no ethical import. For instance, a U.S. maker of shaving razors sells a discontinued razor around the world. This razor is a perfectly safe product; it is just not the most advanced product of its kind.

Sometimes, however, product dumping can have a very important ethical dimension. If, for instance, the manufacturer sells a product that is outlawed or restricted in the home country because it has not been shown to be effective or safe to the satisfaction of the home country's regulatory agencies, that is a question worthy of ethical investigation. The common instances of this situation involve the sale of chemicals and drugs.

How does this relate to technical communication? The information that accompanies the product distributed outside the home country is different from the information that is distributed at home. In the case of drugs, for instance, the list of "indications," those conditions for which the drug is appropriate, is longer in the home country, and the list of warnings is shorter. In other words, the information outside the home country suggests that the drug can be used to cure more conditions and have fewer side effects than does the information distributed in the home country. (See Boatright [2000] for examples of this kind of information tailoring.)

An immediate reaction in cases such as this is to condemn the host country for product dumping. If the product and its information are not good enough for consumers in the home country, they are not good enough for anyone else. The warrant for this conclusion is obvious: the Golden Rule or Kant's second formulation of the categorical imperative.

However, sometimes what looks like an ethical problem is not. As Boatright (2000) explains, different conditions in two countries can call for the use of different drugs and different drug information. For instance, the anti-diarrhea drug Lomotril has been declared by the World Health Organization to be ineffective in curing the causes of diarrhea; it merely stops the diarrhea. In addition, the drug has been declared unsafe for children younger than 2 years of age because of potential side effects. For these reasons, it is not widely used in the United States for treating conditions that cause diarrhea, especially in infants. Still, the manufacturer of the drug distributes it in many developing countries and fails to include the same warnings in the product information that it provides in the United States, the home country.

Why the disparity? Because the general level of health of children is better in the United States, and there are more drugs available to attack the underlying condition that causes the diarrhea. In developing countries, children are less healthy. A far greater number of young children die of dehydration caused by diarrhea. For these children, the diarrhea is not an annoying symptom but a life-threatening condition, and the first priority is to stop it. In addition, local physicians might not have access to the drugs necessary to cure the underlying condition.

I am not saying that all instances of product dumping or tailoring of information are ethically justifiable. There is no justification, for instance, in tailoring information to downplay the safety hazards of a product if the only reason for doing so is that regulations in the country of sale are less rigorous than in the home country. Tailoring the information in this way might in fact tend to increase sales, but it would be wrong, for the simple reason that doing so would violate the Golden Rule, Kant's second formulation, and Donaldson's statement of the international right to physical security.

The situation is somewhat more complex if the home country distributes a nonessential product that has been withdrawn in the home country because of safety concerns. For example, a power lawnmower without a kill switch—a product no longer sold in the United States—is still sold in some developing countries. Lacking this safety feature, the mower is less expensive and therefore popular in the developing countries. Is it ethical to continue to sell it? This question has to be answered on a case-by-case basis. If the only other way to cut grass in that developing country is by scythe, a far more dangerous method, selling a power mower that is outmoded in the developed world seems perfectly ethical. However, if there is an available method that is safer than the outmoded power mower, selling it is ethically suspect.

Of course, a related question—giving the consumer a choice—needs to be addressed. A reasonable argument can be made that a manufacturer is entitled to sell the product so that the consumer can decide what technology to use in cutting the grass. In this instance, the technical communicator can do much to remove the ethical dangers inherent in the situation. If the manufacturer is selling a product that is known to be less safe than it could be, the technical communicator's ethical responsibility is to do a thorough and fully professional job in instructing and warning the consumer. (See Chapter 9 for a full discussion of this topic.) The fact that such instructions and warnings may not be required in the developing country is, naturally, irrelevant in a discussion of the ethics of the situation.

Discrimination in Product Information

A second problem confronted by technical communicators is that the culture in which the goods or services are sold might have very different views from the home culture on the issue of discrimination. Most commonly, the home culture is a developed nation that outlaws discrimination on the basis of sex or race, whereas the target country has cultural traditions that sanction discrimination against women or people of certain races. The question, then, is this: Should the technical communicator accommodate the target culture's views on sex or race by, for example, excluding women from the product information?

Technical-communication research on this topic favors avoiding cultural variables that can impede the communication. For example, William Horton (1993) notes that because men and women play different roles in different cultures around the world, the best approach is to avoid overt gender roles in creating graphics. It would be unwise, therefore, to present a photograph of men and women in a workplace setting. Similarly, it is smart to "stylize the hands so they are not clearly male or female" (p. 689). In addition, "Do not show skin color or else vary skin color throughout a long document. This is true for showing people as well" (p. 689). Nancy L. Hoft (1995) comments that areas "of particular sensitivity" for the technical communicator "include gender, gender relationships, ethnic dress, and hand gestures" (p. 264), and recommends that communicators either research the areas well or avoid them altogether in product information.

In the business-ethics literature, no scholars that I am aware of have addressed the subject of discrimination in product information. However, numerous scholars have addressed the somewhat broader issue of discrimination in business practices in host countries. The consensus is that discrimination of any form is unethical, as explained by Donaldson. De George (1995), for instance, argues that MNCs have an obligation not to discriminate either at home or in a host country. However, he adds, MNCs are not obliged to practice affirmative action in host countries, unless they have a history of past discrimination in those countries.

While the U.S.-based company with integrity cannot discriminate, it is not clear that it must take the lead in breaking down such discrimination by means other than its example and its practices. If the women that it promotes to executive positions have difficulty working effectively with other companies that have a tradition of male domination, it must do the best it can to balance fair treatment of the women and the financial interests of the company. (p. 519)

Schlegelmilch (1998), noting that gender discrimination in Islamic countries is viewed as an effort to protect the livelihood of men, who are traditionally the heads of households, argues that, regarding such phenomena as sexual discrimination,

the answer seems to lie somewhere in between these two extremes [ethical relativism and ethical imperialism]. Thus, it appears impossible to provide a definite answer; corporations will have to resolve such ethical dilemmas on a case by case basis, very carefully balancing the interests of all stakeholders, both those in the host and those in the home countries. (p. 136)

To extrapolate from comments such as these, it is reasonable to suggest that technical communicators are ethically obliged not to reinforce patterns of discrimination in the product information. For example, if the culture of the audience discriminates against women, it would be wrong for the communicator to include a photograph or drawing of a workplace setting that excludes women.

However, I see no reason that the communicator is obliged to actively challenge the prevailing prejudice by, for example, including a photograph that shows women performing roles that they do not perform in that culture. Similarly, the technical communicator is not ethically obliged to portray women wearing clothing, makeup, or jewelry that is likely to offend local standards. Although the communicator should avoid the sexist "he," just as in writing in the United States, the communicator need not use "he or she" in writing to all cultures. Rather, the communicator should find nonsexist ways to avoid the problem altogether, such as those suggested by Maggio (1997). If the communicator can convey the message without risking offense, that is all that is ethically required; it is not necessary to confront the prejudice actively.

The approach I am describing is what the business ethicists call the moral minimum: the least that can be expected of an MNC to justify its existence as a corporate entity. But certainly there is nothing to prevent the MNC from adopting a more activist stance. If an MNC wishes to send a message that it opposes discrimination, that is admirable.

CASE AND ANALYSIS

The following fictional case is intended to dramatize some of the issues described in this chapter. Following the case is my analysis of it.

Case

Crescent Petroleum, an oil-refining corporation based in Riyadh, Saudi Arabia, has issued a request for proposals for constructing an intranet that will link its headquarters with its three facilities in the United States and Europe. McNeil Informatics, a networking consulting company, is considering responding with a proposal. Most of the work will be performed at the company headquarters in Riyadh.

Crescent Petroleum was established 40 years ago by family members who are related by marriage to the Saudi royal family. At the company headquarters, the support staff and clerical staff include women, most of whom are related to the owners of the company. The professional, managerial, and executive staff is all male, which is traditional in Saudi corporations. Crescent is a large company, with revenues in the billions of dollars.

McNeil Informatics is small firm—12 employees—established two years ago by Denise McNeil, a 29-year-old computer scientist with a master's degree in computer engineering. She is working on her MBA while getting her company off the ground. Her employees include both males and females at all levels. The chief financial officer is female, as are several of the professional staff, and the technical writer is male.

Denise McNeil traveled to New York from her headquarters in Pittsburgh to attend a briefing by Crescent. All the representatives from Crescent were middle-aged Saudi men; Denise was the only female among the representatives of the seven companies that attended the briefing. When Denise shook hands with Mr. Fayed, the team leader, he smiled slightly as he mentioned that he did not realize that McNeil Informatics was run by a woman. Denise did not know what to make of his comment, but she got a strong impression that the Crescent representatives felt uncomfortable in her presence. During the break, they drifted off to speak with the men from the other six vendors, leaving Denise to stand awkwardly by herself.

On her flight back to Pittsburgh, Denise McNeil thought about the possibility of gender discrimination but decided to bid on the project anyway, because she believed her company could write a persuasive proposal. McNeil Informatics had done several projects of this type successfully in the last year.

Back at the office, she met with Josh Lipton, the technical writer, to fill him in.

"When you put in the boilerplate about the company, I'd like you to delete the stuff about me founding the company. Don't say that a woman is the president, okay? And when you assemble the résumés of the project team, I'd like you to just use the first initials, not the first names."

"I don't understand, Denise. What's going on?" Josh asked.

"Well, Crescent looks like an all-male club, very traditional. I'm not sure they would want to hire us if they knew we've got a lot of women at the top," Denise replied.

"You know, Denise, there's another problem."

"Which is?"

"I'm thinking of the principal investigator we used in the other networking projects this year—"

"Mark Feldman," she said, sighing. "What do you think we ought to do?"

"I don't know," Josh replied. "I guess we could use another person. Or kind of change his name on the résumé."

"Let me think about this a little bit. I'll get back to you later."

What should Denise do about the fact that the person she wishes to describe as the principal investigator has an ethnic last name that might elicit a prejudiced reaction from her readers? Is Denise's idea of disguising the sex of her employees—and covering up her own role in founding her company—a reasonable accommodation that is justified by common sense, or is it a capitulation to what she perceives as prejudice? Should she assign someone other than Mark Feldman to run the project? Should she tailor his name to disguise his ethnicity?

Analysis

This is a challenging case because Denise McNeil cannot be certain that Crescent Petroleum would act prejudicially if the company were aware of the ethnicity of the principal investigator or the sex of the company president. For all Denise knows, her company has already been eliminated from contention simply because she is female.

By deciding to submit a proposal, Denise is betting that any prejudice by Crescent has not already eliminated her. She now has to decide the appropriate amount of accommodation to make to the culture of Crescent.

In my view, it is appropriate for her to use first initials rather than first names to disguise the sex of her employees, and it is appropriate for her to "remove" herself from the boilerplate history of her company. My reasoning is that neither of these actions involves lying. Rather, these actions involve withholding unnecessary information. By disguising the sex and eliminating the story of her involvement with the company, Denise is choosing to offer less information that she traditionally offers, but she is not providing false or misleading information. What is most important, she is not acceding to what she perceives as a prejudicial attitude by being prejudicial toward any of her employees. In other words, she is not firing her employees or making them less valuable at her own company. If Crescent were to explicitly ask her about the sex of her employees or inquire about why she has the same last name that appears in the name of her company, she should tell the truth.

However, it would be inappropriate for her to tailor the last name of Mark Feldman to disguise his ethnicity. Doing so would be lying. In this case, lying would be inappropriate, not primarily because it would violate a Kantian principle or even the Golden Rule, but because it would represent too great an accommodation of what she perceives as a potentially prejudicial reaction by Crescent. She would in effect become an accomplice of Crescent.

Alternatively, if Denise has an available person other than Feldman to run the project, it would be ethically permissible to assign this other employee so long as doing so does not work against Feldman in his professional career. Before making such a decision, she should discuss the matter with Feldman to learn his feelings about being replaced. If he objects—that is, if he wants to be included in the proposal even if that would decrease the company's chances of winning the contract—Denise should seriously consider his feelings. In this case, following Feldman's wishes would be the right thing to do (from the care perspective), as well as the smartest business decision. Maintaining his trust is more important than winning this one contract, if he has given McNeil no reason to doubt his professional competence and character.

11

Intellectual–Property Issues

The Internet is now an essential tool for technical communicators. Software is sold not only in packages in stores but also as downloadable products on the Internet. Most software is supplemented by ancillary products and services on the Internet—from demos to patches to drivers to technical support. Most technical communicators subscribe to discussion lists and connect to electronic bulletin boards to stay current with general professional subjects and to find answers to specific questions about tools and practices. And, of course, there is e-mail, which technical communicators routinely use to distribute information and products to customers, as well as to solicit information from them. It is difficult to imagine the day-to-day life of the typical technical communicator without thinking of the Internet as a communication medium.

The rapid growth of the Internet over the past few years has focused attention on the always-complex question of intellectual property. Intellectual property—"property" that is created primarily in a person's mind, such as a book or a song or a software program—has always been a contentious subject, because it marks the intersection of two competing impulses. The first impulse is to treat it like real property, such as a house. I wrote the song, and therefore it is mine to do with as I wish. Only I can sing it in public, or sell it, or give it away, or make a recording of it. The second impulse is to treat intellectual property as a commodity that has value only when it is made freely available. What good is a song if nobody can hear it? What is the value of information that nobody can use and transmit to others?

In this chapter, I introduce the central issues of intellectual property that are of most concern to technical communicators. I discuss the main forms of intellectual-property protection—copyrights, patents, trademarks and service marks, and trade secrets—then offer brief discussions of specific issues that technical communicators need to consider, focusing on new questions raised by the growth of digital information. I conclude with a case and my analysis of it.

My goal in this chapter is particularly limited. For two reasons, I seek only to provide a broad outline of the important intellectual-property issues that technical communicators face in the digital age. First, I am not an attorney. Nothing in this chapter should be interpreted as constituting legal services or advice. People who are creating information products should seek the advice of experienced counsel. Second, intellectual-property law and practices are evolving radically and swiftly. Most of the issues I discuss in this chapter are in flux. No book can provide a sure guide to current law on intellectual property. My intent here, then, is to sketch some of the major issues and encourage technical communicators to seek legal counsel when they enter the complex world of intellectual property.

THE COMPLEXITY OF INTELLECTUAL-PROPERTY ISSUES IN THE DIGITAL AGE

The fact that most information today is created and transmitted digitally seriously complicates the already imprecise body of law that is meant to reconcile the impulse to protect intellectual property and the impulse to make it freely available. One obvious example is the fundamental idea in our copyright law that a work is copyrighted as soon as it is fixed in a tangible form. Does that mean that my post to a discussion list is copyrighted? Does its appearance on the discussion list's server constitute a "fixed" form? Is a Web page ever fixed in a tangible form? After all, it displays differently on each person's computer. Another example: when I copy a Web page to my hard drive, am I copying it? When I merely view a Web page, am I copying it? Perhaps, because I am directing my computer to copy the site's files to my RAM.

Is the "look and feel" of a software product protected by intellectual-property law? Are the overall design of the screen, the design of the menus, and the design of the icons "original works" (and therefore protected) or merely a "method of operation" (and therefore not protected)? This question has been contested in several highly publicized lawsuits, and it is likely to be contested again. Proponents of protection for the interface argue that failing to protect it gives other manufacturers an unfair opportunity to copy the original product's unique features, thus undermining the original company's motivation to assume high research-and-development costs. Opponents of protection respond that forcing every company to create a unique interface "impedes the adoption of widely shared conventions, frustrating users, unnecessarily requiring programmers to reinvent the wheel, pushing up development costs, and inhibiting the compatibility that encourages a competitive marketplace" (Anne Wells Branscomb, 1994, p. 146). (See Rosch [1990] and Machrone [1990] for discussions of the legal and technical issues involving "look and feel.")

Another set of complications surrounds the question of authorial responsibility. To what extent should the person or organization that owns the communication pathway be held legally responsible for the content of the information carried on that pathway? Should America Online or some other Internet service provider be expected to monitor the information it carries and be held responsible for instances of fraud, illegal hacking, or libel? Is the Internet like a telephone company (simply a conduit for people's conversation) or like a television station (the owner of the conversation)?

One more complication: the World Wide Web is rapidly becoming truly international. What this means, in terms of intellectual property, is that any information product that appears on the Internet will need to be considered as if it is being literally shipped to every country in the world that has Internet access. A software manufacturer that puts a product demo on its Web site needs to think about whether anything on that demo violates any intellectual-property laws in Denmark, South Africa, France, Indonesia, and perhaps some 150 other nations. The World Intellectual Property Organization (WIPO) or another body might someday develop into a truly international body whose policies supersede those of the world's individual nations, but the experience of the United Nations, now a half century old, suggests that this development is unlikely to be either rapid or totally effective. It is probably safe to say that, during our working lifetimes, intellectual-property issues in the United States and the rest of the world will remain fluid and unresolved.

Complicating these questions even further is the fact that the culture of the Internet is undergoing fundamental, wrenching pressures. Many people who were responsible for creating the Internet a decade ago wish to do away with copyright altogether for digital information; they see the Internet as an alternative to traditional business-oriented media. Their attitude is that "information wants to be free." (See, for instance, Barlow [1996], who calls this phrase *an elegant statement of the obvious* [p. 20]). Recently, however, the giants of American capitalism have discovered the tremendous potential of the Internet as a way to do business. Today's intellectual-property conflicts are the growing pains of a medium that began as a utopian manifestation of noncommercial communication but is now rapidly becoming dominated by e-commerce. Although it is still true that, today, some people want information to be available for free—and are willing to make their own information products available without cost to the whole world—the major players of corporate America now see the Internet primarily as a way to reach more customers.

As complex as intellectual-property issues are, there is no doubt about their importance. If the evolving court cases and legislation do not manage to keep pace with the technological advances that complicate the issues, the health and vitality of the intellectual engine of the information age are at risk. "What is at stake," writes Anthony Lawrence Clapes (1993), " . . . is the computer industry itself" (p. 4). Unless a reasonable compromise can be devised between the rights of the creators of modern intellectual property and the utility of the numerous users of that property, much of the motivation that fuels the remarkable technological innovations of the digital age will disappear.

The problem with intellectual property in the digital age is that the law cannot keep up with the evolving technologies and business practices. Anne Wells Branscomb (1994) uses a common metaphor in describing this problem:

The law will lumber along like an unwieldy dinosaur wending its way to extinction if it cannot keep up with the pace of change in this new interactive, informa-tion-intense environment. But the law is by nature conservative, attempting to bring order only as fast as consensus can be reached among social groups willing to conform to norms they believe are fair and workable. (p. 5)

At its heart, intellectual property is a matter of ethics, a conflict between rights and utility. From the perspective of rights, the person who creates an original work or invents a useful device has the right to determine how that work or device is used, just as a person who buys a car has the right of ownership of that car. And in one limited way, the law accommodates this right: if you don't want anyone to see, use, or copy the program you have written or the device you have invented, just be very quiet, and nobody will know about your efforts. You can use trade-secret laws to protect your creation. However, conflict arises because most people don't want to hide their products from the public. Rather, they want the public to buy the book they have written, the program they have created, or the device they have invented.

When the creator of a work goes public with that work, he or she can no longer insist on a purely rights-based ethic; when the work is made public, the interests of the public must also be addressed. At this point, a util-ity-based perspective seems appropriate, not as a substitute for rights but as a complement. The legal system is our attempt to create a reasonable balance between the rights of the work's creator and the interests of the whole society, including that creator.

Although many of the arguments advanced about intellectual-property issues are causal—about whether a certain change in law will increase the public's access to information and therefore be a good change, or remove a creator's motivation to innovate and therefore reduce the public's access to information and be a bad change—there is little disagreement about the need to balance the rights of the creator and the utility of the whole society. Just where the fulcrum should be placed to achieve the proper balance, however, is the big, unresolved question.

COPYRIGHT LAW

Copyright is the principal means of protecting the information products used by and created by technical communicators. Understanding the basics of copyright law is crucial for technical communicators for two reasons:

- Technical communicators need to be sure they are not infringing another's copyright when they create their products. Although this knowledge has always been necessary, copyright issues for simple text documents are generally quite simple. For complex multimedia products that include music, graphics, or software—content that is itself protected by copyright—copyright issues can be extremely complex.

- Communicators need to understand how to protect the work they create.

In this section, I present the basics of copyright law, discuss the two instances in which permission to use copyrighted material is unnecessary (*fair use* and *works-made-for-hire*), present a recommendation for a corporate policy on copyright, and speculate on the future of copyright for Internet-based materials.

According to Article I, Section 8 of the U.S. Constitution, Congress is authorized to pass legislation "to promote the Progress of Science and useful Arts by securing for limited Times to Authors and Inventors the exclusive Right to their respective Writings and Discoveries." On the basis of this statement, Congress in 1790 enacted the Copyright Act, which has been amended many times and is now found in Title 17 of the U.S. Code.

In this brief statement from the Constitution, we see the two ethical rationales offered for copyright and patent law: rights and utility. The overarching principle is utility: the need to create a policy that will promote "the Progress of Science and useful Arts" in the new nation. As a means to this end, the Constitution stipulates that authors and inventors be given exclusive rights to their intellectual property for a limited period. The word *right* in the statement—interestingly, the only use of that word in the Constitution—suggests clearly that the authors of that document saw the products of a writer's or inventor's labor as actual property, like land or other tangible goods, and therefore deserving of protection.

Works protected by copyright law include musical, dramatic, pictorial, graphic, sculptural, and literary works. This last category includes not only such works as novels and plays and short stories, but also such categories as software, software documentation, brochures, catalogs, print ads, and business directories. In short, "literary" refers to documents consisting largely of words.

The copyright owner has five exclusive rights:

- *the reproduction right:* to copy, duplicate, transcribe, or imitate the work
- *the modification right:* to make a new work based on the work (this product is called a *derivative work*)
- *the distribution right:* to sell, rent, lease, or lend the work
- *the public-performance right:* to recite, play, dance, act, show, or transmit the work in public
- *the public-display right:* to show a copy of the work directly or indirectly to the public

If a right is infringed, the copyright owner may attempt to recover damages from the infringer or seek to have a court issue an injunction to prevent or restrict the infringement.

For works published before 1978, copyright expires 75 years from the date of publication (except if the copyright has already expired or has not been renewed, in which cases the work is not protected). For works published since 1978 and copyrighted by an individual, the copyright will expire 50 years after the death of the author (or of the last surviving author). For works published since 1978 and copyrighted by an organization (such as in the case of a work-for-hire written by an employed technical communicator), the copyright will expire 75 years after publication or 100 years after the date of creation, whichever comes first.

Protection begins when an original work is fixed, that is, when the work is made "sufficiently permanent or stable to permit it to be perceived, reproduced, or otherwise communicated for a period of more than transitory duration" (U.S. Copyright Office, 1998). An *original work* is a work that originated with the author, that is, a work that the author did not merely copy from an existing source. The word *original* is descriptive, not evaluative. It does not mean that the work is highly creative or groundbreaking or that it exhibits intellectual rigor. *Original* means only that the work isn't copied.

Copyright covers the "expression" of an idea, not an idea or fact itself. In general, this concept means that the actual words (and photographs, multimedia items, etc.) themselves, not the facts and concepts expressed by those words, are protected. For instance, copyright law does not "protect" the fact that water freezes at 32° Fahrenheit or the idea that collaborative work groups can help a new employee become acclimated to a company.

However, infringement can occur even if an author has not copied the exact words of another person; infringement occurs if the new work is found to be "substantially similar" to the original work. There is no precise definition in copyright law of this concept of "substantial similarity"; disputes are resolved on a case-by-case basis.

One technique used by authors to protect a work against copying is to build in ways to prove a claim that an infringer has deliberately copied the work. For instance, publishers of maps routinely insert minor errors, such as misspellings, in their maps to discourage copying by competitors. Computer programmers put nonfunctioning, invisible subroutines in their programs; in court, the programmers can reveal these subroutines in the infringer's programs.

Understanding four points about copyright law can help technical communicators avoid infringing copyright law unintentionally and help them secure legal protection of their copyrighted property:

- Ignorance is no defense. Because copyright law is widely published in books and on the Internet, courts are not receptive to the argument that an organization ignorantly violated the law when it infringed. Courts assume that companies are obliged to learn the law. For instance, many people believe (incorrectly) that any information on the Internet is not copyrighted, and that the people who created it do not care how it is used. However courts do not believe it.

- Although placing a copyright notice on the work and registering the work with the U.S. Copyright Office are not required, doing so makes it easier to take legal action against an infringer. For one thing, it deprives an infringer of the right to claim that the infringement was unintentional. In addition, registering a work is necessary before courts will prevent an infringer from violating copyright or before the copyright holder can receive statutory damages and attorney's fees from unauthorized use of the work. (If the work is not registered, the plaintiff can be awarded only actual damages and lost profits.)

- Citing a work is not a defense against copyright infringement. Citing means only that the infringer is not also a plagiarist. In a survey published on TECHWR-L, a technical-communication listserv, Foster and Loew (1997) found that most respondents incorrectly believe that citing a copyrighted source permits copying of that source.

- Copyright law does not trump libel law. Although a libelous e-mail message is protected by copyright, the author who sends it risks being sued for libel (Field, 1998).

There are three main instances in which it is not necessary to obtain permission to use existing material. The first instance is when the material is in the *public domain*. Works enter the public domain when the copyright expires, when the owner of a work copyrighted before March 1, 1989, fails to use copyright notice properly, and when the owner of a work fails to renew the copyright under the Copyright Act of 1909 (Brinson & Radcliffe, 1996). Anyone is permitted to use public-domain works in print or electronic documents. However, as O'Mahoney (1998a) points out, a compilation of public-domain works, being itself an original work, can be copyrighted by the person who made the compilation.

The other two instances in which it is not necessary to obtain permission to use existing material apply to copyrighted material. It is not necessary to obtain permission when the copyrighted material qualifies as "fair use" and when the material qualifies as "work made for hire."

Fair Use

The fair-use provision of the copyright law (U.S. Copyright Office, 1998), less than a page long, states that "for purposes such as criticism, comment, news reporting, teaching (including multiple copies for classroom use), scholarship, or research," copying is permitted. However, the law does not give complete permission to copy. The wording is deliberately vague:

In determining whether the use made of a work in any particular case is a fair use the factors to be considered shall include—

1. the purpose and character of the use, including whether such use is of a commercial nature or is for nonprofit educational purposes;

2. the nature of the copyrighted work;

3. the amount and substantiality of the portion used in relation to the copyrighted works as a whole; and

4. the effect of the use upon the potential market for or value of the copyrighted work.

In other words, the law intends that rulings be made on a case-by-case basis; there is no formula for determining what is fair use and what is an infringement of copyright.

Recent cases involving "coursepacks" illustrate the complexity of fair use. In a 1996 case, for instance, a court found that coursepacks—anthologies of copyrighted articles and book chapters used in college courses—are not covered by fair use. The defendant, a copying company, argued that under the first clause of the fair-use rule, coursepacks are covered because they are to be used for nonprofit educational purposes. The judge, however, found for the plaintiffs, a consortium of publishers, arguing that copyright fees are an important source of income for publishers, and that depriving them of this income removes their incentive to invest in publishing educational materials. (See "Publishers Win" [1996] for details of this case.)

In cases such as this, the court sometimes finds in favor of the plaintiffs because the copying service makes a profit from the coursepack—and the professor ordering the coursepack actually receives a "royalty"—whereas the true copyright owners (the authors or publishers of the content of the coursepacks) receive no payment. Sometimes, however, cases like this do not involve an obvious inequity. Rather, they present a true dilemma: the professor is trying to make the copyrighted materials available to students at the lowest cost, and the publisher is trying to protect its investment in having subsidized the making of the copyrighted material in the first place. In these cases, courts tend to find in favor of rights over utility; that is, they protect the rights of the copyright holder rather than the utility of the numerous students who would benefit from the less-expensive publication of the copyrighted materials.

Works Made for Hire

Material created by an employee as part of his or her regular employment is called a *work made for hire*. The employer owns the copyright to works made for hire.

Although this would seem to be a simple concept, things get complicated fast. For instance, for a regular employee, the assumption is that the material produced is a work for hire; for a consultant, the assumption is that the material is *not* a work for hire (Field, 1996). In the world of technical communication, however, these categories can be slippery. Subcontracting, and even sub-subcontracting, are common. It can be very difficult to determine whether a particular person is, in a given instance, acting as a regular employee or a consultant, or whether that particular person is working for the subcontractor or the subcontractor's supplier. As I suggest later in this chapter, it is wise to clarify this sort of question *before* work begins. Keep in mind, too, that laws regarding works made for hire vary greatly from one country to another.

Rights in work for hire last 100 years from the date of creation or 75 years from the date of publication, whichever is shorter. See Section 101 of the Copyright Statute for the official wording of the law on works for hire, and see Brinson and Radcliffe (1996) for a discussion of a works-made-for-hire conflict in the software industry.

Suggestions for Creating a Corporate Policy on Copyright

The nonprofit organization Copyright Clearance Center (1997) publishes a document template titled "Guidelines for Creating a Policy for Copyright Compliance," for use by organizations that wish to frame a policy statement "as a matter both of moral integrity and of adherence to U.S. copyright law." (This template contains a useful set of links to organizations interested in copyright matters in photography, music, motion pictures, and software.)

This document suggests that organizations take seven steps to reduce the incidence of copyright infringement for which they might be held liable:

1. Develop a corporate copyright policy. Even though the law is unclear and fluid, "honoring copyright is a matter of respect and integrity."

2. Involve everyone who has an interest in using copyrighted information.

3. Publish your corporate policy and keep your constituency well informed. Ignorance of the law is not considered a valid excuse.

4. Ensure protection of information created within your company. Put a copyright notice on all your company materials and register the most important documents with the U.S. Copyright Office.

5. Remind users that not all information on the Web is free. "There is a difference between information that is freely available and information that is available for free."

6. Encourage your constituency to use good common sense. "If you can't do it legally offline, you can't do it legally online either."

7. Do not hesitate to act. If you suspect an infringement by someone in your company, investigate it immediately and decide whether you need to take action. Doing nothing can increase your liability should the matter be contested legally.

Future Directions for Copyright Evolution on the Internet

Nobody can predict what copyright law for Internet-based electronic documents will look like in five years, and nobody can predict how changes in technology will affect common practices. Weiner (1998) sees four possible models for the future of electronic copyright:

- *Clearance centers*. People who wish to use copyrighted material will go through organizations such as the Copyright Clearance Center to secure permission.

- *Subscriptions*. Copyright holders will adopt a subscription model for their protected information. Some reference books and journals today use password protection, but the practice is still rare.

- *Meters*. Copyright holders will use technological meters that measure a person's use of copyrighted material and charge for that usage.

- *Barriers*. Copyright holders will use hardware and software that physically prevent unauthorized users from copying, changing, or transmitting copyrighted material.

PATENT LAW

Patent law is relevant to technical communicators primarily because some software can be patented. Whereas copyright is the primary means of protecting software (software, especially the source code written by programmers, is a "literary work"), several thousand software programs have received patents, a stronger form of protection than copyright.

Patent protection, mentioned in the same sentence in the Constitution as copyright protection, was enacted into law in 1790. Abraham Lincoln wrote that, before the patent provision of the Constitution, "any man might instantly use what another had invented; so that the inventor had no special advantage from his own invention. . . . The patent system changed this; secured to the inventor, for a limited time, the exclusive use of his invention; and thereby added the fuel of *interest* to the *fire* of genius, in the discovery and production of new and useful things" (qtd. in Novak, 1996, p. 6). The current law, enacted in 1952, is expressed in Title 35 of the U.S. Code (United States Code, 1998a).

A patent is defined by the U.S. Patent and Trademark Office (1998a) as "a grant of a property right by the Government to the inventor." A patent confers "the right to exclude others from making, using, offering for sale, or selling" the invention in the U.S. or importing it into the country." Although there are several categories of patents, the main one of interest here is called a *utility patent*. A utility patent protects devices and processes. Recent utility patents include those for hundreds of different genetically engineered microorganisms, for a tuning device for string instruments, and for a charging-station system for electric vehicles.

To qualify for patent protection, a device or process must meet three criteria. It must be:

- *New.* Either of two conditions would make it impossible to obtain a patent: if the device or process was known or used by others in this country, or patented or described in a printed publication in this or a foreign country, before being invented by the patent applicant; or if the device or process was patented or described in a printed publication in this or a foreign country or in public use or on sale in this country more than one year prior to the application for patent in this country.

- *Useful.* To be useful, the device or process must enable the user to carry out a real task. Implicit in this statement is that the device or process must be operational; that is, it must be in working condition.

- *Nonobvious.* To be nonobvious, the device or process must be sufficiently different from an existing means of carrying out that task, according to "a person having ordinary skill in the area of technology related to the invention." No precise meaning is offered for the phrase "sufficiently different."

The term of protection of a patent is limited. Before June 8, 1995, utility patents were granted for 17 years. After that date, the term is 17 years after the patent is issued or 20 years after the patent application is filed.

Because the process of obtaining a patent is lengthy and expensive (sometimes costing more than $1 million), relatively few programs are in fact patented. However, those that do receive a patent enjoy far greater protection than those that are merely copyrighted. Whereas copyright law does not protect the copyright holder from simultaneous independent creation, a patent prevents someone other than the patent holder from making, using, or selling the patented item, even if that other person invented the device or the procedure independently.

There is considerable controversy over the practice of granting patents to software. Many commentators argue that software should not be patentable because it is really just a mathematical algorithm, which is not patentable. Others argue that software should not be patentable because patents retard innovation. Mitch Kapor, f0or instance, the former head of Lotus Development Corporation, calls patents the "toxic waste" of the computer industry, lying below the surface and poisoning the spirit of innovation (qtd. in Clapes, 1993, p. 104). For a full discussion of the controversy about patenting in the software industry, see Clapes (1993); Garfinkel, Stallman, and Kapor (1996); and Heckel (1996).

TRADEMARKS AND SERVICE MARKS

A trademark or service mark is defined by the U. S. Patent and Trademark Office (1998a) as

any word, name, symbol, or device which is used in trade with goods and services to indicate the source or origin of the goods and services and to distinguish them from the goods and services of others. Trademark rights may be used to prevent others from using a confusingly similar mark but not to prevent others from making the same goods or selling them under a non-confusing mark. Similar rights may be acquired in marks used in the sale or advertising of services (service marks).

Trademarks are used to designate a particular company's product (such as WordPerfect), not a general class (such as word-processing software). Trademark law protects a company from another person or company that uses the trademark to confuse the public into thinking that the product or service is associated with the protected company.

Technical communicators should know the difference between two related terms: *trademarks* and *registered trademarks.* According to the U.S. Patent and Trademark Office (1998b),

Anyone who claims rights in a mark may use the TM (trademark) or SM (service mark) designation with the mark to alert the public to the claim. It is not necessary to have a registration, or even a pending application, to use these designations. The claim may or may not be valid. The registration symbol, ®, may only be used when the mark is registered in the PTO. It is improper to use this symbol at any point before the registration issues.

Claiming a trademark gives a company the right to associate its product with its mark within a certain geographical area, usually the state. The state may then take legal action to prevent competing companies from using that mark (or a very similar one) within that same state. But the competing company may use that mark in a different geographical area. Only a registered trademark, however, provides federal protection throughout the country.

Communicators are responsible for using the trademark and registered trademark symbols accurately when referring to the items. Unfortunately, doing so is not always easy, because companies often inappropriately claim registered-trademark status for their products. The U.S. Patent and Trademark Office site (www.uspto.gov) describes how to research trademark status.

Trademark law is also of special interest to technical communicators because of recent suits involving deep linking, the process of creating a hyperlink to a lower-level page on a Web site. This issue is discussed later in this chapter.

TRADE SECRETS

A trade secret is "information of any sort that is valuable to its owner, not generally known, and that has been kept secret by the owner" (Brinson & Radcliffe, 1996). There is no federal trade-secret law; it is handled only by individual states.

Technical communicators often use trade-secret law to protect databases and lists of customers, manufacturing processes, and software-development techniques. In addition, companies often use trade-secret laws to protect inventions while they wait for patent applications to be approved.

Trade secrets are protected automatically; there is no application process. Although competitors are not permitted to use industrial espionage to uncover trade secrets, they are permitted to research publicly available information and to use reverse engineering (the process of disassembling a product to understand how it operates). (See Clapes [1993] for a detailed discussion of trade secrets.)

Disputes about trade secrets pit the company's right to protect valuable competitive information against the worker's right to make a living. Trade-secret law is sometimes a serious problem for technical communicators who freelance or who move from one company to another. To prevent technical communicators from violating trade-secret law, companies often ask them to sign non-compete contracts: contracts that state that the com-

municator may not work for any competing companies for a specified period of time after leaving the contracting company. Although non-compete
contracts are not, as a category, illegal, courts have ruled that some
non-compete contracts are not "reasonable" and therefore not valid (see
Ryan [1998] for a discussion). A non-compete contract might be invalid, for
example, if it prevents workers from seeking employment in a certain industry, if it prevents workers from seeking employment for an excessive
length of time, or if it prevents workers from using their skills and knowledge in a new position.

INTELLECTUAL-PROPERTY ISSUES FOR INFORMATION DEVELOPERS

In this section, I describe nine intellectual-property issues that technical
communicators need to understand as they create their information products:

- copyright registration of Web sites
- the uncertain legal status of the "first-sale doctrine"
- implied and express licenses for e-mail lists
- works made for hire and the authorship question
- trademarks and service marks
- copying the design of Web sites
- deep linking, improper framing, and misleading metatags
- conflicts of interest
- rights of publicity and of privacy

I decided against using the word *guidelines* in the heading for this section
because so many of the issues discussed here are still in legal limbo. It will
be some years, at the earliest, before a technical communicator will be able
to find a clear set of acceptable—ethical and legally permissible—practices
about these issues. For this reason, I offer only one central guideline: consult an experienced intellectual-property attorney before embarking on
any project that involves any of these issues.

One other suggestion: remember that any information product to be
published on the Internet requires worldwide permissions for every copyrighted item it contains. Acquiring these permissions might be extremely
challenging because of the great differences in intellectual-property laws
from one country to another.

Copyright Registration of Web Sites

Copyright law suggests that a Web site, like any other sort of "literary work," is protected as soon as it is fixed in some tangible form; presumably, storing the files on a server meets this standard. Therefore, it is not legally required to register the site with the U.S. Copyright Office. However, attorney Thomas G. Field, Jr. (1998) recommends that important works such as Web sites be registered promptly. As he points out, although the law is imprecise in stating when an item must be registered, in order to recover statutory damages and attorney fees, a period of no greater than three months would be a good estimate.

However, copyright law does not stipulate how to register a Web site. The guidelines in the law are written to refer to tangible items, such as books, that have pages. Web pages are not fixed in the same sense as books: the same site, when printed out on two different computer systems and printers, could appear quite different. Therefore, it is unclear what information should be provided with the registration form: printouts of the contents of the site or source code of the files. For small sites, this problem is trivial: provide both. For large sites containing hundreds or thousands of pages, registration can be a problem.

Another obvious problem is that sites change, sometimes every day. How can a technical communicator register a dynamic site? Must a site be re-registered every time a change is made or every time a *major* change is made? The law does not address this issue.

The Uncertain Legal Status of the "First-Sale Doctrine"

The *first-sale doctrine* is the concept that after you legally acquire a copyrighted work, you have the right to give it away or sell it. After you buy a book, for instance, you are free to sell it to a book dealer. The copyright owner received a royalty in selling the book to you but does not (and should not) receive another royalty when you sell it to a used-book dealer.

The first-sale doctrine regarding digital information, however, is, at this time, legally uncertain. The complication posed by digital information is, of course, that it is very easy and very inexpensive to create and sell an exact duplicate of electronic information, such as software programs. Theoretically, a person could buy a legal copy of a piece of software and sell thousands or millions of copies of it, thus undermining the copyright owner's market. Something very close to this situation exists in many countries, where virtually all copies of popular, expensive programs such as AutoCAD are pirated.

The software industry's response to this problem is, whenever possible, to license its products rather than sell them. That is, manufacturers claim that when you "buy" a piece of software, you are in fact purchasing only a license to use the software. Because you are not buying that copy of the software, they claim, you are legally obliged to abide by the terms of the license. By using a license agreement rather than a purchase agreement, the software industry is attempting to reduce the piracy problem, as well as restrict many consumer rights that are normally held by the purchaser of a product. (You see these so-called "shrink-wrap licenses" when you open a new software package; you see "click licenses" when you encounter a license agreement on the screen as you install a program and are asked to "click to accept" the conditions of the license.)

Advocates of computer users strongly protest manufacturers' claims that such licensing agreements are legally binding. Kaner and Pels (1998), for example, argue that these licenses are not binding because they violate a central concept of the Uniform Commercial Code: the potential consumer's right to inspect the item carefully before deciding whether to make the purchase. For this reason, consumer advocates argue that, although there is nothing illegal about licenses in general, these particular kinds of licenses are not legally binding, despite the claims of the manufacturers. See Kaner and Pels (1998) for a detailed discussion of Article 2B, a proposed amendment to the Uniform Commercial Code that would significantly increase the rights of software manufacturers and reduce the right of users.

Implied and Express Licenses for E-mail Lists

Some commentators believe that anyone who posts a message to a listserv or bulletin board is implicitly giving the systems operator permission to archive or forward that message. Thomas G. Field, Jr. (1998) recommends that systems operators of listservs or bulletin boards explicitly state their copyright policies, as in the following:

Those who post to this list retain their copyright. However, subscribers grant a non-exclusive license to the list owner, directly or indirectly, to archive, and to other subscribers to forward, any message posted here.

All archiving of messages posted to this list is forbidden without express permission of their authors or the list owner! No site that conditions access on payment of a fee will be approved by the list owner as an archive.

No subscriber, by merely posting to this list, grants implied permission to associate his or her message directly with any commercial product or service. Nevertheless, subscribers should bear in mind that virtually anyone will have access to their messages. If there is *anyone* you would not want to see some message, do not post it here!

Field adds that people should not regard his model statement as legal advice. "I certainly do not suggest it as a fool-proof way to avoid copyright (much less any other) problems."

Works Made for Hire and the Authorship Question

The question of works made for hire can be approached as either a legal question or an ethical question.

The legal question, as I mentioned earlier in this chapter, hinges on whether the person who did the work was a regular employee or a consultant at the time the work was done. I pointed out that even this apparently simple distinction can be a source of controversy, and it often is, especially when the product turns out to be successful in the marketplace. (See Brinson and Radcliffe [1996] for a discussion of these controversies.) The obvious solution is to work out the ownership question in advance, and in writing.

The ethical question is somewhat different. Although the law states that a regular employee who writes, for instance, a user's manual has no legal right to ownership and therefore has no right to have his or her name displayed on the manual, most writers take pride in their craftsmanship; the fact that they received a paycheck in exchange for their work is important, naturally, but it not the same as a credit. Complicating this issue is the fact that modern information products are usually created collaboratively, then revised or updated by a different set of authors. Figuring out whom to list as a contributor to the product can be difficult and cumbersome. Still, many complex information products such as manuals do in fact list the major contributors, as do many software programs. If it is possible to cite major contributors to a product, fairness dictates that it be done.

Trademarks and Service Marks

The following discussion is based on an excellent article by E. Sanford Branscomb (1993) and Gregory H. Guillot's unusually comprehensive Web site, "All about Trademarks" (1998). To protect your own company's trademarks, follow these four guidelines:

- *Distinguish your trademarks from other material.* Use text attributes such as boldface, italics, or a different typeface to distinguish the trademarked term.

- *Use the registered trademark symbol.* At least once in each document—preferably, the first time—use the ® symbol after the name or logo, followed by an asterisk. At the bottom of the page, include a statement such as the following: "*COKE is a registered trademark of the Coca-Cola Company." An alternative to footnoting is to include a section in the front matter listing all the owners of registered trademarks mentioned in the product.

- *Use the trademarked item as an adjective, not a noun or verb.* Trademarks can get confused with the generic term they refer to; Xerox routinely runs ads explaining that you cannot "xerox" anything, even on a Xerox® photocopier; you can only photocopy something. Therefore, use the trademarked item along with the generic term: LaserJet® printer.

- *Do not use the plural or possessive form of the term.* Using plurals or possessives reduces the uniqueness of the item and encourages the public to think of the term as generic.

Incorrect:	purchase three LaserJets®
Correct:	purchase three LaserJet® printers
Incorrect:	the LaserJet's® fine quality
Correct:	the fine quality of LaserJet® printers

Copying the Design of Web Sites

Open any tutorial on Web-page design and you are likely to find the advice that the best way to learn design principles for Web sites is to look at a lot of sites and identify what works and what doesn't. I know of nobody who has made a site who has not spent many hours analyzing many designs. The common practice, when you find a site that you really like or one that contains features you do not know how to create in HTML, is to view the document source: the code that displays what appears on the screen.

Many Web designers go one step further: they actually copy the HTML code to their hard drive, modify it for their own content and audience, then launch the site as their own. One reason to create a site by modifying an existing one is to save time. HTML standards require a number of tags, particularly at the start and at the end of each file, that are the same for every page ever created for the Web. Another reason to copy and modify a site is to avoid having to learn the sometimes complicated syntax for creating elements such as tables and frames. With a printout of the Web page sitting beside your keyboard, and the HTML code on the screen, you can usually figure out how the designer created the effect you like.

Is the practice of modifying an existing Web page, then publishing it as your own, illegal? Nothing in the law answers this important question. The Web page that was copied and modified is copyrighted, regardless of whether the creator attached a copyright notice to it or registered it with the U.S. Copyright Office, and one of the rights reserved for the copyright owner is to make derivative copies of that work. This right means that the owner can modify the site, then publish it as another site or sell it to a customer. But does the fact that someone else downloads the HTML code of a copyrighted site, then modifies it, mean that that person has necessarily violated the copyright of the original designer? I would think not.

The important factor is not the method by which a person writes or acquires the code, but rather the use to which the person puts the code. In other words, what does the new site actually look like? If the new site copies text or includes original multimedia elements from the original site, then certainly the designer of the new site has infringed copyright. But if the new site uses navigation buttons in a narrow frame on the left side of the screen, just like the original site does, that probably does not constitute copyright infringement; the use of a narrow frame on the left side is a very common and very obvious design technique.

However, if the design of the whole page is strikingly similar to that of the original site, the owner of the original site might indeed have good cause to pursue legal redress on the grounds that the new site is an unauthorized derivative work. Of course, the chances that a suit would succeed rise if the alleged infringer is a business competitor of the plaintiff. In such a case, the court might find that the copying of the original design is not coincidental or unintentional.

The ethical implications of copying a Web design align with the legal implications. Just as a novelist reads other authors' novels and tries to learn from them, a Web author studies other people's sites. The actual downloading of code in order to save the time of writing it oneself might, in fact, be a technical violation of the law—the law is not yet clear on this question—but as a practical matter, nobody would know that you have done so unless you actually do something with that code: either publish it as your own, modify it and then publish it, or sell it. In any case, the ethical implications of the situation flow from your decision. If your own design is merely inspired by that of the original site, there is no problem. But if you publish it as your own work when it isn't, or modify it so little that it is essentially a copy, then you are stealing—and stealing is wrong.

Deep Linking, Improper Framing, and Misleading Metatags

A number of design practices related to creating Web pages are currently the subject of intellectual-property lawsuits. These actions involve allegations that defendants are unfairly suggesting that they own intellectual property that actually belongs to the plaintiffs. Three main areas are currently under scrutiny:

- *Deep linking*. Deep linking is the process of hyperlinking to a lower-level page on another organization's site, rather than to the organization's home page. Many Web-site designers routinely use deep linking, especially when they want to direct their readers to a page buried deep in the other organization's site. Deep linking saves time and effort for both the designer and the user: the designer doesn't need to include instructions on how to navigate all the way down to the desired page on the other site. And the user doesn't have to write down or try to remember the path to the desired page.

What is the intellectual-property problem? The problem is that deep linking enables the user to bypass all the site's trademarks, service marks, policy statements, and advertising. This bypassed information is the means by which an organization defines its own corporate identity, states its policies on how its site operates, and finances the operation of the site itself. In different lawsuits being tried now, plaintiffs are accusing defendants of numerous infringements of federal and state laws concerning copyrights and trademarks. However, it will be years before the courts reach consensus on rational policies on deep linking.

- *Improper framing.* Framing is the process of dividing a Web display into different sections, called frames, each of which operates independently. In a Web site that does not contain frames, the user who links to a new site "goes to" the new site; that is, the old site is replaced on the screen by the new site. In a framed Web site, the user who links to a new site usually sees the new site displayed in a frame of the old site. The new site is displayed "in" the old site.

  The problem here is that the contents of the new site appear to be contents of the framed site. For instance, a small newspaper with a framed site can link to a story in a major newspaper, such as the *New York Times,* and the *Times* story will appear in the small newspaper's frame, perhaps without any indication that the story is copyrighted property of the *Times.* This confusion is made more likely by the fact that one of the major reasons that a site might use frames is to display its own trademarks and advertising on the screen in a frame that never changes. No matter where the user is sent, or how far down the user scrolls on a page, the frame with the trademarks and the ads remains visible. Plaintiffs are arguing that defendants are deliberately misleading users into thinking that the defendants, not the plaintiffs, own the intellectual property that rightfully belongs to the plaintiffs.

- *Misleading metatags.* Metatags are keywords that a Web designer includes in the source code of the site to help search engines "find" their sites. The user of the Web site doesn't see the metatags, but search engines use them to classify sites by content area. (You can see the metatags in any site by viewing the site's source code.) As a result, someone who uses a search engine to find sites featuring the plaintiff's products is improperly directed to the defendant's site, even though the defendant has no relationship with the plaintiff. For example, if a Ford dealer listed "Chevy" and "Chevrolet" in its metatags, a user who searches for "Chevrolet dealers" might find the Ford dealer listed as one of his or her "hits" on the search.

Because of the slow pace with which courts rule in cases related to these rapidly changing high-tech issues of intellectual property, clear direction is some years off. Waiting for clear direction in fact might be futile, for the rate of technological change is accelerating, and statutory and case law is falling further behind every year. For this reason, some organizations are turning to technology itself as a means of protecting its intellectual property: software is being developed that blocks access to certain pages, thus enabling the organization to control, at least to some degree, other people's access to its site.

Common sense suggests, however, that one way to cut down on litigation and, in the process, to reduce unethical use of Web-based intellectual property is to communicate carefully with your users and with the organizations to which you wish to link.

For instance, if you want to link to a deep page on another organization's site, ask its Webmaster how to handle the situation. If he or she wants you to link to the main page, you should do so, for the organization's right to control access to its information outweighs the utilitarian concerns caused by the inconvenience.

To reduce the problem of improper framing, state clearly and prominently on your site that you are linking to different sites that own the copyright to their own intellectual property. Avoid placing a frame containing your own organization's information directly above the frame in which the other organization's content will appear; avoiding this practice will cut down on the chances that the user mistakenly thinks that your organization is the owner of the other organization's intellectual property.

To reduce the problem of misleading metatags, don't use them. Don't use a competitor's name or trademark in your metatags.

In general, ethical use of the Web correlates strongly with common netiquette. As O'Mahoney (1998b) suggests, if you wish to link to an organization's site, ask permission first. And state clearly on your site that if an organization to which you link objects to the link, or to the way you have linked to its site, you will eliminate or alter the link to conform to that organization's wishes. That organization's site is its own property; therefore, it has the right to determine whether, and in what ways, others may visit. See Kuester and Nieves (1998) for a discussion of the current status of these issues.

Conflicts of Interest

As I discussed in the section on trade secrets, many companies for which technical communicators work are concerned that the communicator will resign and take trade secrets to a competitor. A related fear is that freelance communicators will reveal trade secrets when they do a project for a competitor. Many companies insist that their employees and freelancers sign contracts that outlaw these actions.

Unfortunately, there is no simple, clear definition of trade secrets that enables either companies or technical communicators to distinguish between a company's trade secret and a person's knowledge and skill derived from working at that company. When a company sues a former worker for revealing a trade secret, the court listens to the evidence and decides on the merits of that particular case.

The best course of action is to consider this question before accepting a job with a company. If you think the language of the contract is too restrictive or in some other way unfair, attempt to get it changed. If the company responds that the language is just some legalese—"nothing to worry about"—insist that it be revised. If necessary, consult an attorney before signing a contract that concerns you.

Rights of Publicity and of Privacy

The right of publicity is a person's right to control the commercial use of his or her name, face, voice, or image. A technical communicator cannot use an image of a person without that person's permission (or, in the case of a deceased person, the permission of the estate). The right of privacy protects citizens—celebrities and noncelebrities alike—from unreasonable intrusion into their personal lives. Rose (1995) cites the case of a woman included in a photograph used in a news story about prostitutes; the woman claimed that the use of that photograph suggested, inaccurately, that she was a prostitute. In another case, a photo of a couple kissing was used without the couple's permission in a magazine article about "love at first sight." The couple sued, claiming that the photograph inaccurately suggested that their love was superficial.

These claims, as reasonable or unreasonable as they may seem, suggest that it is unwise to publish in a product any photographs, videos, sound clips, or other media that might violate a famous person's right of publicity or anyone's right of privacy. The best course is to create original media.

CONCLUSION

James Madison, writing for the *Independent Journal* in 1788, wrote

The utility [of copyright and patent protection] will scarcely be questioned. The copyright of authors has been solemnly adjudged, in Great Britain, to be a right of common law. The right to useful inventions seems with equal reason to belong to the inventors. The public good fully coincides in both cases with the claims of individuals. (qtd. in Clapes, 1993, p. 24)

Madison's view, that the public good meshes with the rights of the writer or inventor, is also that of the framers of the Constitution. Even amidst the turmoil caused by the rapid growth of digital information, few people question the ethical underpinnings of current intellectual-property law. Those who say, like John Perry Barlow, that "Intellectual Property is an oxymoron" (qtd. in Ryan, 1998, p. 171) usually are referring to digital information in the form of electrons, not digital information that has been printed. And I am not aware of any recent commentators who argue seriously that the recent chaos surrounding digital information should impel us to overturn traditional ideas and laws about older formats such as books and paintings or about inventions. I know of nobody who is advocating, for instance, that everyone be permitted to make and sell copies of John Updike's latest novel.

The controversy, for the most part, is tactical, not strategic. That is, most of the disputes concern such questions as whether viewing a Web site constitutes copying it—in one sense, it clearly does; in another sense, it doesn't—or how much of the design of a Web site is protected by copyright. The fact that they are tactical rather than strategic, of course, does not make them any less important.

As Paul Saffo has written, "The one thing about intellectual property that will not change is the complete chaos of intellectual property laws" (qtd. in Ryan, 1998, p. 171). Technical communicators need to be aware of the general outlines of the intellectual-property issues that affect their field—both the traditional questions and the newer ones spawned by the digital revolution. But technical communicators also need to understand that good will and a general desire to avoid infringing another's rights is probably inadequate, given the complexity of intellectual-property law and the rapidity with which it is changing. The best approach to intellectual-property issues is to know when to consult experienced counsel.

CASE AND ANALYSIS

The following fictional case is intended to dramatize some of the issues described in this chapter. Following the case is my analysis of it.

Case

John Wexell is Acquisitions Editor for Adams Associates, which publishes books about how to use new versions of operating systems and applications software, such as word processors and spreadsheets. Authors working for Adams, like authors working for its competitors, get early access to beta versions of the products they are describing, so that the how-to books appear on the market when the new software products are introduced. Also like its main competitors, Adams subcontracts its books. It does not have authors on staff; it receives proposals from freelance authors who wish to submit manuscripts to be published by Adams.

Adams is studying proposals from a number of experienced freelancers who wish to write its book on how to use the upcoming release of a major operating system for personal computers. Among those who have submitted proposals is Rajiv Gupta, who wrote an extremely successful guide to the previous version of the operating system. That guide was published by RTR Publishing, a competitor of Adams Associates.

Gupta's book for RTR Publishing won a number of industry awards, primarily for its innovative use of a flowcharting method that combined elements of several different varieties of structured writing. One of the awards cited "Gupta's groundbreaking design, which promises to revolutionize an industry not known for its willingness to change."

In the letter accompanying his proposal to Adams Associates, Gupta quotes some of the complimentary reviews of his last book. In addition, he explains the reason he is interested in working for a company other than RTR Publishing for his next book: although RTR did provide a graphic designer full time for over a month to help Gupta refine his design for the main pages of the book, Gupta was unsuccessful in reaching an agreement with RTR about a royalty rate for the book on the new version of the operating system. Therefore, Gupta approached Adams Associates to see if they were interested in signing him to write the book on the new version of the operating system.

As Acquisitions Editor at Adams, John Wexell is extremely interested in talking with Gupta, whom he sees as a bright young star in the world of software books. Wexell would love to sign Gupta to a contract that would have him do a whole library of titles on the new version of the operating system, a complex version that is sure to support several different books for different levels of users.

Given the fact that RTR partially subsidized the graphics used in Gupta's previous book, and that therefore RTR could claim that the graphic designer helped Gupta develop his flowcharting technique, would Adams Associates be in violation of any laws if it signed Gupta to write a book and he used that flowcharting technique?

Analysis

Maybe. Wexell should consult the legal staff at Adams Associates because of the risk that RTR would seek legal redress if Adams Associates published a book in which Gupta uses a design similar to the one he used in his RTR book. The legal staff might wish to advise Wexell on how to proceed, or might take over the negotiations itself.

There might in fact be a legal issue in this case. If the design devised by Gupta in his RTR Publishing book was sufficiently novel—a claim that might be strengthened by the positive reviews that mentioned the innovative design—RTR might well take legal action against Adams Associates for copyright infringement. As is common in the industry, copyright for Gupta's RTR book is probably held by RTR, not by Gupta himself. RTR might claim that the Adams Associates book is in fact a derivative work because it relies heavily on the design of the RTR book. RTR's case for copyright infringement might be strengthened by the fact that the designer worked full time with Gupta for more than a month on the design.

And, certainly, the fact that Gupta mentioned in his cover letter to Adams Associates that he could not reach an agreement with RTR suggests that RTR would likely be motivated to seek legal redress from Adams Associates if it thinks there is a case to be made.

First, however, Wexell could discuss with Gupta whether the flowcharting technique could be changed sufficiently to prevent any claim of copyright infringement. Gupta might have devised a new technique since the publication of the RTR book.

Wexell needs to find out, too, whether the designer who worked on the RTR book was a regular, salaried employee of RTR at the time he or she worked with Gupta. That information will help Adams Associates determine whether the ownership of the flowcharting technique resides with RTR (if it was a work-made-for-hire arrangement) or the graphic designer (if it was not). If the designer owns the copyright, Wexell could negotiate with him or her, and RTR would not be a party to the negotiations.

For these reasons, Wexell should meet with his company's legal department. The legal staff will probably want to examine Gupta's contract with RTR, as well as the book he wrote for them and a large sample of competitors' books on the same subject. Until Wexell gets legal counsel, he will not know how to approach Gupta.

12

Codes of Conduct

Codes of conduct are written statements, created by individual corporations or professional organizations, meant to encourage readers to act ethically on the job. Although codes vary significantly, most of them address several or all of the following issues:

- values of the corporation or professional organization
- practices that are permissible and impermissible for employees or professionals
- sanctions that the organization might impose if it finds an employee or professional guilty of an impermissible practice
- aspects of the law that affect employees or professionals

I will use the term *codes of conduct* to refer generically to the broad range of these statements. Different terms are used in the literature, including *credos, values statements,* and *ethics codes.* Although some scholars distinguish among these terms on the basis of factors such as specificity, length, and subjects addressed, I have not been able to discover a clear and uniform taxonomy. The only clear distinction seems to be between codes written and published by individual corporations and by professional organizations, because, despite many superficial similarities, the codes have different purposes, which I will address later in this chapter.

Codes of conduct are an appropriate subject of this book for two reasons. First, technical communicators are often involved, along with senior executives and legal staff, in creating codes. An introduction to codes—what they are intended to do, and what they can be expected to do—can help technical communicators in this task. Second, a discussion of codes summarizes a number of major themes of this book. The major theoretical question concerning codes—namely, whether they positively affect behavior—is a form of the basic question that this book addresses. Does the study of ethics have any real value beyond mental exercise? Are people's ethical values already fixed by the time they enter the workforce? Does the economic sphere respond only to the value of expediency? Should employees feel obliged to act ethically if doing so jeopardizes their own interests within the organization?

Obviously, I think the study of ethics is important for technical communicators (or I would not have written this book), but I am aware of the persistence and complexity of the questions surrounding a serious discussion of ethics as a practical body of thought. I don't know the answers to these fundamental questions; at this point, I hope only that this discussion of codes of conduct serves as a useful introduction to the subject and as a summary of some of the major themes of this book.

In this chapter, I begin by presenting a general description of codes, then discussing some of the major differences between corporate and professional codes. Next, I explain the various rationales offered to justify using codes, the process of creating them, their content, and the process of implementing them. I discuss the major criticisms of codes and the complex question of whether they are effective. Finally, I present a case and my analysis of it.

A BRIEF INTRODUCTION TO CODES

Figures on the prevalence of codes of conduct are not precise. One scholar estimates that some 90 percent of the country's 10,000 largest corporations have codes, but that only 5 percent of the country's 3.7 million other corporations have them (Manley, 1991). Another scholar places the figure somewhere between 70 and 90 percent of large corporations (Murphy, 1995). By contrast, almost all professional societies have codes, for the first question that has to be answered when people get together to form a professional organization is an obvious one: Why should we create an organization? Unlike a corporation, which has the underlying rationale of making a profit, a professional organization more likely exists to define and protect the interests of its members and to further the good of society.

Some professional codes, such as that of the Society for Technical Communication, are a few hundred words; others, like that of the American Institute of Certified Public Accountants, are a few hundred pages. Codes are distributed in different ways. Some corporations distribute them only to selected employees, although it is more common now to include all employees and, often, the general public. Codes are published as separate statements on Web sites, as parts of employee manuals, and as parts of new-employee orientation materials.

Codes are a relatively recent phenomenon. Although the J.C. Penney code dates to 1913, and Johnson & Johnson's famous Credo first appeared in the 1940s, most codes date from the 1970s and 1980s. Several events in the 1970s led a number of corporations to create their codes. Against the general backdrop of corruption related to Watergate, many large military suppliers and major industrial manufacturers were discovered to be bribing potential customers. A major investigation in 1973–1976 by the Securities and Exchange Commission, the Internal Revenue Service, and the Justice Department found that one third of the 900 corporations they investigated had slush funds for bribing domestic and foreign government officials. Investigations also revealed that, from 1971 to 1975, 34 corporations with gross revenues of $1 billion or more had made almost $94 million in illegal or questionable political payments domestically and abroad. These abuses led to the 1977 Foreign Corrupt Practices Control Act, which outlawed bribery of foreign customers, including government officials (Benson, 1989).

Another major impetus for many corporations to create codes of conduct came in the 1980s. The Treadway Commission (the National Commission on Fraudulent Financial Reporting) was created in 1985 by the American Institute of Certified Public Accountants and other organizations to prevent and detect improprieties in the financial-reporting process. This commission recommended in 1987 that all accounting firms create ethics codes. The Defense Industry Initiative on Business Ethics and Conduct, begun in 1986, encouraged the nation's 46 largest defense contractors to create codes of ethics, conduct ethics training programs, and institute hotlines (Raiborn & Payne, 1990).

Scandals and the resulting bad publicity are not the only events that motivate organizations to create codes. Many write codes when a new chief executive officer joins the corporation, when the corporation goes public, when new technologies raise new ethical issues, when the corporation enters a new market or increases rapidly in size, or when the corporation wishes to raise awareness of social issues such as cultural diversity.

As Stevens (1994) points out, modern codes of conduct derive from the ancient idea of *respondeat superior*: "Let the master answer." This concept immediately introduces one of the large, unresolved theoretical issues about business: the question of agency. A corporate code of conduct is, of course, a statement meant to influence the behavior of employees of that corporation and, to some extent, that of people who do business with that corporation, such as customers and suppliers; a professional code is a statement meant to influence the behavior of people working in that profession, such as lawyers or physicians.

But what precisely is the relationship between the individual and the corporation or professional body? Does it make sense to discuss the ethical responsibilities of, say, Sun Microsystems as a corporation, or only of the individuals who work for Sun? Is a corporation or professional organization entitled to stipulate ethical responsibilities for its employees or members? Business ethicists have not settled these questions, and, as I will discuss later in this chapter, some commentators consider the nebulous ethical status of organizations a serious impediment to the whole process of creating and distributing codes.

For our purposes at this point, it is enough merely to acknowledge the precarious theoretical framework on which codes rest. Because codes of conduct are extremely popular, and because corporations and professional organizations are routinely treated as entities by the legal system, discussing them is justified, even though, in some important ways, they are problematical.

CORPORATE CODES AND PROFESSIONAL CODES

To understand the difference between a corporate code and a professional code, it is necessary to understand what a profession is. Although there is no single definition accepted by all scholars, most accept the general outline of the definition provided by Bayles (1989), who sees six essential characteristics of professionals:

- *Professionals require extensive training.* Most professionals earn at least a baccalaureate degree, and many, such as physicians and attorneys, earn additional degrees.

- *Professional work involves a significant intellectual component.* Professions are primarily intellectual work. Although trades such as woodworking and plumbing require intelligence, the work is often less intellectually demanding than physically demanding.

- *Professionals provide a valuable service to society.* Lawyers, teachers, engineers, and physicians provide important services that everyone uses, whereas chess experts do not.

- *Professionals earn credentials certifying their qualifications.* Physicians receive certification in a branch of medicine, such as psychiatry, and attorneys earn licenses to practice in particular states by passing bar exams.

- *Professionals join professional associations.* Although tradespeople join unions, professionals join organizations that work to secure not only their own economic interests but also the interests of the greater society, such as high standards of medical care or safe practices in engineering.

- *Professionals often work autonomously.* More than other kinds of workers, professionals exercise their own discretionary judgment as they do their work.

These six characteristics of professionals are only generalizations. Many attorneys, for instance, do not work autonomously but are employed by large corporations that have a hierarchy as rigid and clearly defined as that of the military. And many physicians work for health-maintenance organizations.

Because most professionals have recognized expertise and credentials and provide valuable services, the general public is willing to let professional organizations control their professions to a much greater degree than is common in the working world. The American Medical Association and the American Bar Association, for instance, tightly control the entrance of new people into their fields. To the extent that this control works to society's advantage, the public tolerates it. After all, the public wants its doctors and lawyers to be highly skilled and highly principled.

When the public senses that the professional organization is seeking only to protect its own economic interests, however, it often takes action against the profession. Jamal and Bowie (1995) discuss a number of recent court cases in which anticompetitive features of professional codes—such as prohibitions against advertising—have been struck down by courts.

A second controversial aspect of some professional codes concerns practices or positions that the public does not understand or with which it disagrees. For example, the code of the American Bar Association contains statements recommending that attorneys be zealous advocates of their clients. Many people, however, wish that defense attorneys were a little less zealous, especially when they know or strongly suspect that the client is guilty. Many people also do not understand the concept of confidentiality when it applies to attorneys or journalists. They wonder why journalists should not be required to tell police valuable information that will help them solve a crime and arrest the criminal.

In a discussion of these aspects of professional codes of conduct, Jamal and Bowie (1995) recommend that professional bodies remove the anticompetitive aspects of their codes and that they explain more clearly their rationale for controversial ethical stances on matters such as confidentiality. This kind of explanation would require a discussion of rule utilitarianism, which holds that the best way to determine the ethicality of an action is, first, to articulate a general rule that leads to the greatest utility, then follow that rule even if, in this particular case, not following the rule would lead to a better outcome.

For instance, in the question of whether an attorney should be forced to violate confidentiality, the general rule that leads to the greatest utility is that all defendants deserve a vigorous defense, which requires that they be free to speak honestly with their attorneys, even though, in some instances, guilty people will be acquitted. Our justice system is based on the premise that it is better for guilty people to be acquitted than for innocent people to be convicted. For this reason, the state assumes the burden of proof in criminal cases; the defense has only to prove reasonable doubt. See Chapter 4 for a discussion of rule utilitarianism.

Although professional codes are limited, the best of them can—at least in theory—serve the public interest better than corporate codes can. Whereas a corporate code is written primarily to serve the interests of a particular corporation, a professional code, by its nature, is meant to serve the whole profession. The interests of the medical community, for instance, are more likely to overlap with the interests of the general public than are the interests of one medical-supply corporation. For this reason, a professional code is more likely than a corporate code to provide for uniform, consistent penalties, and more likely to resolve disputes in favor of the ethical action than the expedient action. See Molander (1987) for an excellent discussion of professional codes of conduct.

RATIONALES FOR WRITING CORPORATE CODES

Two main rationales for writing corporate codes have been offered. The first, the social-responsibility rationale, is that market forces and the legal system need to be supplemented by business itself if business is to fulfill its responsibility to its stakeholders. The second rationale, which might be called the commonsense rationale, focuses on the positive results that codes are intended to effect.

The social-responsibility rationale is based on the idea that the function of business is not merely to increase the profits of its owners. Rather, business has a responsibility to the greater society. This idea, frequently called the stakeholder model, holds that a business is connected with all the people and entities with which it interacts, including employees, owners, customers, the broader public, and the communities in which the business is located. The market economy and the law are insufficient to regulate businesses and prevent widespread and significant economic abuses. Business has a responsibility to regulate itself, to go beyond the profit-maximizing impulses of the market system and the slow and sometimes inconsistent dictates of the legal system.

Kenneth Arrow (1973), for instance, argues that businesses should be regulated in two circumstances: first, when they hurt the public and there is no market mechanism or law for fixing the damage (as in the case of environmental pollution); and second, when they have considerably more information than the public (as in the case of product information and safety issues).

Christopher Stone offers a similar social-responsibility rationale for corporate codes. In his book *Where the Law Ends* (1975), Stone counters Milton Friedman's argument that the social responsibility of business is to increase profits (see Chapter 2 in this book). Stone argues that Friedman's central premise—that corporations have made a commitment to their shareholders or owners to maximize profits, and that devoting any resources to any other goal violates that commitment—is vastly oversimplified and inaccurate. In addition, Stone sees the legal system as an ineffective guardian of the public's interest. Legal remedies are time-consuming and costly, and many ethical standards are impossible to translate into clear, objective law. Stone writes that

there is something grotesque—and socially dangerous—in encouraging corporate managers to believe that, until the law tells them otherwise, they have no responsibilities beyond the law. . . . We do not encourage human beings to suppose so. And the dangers to society seem all the more acute where corporations are concerned. (p. 94)

Arrow and Stone are representative of a number of business ethicists who think that the business community can most effectively fulfill its responsibilities to society if it complements market forces and the legal system with self-regulation.

The commonsense rationale for writing codes of conduct is that codes can benefit employees, individual businesses, and whole industries. Proponents of codes assemble lists of positive effects that codes can have (see Manley [1991] for the most comprehensive list, as well as excerpts from numerous codes).

Codes can help individual workers in four main ways:

- Codes can improve workers' morale and pride. People want to work for corporations that believe in positive values.
- Codes can help workers understand their rights and responsibilities. Workers therefore are less likely to commit unethical actions.
- Codes can help workers resolve ethical dilemmas, especially when their job requires that they supervise others.
- Codes can help workers resist unreasonable requests from supervisors, subordinates, clients, and suppliers.

Codes can help corporations in five main ways:

- Codes can help corporations clarify their own values and do strategic planning.
- Codes can help corporations reduce practices that are inefficient or that are causing negative publicity (such as bribery, sexual harassment, or

theft) by clarifying why the practices are undesirable and by spelling out a procedure for penalizing employees.

- Codes can help corporations reduce their vulnerability to lawsuits.
- Codes can help corporations integrate their headquarters with other domestic and international facilities, especially during mergers and acquisitions.
- Codes can help new employees understand the corporation's values.

Codes can help industries in two main ways:

- Codes can help reduce the chances of government regulation by showing that the industry is willing to regulate itself.
- Codes can help restore public confidence in the industry.

Obviously, this list of rationales for writing codes is a mixture of guesses and wishful thinking. All the rationales are plausible, but none of them is empirically verifiable. I will discuss this point in some detail later in this chapter.

THE PROCESS OF WRITING CODES

Perhaps the chief benefit of having a code of conduct derives directly from the process of writing it. The process of writing the code is fundamentally important because one of the main goals of the whole enterprise is to generate a serious discussion within the organization about its values and priorities. If the process of writing the code does not seem to give voice to the different constituencies that will be most affected by the code, the resulting code will be suspect. If employees do not have an opportunity to contribute to the process of creating the code, any high-minded claims in the code about the organization's respect for the innate worth of all the employees will ring false.

Joanne Ciulla (1992), who serves as an ethics consultant to corporations, makes this point when she writes about the practice of having an outsider draft a code.

I'm not sure that it is ethical for a consultant to author a code of ethics for a firm. I have my doubts about the authenticity of a company that goes out and buys a code of ethics. Codes aren't important on their own. What is important is how they were developed, implemented and understood inside the organization. (p. 178)

Who in fact does write ethics codes? Almost every conceivable person and entity within a corporation or professional organization: the chief executive officer, the board of directors, the legal department, finance, human resources, and technical communication. Codes are also written by task forces and by committees of employees. On the basis of a 1991 survey of American and European corporations, Laura Nash (1992) observes that, in recent years, fewer outsiders are involved in writing codes, suggesting that codes are becoming more central to the actual operations of corporations. Another possible explanation of this trend, however, is that businesses are becoming more comfortable with the process of writing codes and therefore see less need to turn to outsiders for assistance.

Of more importance than the question of who actually drafts the code are two other factors: the involvement of the organization's leader, and the opportunity for commentary before the document is finally published.

The organization's leader—the chief executive officer or the president of the organization—has to be involved to give the code credibility. For the code to have any effect, employees and members of professional organizations need to believe that the process of creating and implementing it is a serious and sincere effort by the organization. Therefore, regardless of who drafted the code, all communication about the code should come from the office of the organization's leader, and that leader should be actively engaged in the process, rather than a mere signatory to the document.

In addition, all employees must be given an opportunity to respond to drafts of the code. Many workers will interpret the drafting of a code to be a cynical attempt to manipulate employees and influence public relations; these workers do not need another reason to distrust management's motives. Many organizations attempt to involve not only their employees and members but also the general public. Publishing drafts on a Web site and soliciting comments can improve the quality of the code and improve the organization's chances of having it perceived positively.

THE CONTENT OF CODES

Deciding on the content to be included in a code of conduct is a challenging task. As with any technical-communication task, content is largely a function of audience and purpose. In planning a code, therefore, it makes sense to determine the audience first. Will the code be addressed to some of the employees or all of them? Will it also be addressed to the public? What will be the purpose of the code? Will it simply describe, in general terms, the values that the organization considers important, or will it also provide detailed explanations of permissible and impermissible actions? Will it review relevant legal strictures?

In their book on ethics and technical communication, Allen and Voss (1997) list six precepts commonly articulated in codes of conduct:

- Avoid not only improper action but also the appearance of improper action.
- Avoid conflicts of interest.

- Meet the quality standards of the industry or profession.
- Deal honestly and fairly with others.
- Address social issues.
- Make the code enforceable.

Allen and Voss are right: these precepts do often appear in codes. The difficult question, however, is how to treat these precepts. Every one of them can pose a problem for the writers of a code. For instance, "address social issues." What precisely does that mean? Does it refer to issues of discrimination and harassment in hiring and employment and, if so, does it call for anything other than a statement that the corporation pledges to adhere to all relevant laws regarding hiring and employment? Or does the precept refer to broader societal issues, such as resource use or environmental pollution, and, if so, how elaborate a description of the organization's position on these issues is required? Does the precept refer to the organization's philanthropic efforts regarding such issues as poverty, support for the arts, and disease prevention? In other words, Allen and Voss's list of common precepts should be viewed not as the outline of a code, but only as the start of a brainstorming list to be used to prompt a comprehensive, serious process of inquiry and deliberation.

Kaptein and Wempe (1998) describe some of the major dilemmas faced by people as they begin this process of inquiry and deliberation. Some of the most important questions that code writers have to resolve concern the following seven polarities:

- *Negative versus positive.* What tone is to be communicated by the code: an exhortation to the highest ideal or a stern warning to prevent unethical behavior?

- *Rules of behavior versus ethical principles behind the rules.* An overemphasis on rules can lead to a negative tone, whereas an overemphasis on ethical principles can seem imprecise and irrelevant.

- *Actual moral intuitions versus ideal moral intuitions.* Is the purpose of the code to describe appropriate and inappropriate behavior, given readers' actual ethical positions, or is the purpose to encourage readers to change their ethical positions?

- *Detailed versus concise.* Is the code supposed to be a kind of employee manual, describing principles and actions in detail, or is it supposed to be a brief statement of general concepts?

- *Internal versus external.* Is the code supposed to be an internal document, intended to bring about changes in operating practices, or an external document, intended to include stakeholders outside the organization?

- *Voluntary versus compulsory.* Is the code a set of ideals or aspirations that readers are invited to think about, or is it a statement of procedures that readers are expected to follow?
- *Education versus enforcement.* Is the code intended primarily to educate readers or to stipulate serious sanctions for transgressions?

The most important aspect of creating a code is likely to be the process by which some of these issues are decided.

In an influential article about codes of conduct, Molander (1987) offers an approach to help organizations write codes. His approach consists of two components: a classification scheme for types of content to be included in a code, and advice for structuring a code. Molander classifies the content of codes into four categories:

- societal values (such as "tell the truth")
- general ethical precepts ("our advertising will always be truthful");
- specific practices ("our television commercials will use only the actual product in testing, not 'lookalike' substitutes")
- law ("unfair methods of competition in commerce and unfair or deceptive acts or practices in commerce are unlawful")

Then, Molander applies this classification scheme in describing the structure of a code. He recommends beginning with a preamble, which has three purposes:

- *To emphasize the corporation's commitment to ethical conduct.* This commitment is necessary to validate the code.
- *To justify this commitment on economic grounds.* Unless this commitment is seen to be consistent with the economic imperatives of the organization—profitmaking for a corporation or survival and prosperity for professional organizations—the code will be dismissed as irrelevant.
- *To acknowledge the diversity of ethical views.* Codes should not perpetuate the fallacy that ethical issues are simple and that all the reader has to do is follow the rules contained in them.

For the body of the code, Molander recommends arranging the content in terms of "ethical distance," starting with those issues that are most central to the operations of the organization, then working outward toward the more peripheral issues. In other words, the code should start by addressing employee relations (issues such as favoritism, discrimination, and affirmative action), then the worker in relation to the organization (issues such as conflict of interest, privacy, and theft), customer relations (deceptive advertising and pricing policies), accounting standards (fraudulent reporting), relations with suppliers (gifts, bribes, receiving stolen merchandise), relations with competitors (price fixing, industrial espionage), and relations with government (improper political contributions, improper gifts to regulators).

Each issue discussed in the code should be approached in terms of one or more of the three categories he established earlier: a general ethical principle, a specific practice, or a review of law. For instance, the discussion of affirmative action should be treated as a general ethical principle (the organization's commitment to affording opportunities to groups of people underrepresented in the organization) and a review of law (affirming the organization's adherence to affirmative-action law).

In drafting a code, it is important to be aware of the tone it communicates. To a large extent, tone is determined by content; if the code describes sanctions for impermissible practices, it will have a different tone than if it presents only idealistic values. To some extent, however, tone is a question of language and emphasis. Lynn Sharp Paine (1996), for example, distinguishes between an integrity strategy and a legal-compliance strategy. An integrity strategy

is broader, deeper, and more demanding than a legal compliance initiative. Broader in that it seeks to enable responsible conduct. Deeper in that it cuts to the ethos and operating systems of the organization and its members, their guiding values and patterns of thought and action. And more demanding in that it requires an active effort to define the responsibilities and aspirations that constitute an organization's ethical compass. Above all, organizational ethics is seen as the work of management. Corporate counsel may play a role in the design and implementation or integrity strategies, but managers at all levels and across all functions are involved in the process. (p. 500)

In a linguistic analysis, Farrell and Farrell (1988) argue that many codes overuse such features as passive voice, nominalizations, and modalities such as *must* and *shall* to create an authoritarian tone.

As texts, the codes examined in this study impose the status quo and the requirements of management: they do not liberate moral and ethical resources within the individual. Rather the codes use language to create or maintain a hierarchical power relationship between addressees and the enterprise and generally indicate a tightened control over employees. (p. 598)

I find this view unconvincing. The first paragraph of the world's most respected code, the Johnson & Johnson Credo (1998), is full of the constructions Farrell and Farrell cite:

We believe our first responsibility is to the doctors, nurses and patients, to mothers and fathers and all others who use our products and services. In meeting their needs everything we do must be of high quality. We must constantly strive to reduce our costs in order to maintain reasonable prices. Customers' orders must be serviced promptly and accurately. Our suppliers and distributors must have an opportunity to make a fair profit.

This passage contains passive constructions, nominalizations, and the modalities singled out by Farrell and Farrell. Although I would make a few editorial changes, the tone communicated by this paragraph does not suggest the oppressive hierarchy suggested by Farrell and Farrell's commentary. Rather, the tone of this paragraph, in my view, is straightforward, clear, and assertive; the passage projects a sense of self-confidence, sincerity, and commitment. We err when we try to indict particular linguistic constructions; it is probably best not to worry too much about tone, at least at the start. If we try to say what we mean, clearly and accurately, the tone will probably reflect our sincerity.

IMPLEMENTATION OF CODES

As I mentioned earlier in the chapter, one point about which all scholars agree is the need to involve as many stakeholders as possible in the creation of a code. After the code has been revised, it is distributed, then implemented. Increasingly, organizations are realizing that codes need to be complemented by other initiatives; otherwise, codes lose their rhetorical power. This section discusses these issues of implementation.

Today, most codes are distributed to all employees or members of the organization. Limiting the distribution to only some segments of the organization—such as managers at a certain level or above—is now generally regarded as unwise in two ways: it is elitist, and it implies that people who do not receive it are exempt from ethical standards. A study by Nash (1992) found that whereas in 1986 only 66 percent of codes were distributed to all employees, by 1991 the figure was 77 percent. Increasingly popular is the strategy of distributing codes not only internally but externally as well. A study by Murphy (1995) shows that fewer than half of corporations responding to a survey distributed their codes to the general public, but that figure will probably continue to increase.

Many codes include sanctions that can be enforced when an employee or member of a professional association violates a statute in the code. Raiborn and Payne (1990) advise that codes that include sanctions be enforceable to allow the employee a chance to decide if the impermissible action is worth the risk of the penalty, and to suggest the seriousness with which management regards the ideas behind the code. Penalties usually include reprimand, termination, suspension, demotion, and unfavorable performance evaluations. In punishing an employee, the organization should consider the employee's level of employment and length of service, familiarity with the code, and the amount of training he or she has received. Although the organization wishes to use sanctions to underscore the seriousness of the code, the sanctions should be proportionate to the infraction. Little good is accomplished if the penalties are so severe that the employee simply leaves the corporation or the professional organization. Except in cases where a professional's conduct is quite literally dangerous to the public, the purpose of imposing the sanction is to encourage the person to act more responsibly, not to quit and join a corporation that tolerates the unethical conduct.

In organizations that include sanctions in their codes, one question that must be considered is how to set up a mechanism for imposing the sanctions. One model has enforcement carried out as part of normal operations in the organization. Another has enforcement carried out by a special disciplinary committee. The first model provides for faster and cheaper enforcement, but the second can increase the chances of detection, improve the uniformity and consistency of sanctions, and lead to more-ethical decisions.

A related question concerns the role of outsiders in the process. Those organizations that include outsiders in the sanction model find that doing so gives their committees a better perspective and leads to good publicity; however, the participation of outsiders can lead to breaches of confidentiality. In addition, the task of educating outsiders about the organization's business can be expensive and time-consuming.

There is growing consensus that, regardless of whether the code includes sanctions, it must be viewed as only part of a more comprehensive ethics program. If the code appears to be simply a piece of paper, it is unlikely to be a significant factor in educating people. Nash's study (1992) found that in the previous five years, one fourth of all corporations that have codes had added other elements, including in-house seminars, videotapes, and speeches from outsiders. The effect of these other elements is to raise the visibility of the issues addressed in the code; whether that increased visibility leads to greater compliance is impossible to determine.

A survey by McCabe, Trevino, and Butterfield (1996) suggests a positive correlation between employees' self-reported ethical actions and their perception that the code is not merely a public-relations gimmick. In addition, the study found a positive correlation between self-reported ethical actions and formal aspects of an ethics program, such as requirements that employees sign a form that they have read and understood the code, that they undergo mandatory training and orientation, that the code is widely distributed, and that the organization has a formal procedure by which employees can communicate with management about ethics questions. Later in this chapter, I discuss the difficulties posed by this sort of empirical research.

Efforts to create an ethics program, rather than merely publish a code, are based on the premise that corporate culture is an especially powerful factor in people's behavior on the job. According to William Frederick (qtd.

in Wartzman, 1987), studies show that "even the most upright people are apt to become dishonest and unmindful of their civic responsibilities when placed in a typical corporate environment" (p. 21).

An important task in an ethics program is to evaluate the code periodically. In Nash's study (1992), more than half of the organizations responding to her survey had revised their codes in the last three years, in response to such factors as new ownership, a new total-quality-management policy, new industry guidelines, or an important instance of employee misconduct. Among the topics most frequently added to codes in recent years are environmental-policy questions and such human-resources issues as privacy policies and drug-testing. Regardless of the directions the revised code takes, the important idea is that codes should be considered as dynamic documents that respond to changes in the ethical, legal, technological, and social environments in which organizations exist, not as static documents that articulate received truth.

CRITICISMS OF CODES

Although the business and professional communities are adopting codes of conduct at a steady rate, there is persistent criticism of codes in general and of particular aspects of codes. Following are the three most common criticisms:

- *Codes are paternalistic, authoritarian, and simplistic.* Cressey and Moore (1983) are the most prominent of those who charge that the premise behind codes of conduct is flawed. Why does the organization assume it has the right to offer advice—or stipulate policies—on a matter as complex as ethics? What is the source of its ethical authority? Another way to look at this question is to ask whether it serves the best interests of ethical thinking and actions to reduce complex dilemmas to platitudes. Offering simplistic bromides only teaches people that it is unnecessary to think about the complexities of the actual situation.

- *Codes are meant only for public relations; they are not intended to improve ethics in the business environment.* Criticism ranges from the claim that codes are mere window dressing to the more radical assertion that codes are cynical exercises meant to disguise cost-cutting measures or to placate citizen's groups or government regulators. For example, Cressey and Moore (1983) observed that code writers have more confidence in their ability to conduct surveillance of their employees than to create an environment that encourages ethical actions. Stevens (1994) makes a similar comment: "First, it is apparent that firms are strongly concerned with self-protection; that is, conflict of interest is a common theme in nearly all the studies. Firms seem primarily concerned with employee misconduct which might damage the firm. Second, the codes seem preoccupied with following laws. While ethical codes should promote law-abiding behavior, it appears that they are preoccupied with law enforcement and self-defense and often do not rise above this plateau to successfully articulate the values, beliefs, and precepts of a desirable corporate culture" (p. 67). Matthews (1987) states, "it cannot be concluded that codes of ethics demonstrate either (1) social responsibility, (2) a corporate culture which promotes anti-criminal behavior patterns or (3) self regulation" (p. 68). And Robert Jackall, in *Moral Mazes* (1988), observes that managers "who find their way out of the crowded, twisting corridors, and into the back room where the real action is, where the big games take place, and where everyone present is a player, shape, in a decisive way, the moral rules in use that filter down through their organizations. The ethos that they fashion turns principles into guidelines, ethics into etiquette, values into tastes, personal responsibility into an adroitness at public relations and notions of truth into credibility." (p. 204)

- *Codes are too general to be of any value.* Although they might be well intentioned, they offer insufficient detail to be of much practical assistance to employees who seek specific advice. Most brief codes would be vulnerable to this criticism. Consider this excerpt from the Society for Technical Communication's "Ethical Guidelines for Technical Communicators" (1998): "We seek to promote the public good in our activities. To the best of our ability, we provide truthful and accurate communications. We dedicate ourselves to conciseness, clarity, coherence, and creativity, striving to address the needs of those who use our products." These are laudable sentiments. But what exactly does it mean to say, for example, that we "seek to promote the public good in our activities?" Does it refer to how we choose clients or corporations to work for, or projects to work on—only those that promote the public good? How do we balance the public good and our own personal good? A sentence that uses the term "public good" without defining it or even suggest the criteria by which it might be characterized is unlikely to help someone determine how to act more ethically. The STC code is not unique in its use of broad sentiments; they appear in virtually every professional code.

Even codes that contain sanctions are subject to the criticism that they are too general. There is no code that can address every conceivable situation. As a result, some critics contend, the code sends exactly the wrong message: if the action is not explicitly proscribed by the code, it must be permissible.

THE EFFECTIVENESS OF CODES

Ultimately, proponents and opponents of codes of conduct need to address the big question: Do codes of conduct have any effect—either positive or negative—on actual behavior? Unfortunately, no clear answer is available, even though scholars have spent decades trying to find one.

For obvious reasons, opponents of codes have been less interested than proponents in trying to test the usefulness of codes. Opponents implicitly place the burden of proof on proponents: "If you would like to make the case that codes work," the opponents say, "go ahead; we're listening." I am aware of no empirical studies that have attempted to prove the hypothesis that codes are ineffective or harmful.

Proponents have tried to show that codes do in fact influence people's behavior in positive ways. In reviewing nine articles that investigate the effectiveness of codes of conduct, Ford and Richardson (1994) conclude that three of these studies reported weak, nonsignificant findings, one had mixed results, and two studies looked only at perceptions, not at behavior. Two more of the nine studies were based on surveys of business students. And the ninth article was a survey of salespeople from one corporation. In their own research, Ford and Richardson asked businesspeople to respond to a survey about their own unethical behavior. The researchers found a significant difference in the amount of unethical behavior reported by those businesspeople who work for corporations that have a code and those who work for corporations that do not.

This sort of empirical research, however, is vulnerable to a number of significant criticisms. Many people, for example, would view any sort of survey data with extreme skepticism. When survey respondents are asked to give their views, there is no way of knowing whether they are reporting their real attitudes or simply expressing what they think they should think, or what they think the researchers want to hear.

An even more serious problem is that this kind of research measures perceptions of reality, not reality itself. Survey research measures what people say they think, or what people say they see; it does not measure what is actually there. If employees of corporations that have codes sincerely report that they act more ethically than do similar businesspeople in corporations without codes, they might be demonstrating nothing more than that they have learned to parrot the language of the codes or to see their own behavior in a more positive light.

There is no way to tell, empirically, whether the behavior in one sort of organization is affected by the presence or absence of a code. One study (Verschoor, 1997) seeks a different approach: a correlation between the presence of codes and the corporation's financial performance. Verschoor's survey of the 500 largest U.S. corporations found that those corporations that discuss ethics in their "statements of internal controls" in 1996–1997 performed better than those that do not: they outperformed the no-code corporations in terms of total returns for one and three years, sales growth for one and three years, profit growth for one and three years, net margin, and return on equity. In addition, corporations that discussed ethics in their statements of internal controls were significantly more likely to make *Fortune* magazine's 1997 "most admired" list.

Verschoor's (1997) data provide interesting evidence supporting the premise suggested in the title of his article, "Principles Build Profits." But this premise requires considerably more support. It would probably be fairly easy to infer different or even contradictory conclusions from the same financial data that Verschoor used. In addition to this uncertainty, there is another complication: perhaps the employees who work at corporations with codes do in fact act more ethically than employees at no-code corporations, and perhaps the corporations with codes do in fact outperform no-code corporations. But perhaps the explanation for these differences is that people with higher ethical standards joined the corporations with codes for reasons completely unrelated to the codes.

The most compelling explanation of Verschoor's data for proponents of codes is that more-ethical workers were attracted to corporations with codes because they liked the corporate cultures that they saw in those corporations. Verschoor himself claims at least this: "While this strong association does not prove causation, it certainly suggests it" (1997, p. 45). If this explanation is valid—and this is a very large *if*—codes of conduct can be said to be only indirectly related to superior financial performance.

This argument for indirect causation can be seen as consistent with a number of studies that discount the importance of codes in influencing behavior. A survey of information-systems professionals by Pierce and Henry (1996), for example, reports no strong agreement or disagreement with the statement that a formal code of ethics acts as a deterrent to unethical behavior. Overwhelmingly, the information-systems professionals indicated that their behavior was influenced by their personal ethical codes: some 80 percent indicated that the personal code was the one they themselves used most often. And Lawrence (1975) found that people are more than twice as likely to follow their own personal codes than a formal code.

Perhaps having a code is a corporation's best way to attract people who want to work in a corporate culture that values ethical conduct. As Cleek and Leonard (1998) speculate, in relation to the personal factors of employees that an organization can influence,

the organization does not have control over the individual factors of their employees, except insofar as they control the factors that result in the people that will be working in their organization; thus their recruiting and selection procedures are the only means the business can use to influence the character of the employees. (pp. 620–621)

My conclusion, then, is that there is insufficient empirical support for the hypothesis that ethics codes actually influence employee behavior—their principal rationale. In drawing this conclusion, however, I am commenting more about the nature of empiricism than about the validity of the hypothesis. There are simply too many confounding variables—factors other than the factors being studied that might influence behavior—to support an empirical conclusion about this subject.

Still, I think it makes sense to create and publicize a code of conduct, as part of a comprehensive ethics program. Ultimately, whether a code of conduct is effective is less a matter of what the code does or does not say than of the broader culture of the organization. An effective statement of this idea is contained in "The HP Way," a credo published on the Hewlett-Packard Web site (1998):

> We conduct our business with uncompromising integrity. We expect HP people to be open and honest in their dealings to earn the trust and loyalty of others. People at every level are expected to adhere to the highest standards of business ethics and must understand that anything less is unacceptable. As a practical matter, ethical conduct cannot be assured by written HP policies and codes; it must be an integral part of the organization, a deeply ingrained tradition that is passed from one generation of employees to another.

The last sentence here is important: ethical conduct cannot be assured (and, what I think the code is intended to say, "cannot be *ensured*") by policies and codes. People have to believe what the code says and act accordingly. If the process of creating and implementing a code of conduct forces people in the organization to think about their ethical responsibilities, that is a good thing.

In the wake of the 1982 Tylenol product-tampering case, Johnson & Johnson president James Burke was widely praised for his decision to withdraw all Tylenol products from store shelves, a decision that cost his corporation $100 million. He said he made the decision because the first line of the corporation's code read, "We believe our first responsibility is to the doctors, nurses, and patients, to mothers, and to all others who use our products and services" (DeGeorge, 1995). When pressed by skeptical reporters, Burke expressed surprise that so many people would consider his decision unusual. He simply did what the code said he should do.

CASE AND ANALYSIS

The following fictional case is intended to dramatize some of the issues described in this chapter. Following the case is my analysis of it.

Case

Sarah Gibson joined the Society for Technical Communication as an undergraduate major in technical communication. She helped organize the student chapter and, for a year, served as the president. An active student with above-average grades, she did two internships, one with the registrar's office at her university, helping write instruction manuals for clerks using the university's new online registration system, and one with a local software manufacturer, writing and editing user manuals. Now in her last semester at the university, she is looking forward to her first full-time job as a technical communicator. One reason she wants to start work is that she is carrying a student loan of over $10,000. Because she has supported herself with part-time work for the last six years, she is eager to start paying off the debt.

One of her interviews is with Haynes Peripherals, a small start-up company founded by Warren Haynes, a 45–year-old electrical engineer who has invented four hardware products used in connecting computers in small office networks.

Warren Haynes is interviewing Sarah Gibson. He is describing the company. There are only six technical personnel and one secretary. Sarah would be joining the company as their technical communicator. In that capacity, she would handle all the documentation for the hardware. In addition, she would start an employee newsletter and a Web site.

Sarah asks to see their documentation. Warren's face brightens as he pulls a few small manuals off the shelf behind him. He hands them to her.

"I don't mind telling you I'm pretty proud of these." Her heart sinks as she pages through one of them. They look like photocopies of typewritten pages. "I wrote them myself," he beams. "The way I figure it, who knows the product better than the people who built it, from the ground up? I believe we owe it to our customers to give them the very best information we can about our products."

The body of the manual she is looking at is a list of descriptions of the different tasks that can be accomplished through the function keys. The body begins with a brief chapter on the F1 key, consisting of a table showing what happens when the user hits the F1 key, the F1 key +<Shift>, the F1 + <Ctrl>, and so forth. Then comes the chapter on the F2 key, and the chapter on F3. In 15 seconds, Sarah can tell that Mr. Haynes has no idea how to create product documentation.

"Tell me, Mr. Haynes," Sarah says, raising her eyes up from the manual, "why you're interested in hiring a technical communicator."

"Well," he replies, "to tell you the truth, it's just a question of time. I don't know if you can tell, but I took a couple of writing courses in college, and I'm one of the few engineers I know who actually likes writing manuals. But I just don't have the time anymore. What I'm looking for is someone who can follow in my footsteps. You know, use these as a template for the new products. Of course, you'll have to work with me and the other engineers to make sure you haven't introduced any errors into the manuals. But other than that, it shouldn't be too hard. We'll give you all the information you need about the new products."

The interview concludes a few minutes later. Two weeks later, Sarah has heard from all four companies with which she interviewed. Two companies selected other applicants. She has received an offer from a health-care company that is offering her an average salary for an entry-level position as a writer/editor. The position would require a 45–minute commute each way, a factor that doesn't please her, especially since her car is two months away from its 20th birthday. In addition, Sarah is not particularly interested in the subject she would be writing about.

Warren Haynes makes his offer in a phone call. The salary is $9,000 higher than that offered by the health-care company. He tells Sarah, "It's a pretty good offer—I've done some checking around—but I think you could do the job, and you've got excellent references."

Sarah isn't prepared for the phone call and doesn't want to have to give him a decision right at the moment. She thanks him for the offer and asks if she can have a few days to make up her mind. He agrees.

After hanging up, she starts to consider the pluses and minuses of the offer. The big plus is a salary differential of almost $9,000. And she likes the idea of working for a small company, where she would have a lot of different kinds of tasks to do. The one sticking point is the horrible documentation that Mr. Haynes showed her. If only someone else had written it, she thinks. How can she do what he wants: use his manuals as a template?

Sarah thinks back to a project she did last year in a technical communication course: analyzing the STC code. She pulls out a copy of the "STC Ethical Guidelines for Technical Communicators" and looks at the section titled "Professionalism:" We seek candid evaluations of our professional performance from clients and employers. We also provide candid evaluations of communication products and services. We advance the technical communication profession through our integrity, standards, and performance. Because writing product documentation is the single biggest part of the job, this problem is important. She wonders if she can take a job where she would have to create documentation that is hopelessly out of date and ineffective.

What should she do?

Analysis

Although the salary offered by Warren Haynes is attractive and the variety of tasks is a selling point, Sarah Gibson should think seriously before accepting the position. Although her only other offer is unattractive in a number of ways, and Sarah wants to start work right away, the question of professionalism is important. If she starts working for Haynes Peripherals and determines that Mr. Haynes is committed to his style of documentation, Sarah will clearly be violating the section of the STC code that calls for offering candid evaluations of information products. Certainly, users of the documentation cannot be satisfied with it, even if Mr. Haynes is not aware of the dissatisfaction. In this case, the comment in the STC code should help Sarah focus on an important point: she needs to balance her own personal needs with those of her readers. She should not take the job if doing so means that she will have to perpetuate the company's tradition of ineffective documentation. The bad documentation does not serve the interests of the users, a fact that would soon demoralize her.

Sarah should see if she can set up an appointment with Mr. Haynes, at which she can thank him for his offer and openly discuss her misgivings about his approach to documentation. If she could explain how she would approach the documentation, possibly by showing him some samples from her own portfolio or by revising a section of one of his manuals, and by discussing some of the advantages associated with effective documentation (decreased support costs, increased user satisfaction), she might be able to persuade him to let her use her own approach to writing the documentation.

If he won't grant her the interview or rejects her ideas, she should not accept the position. If he seems willing to go along with her ideas, or at least to let her try out her ideas on the job, she should accept the position.

A FINAL THOUGHT

I would like to take a moment now to expand this discussion of codes of conduct to include the subject of this book: ethics and the technical communicator. In the first part of this book, I have tried to introduce some of the main currents of Western ethical theory, providing enough detail to suggest some of the enormous complexity of ethical thought and highlighting some of the major conceptual shortcomings of the different ethical theories. And I have tried to sketch an approach to ethical decision making that combines the best elements of rights, justice, utility, and care with the consensual decision-making approach of contemporary discourse ethicists such as Habermas. (This Habermasian approach, which I explain in Chapter 7, would be the best way to begin a discussion of codes of conduct in an organizational context, because it would provide the greatest opportunity for the organization to discover its own culture.)

In Part II of this book, I have tried to provide a brief overview of some of the ethical issues that are central to the lives of technical communicators, such as liability issues and intellectual-property issues. My goal in this part of the book has been merely to suggest the kinds of ethical and legal implications inherent in these issues so that technical communicators can be aware of the issues and seek further counsel.

Asking whether this book will influence a reader's behavior is similar to asking whether a code of conduct will do any good. My hope is that this book has, on occasion, prompted readers to think about ethics and technical communication in new ways, to see the many complex and significant ties between the two fields, and that this thinking will, in some positive way, be reflected in readers' working lives. I don't know whether this book will fulfill even this modest goal. However, I am reasonably confident that, as the saying goes, it can't hurt.

References

Allen, L., & Voss, D. (1997). *Ethics in technical communication: Shades of gray.* New York: Wiley.

Allen, N. (1996). Ethics and visual rhetorics: Seeing's not believing anymore. *Technical Communication Quarterly, 5,* 87–105.

Andrews, D. (1998). *Technical communication in the global community.* Upper Saddle River, NJ: Prentice-Hall.

Aristotle. (1953). *Nicomachean ethics* (J. A. K. Tomson, Trans.). Baltimore: Penguin Books.

Arrow, K. J. (1973). Social responsibility and economic efficiency. *Public Policy, 21,* 303–317.

Ayer, A. J. (1936). *Language, truth and logic.* London: Gollancz.

Baier, A. C. (1987). Hume, the women's moral theorist? In E. F. Kittay & D. T. Meyers (Eds.), *Women and moral theory* (pp. 37–55). Totowa, NJ: Rowman & Littlefield.

Baier, A. C. (1993). What do women want in a moral theory? In M. J. Larrabee (Ed.), *An ethic of care: Feminist and interdisciplinary perspectives* (pp. 19–32). New York: Routledge.

Barlow, J. P. (1996). Selling wine without bottles: The economy of mind on the global net. In P. Ludlow (Ed.), *High noon on the electronic frontier: Conceptual issues in cyberspace* (pp. 9–34). Cambridge, MA: MIT Press.

Barton, B., & Barton, M. (1981). Ethos, persona, and role confusion in engineering: Toward a pedagogy for technical discourse. In J.C. Mathes & T. E. Pinelli

(Eds.), *Technical communication: Perspectives for the eighties* (pp. 447–453). Hampton, VA: National Aeronautics and Space Administration.

Bathon, G. (1999, May). Eat the way your mama taught you. *Intercom*; 22–24.

Baumrind, D. (1993). Sex differences in moral reasoning: Response to Walker's (1984) conclusion that there are none. In M. J. Larrabee (Ed.), *An ethic of care: Feminist and interdisciplinary perspectives* (pp. 177–192). New York: Routledge.

Bayles, M. D. (1989). *Professional ethics* (2nd ed.). Belmont, CA: Wadsworth.

Beauchamp, T. L. (1993). Manipulative advertising. In T. L. Beauchamp & N. E. Bowie (Eds.), *Ethical theory and business* (4th ed., pp. 475–483). Englewood Cliffs, NJ: Prentice Hall.

Beauchamp, T. L., & Bowie, N. E. (Eds.). (1993). *Ethical theory and business* (4th ed.). Englewood Cliffs, NJ: Prentice Hall.

Benhabib, S. & Dallmayr, F. (Eds.). (1990). *The communicative ethics controversy.* Cambridge, MA: MIT Press.

Benson, G. C. S. (1989). Codes of ethics. *Journal of Business Ethics, 8*, 305–319.

Bentham, J. (1948). *An introduction to the principles of morals and legislation.* New York: Hafner. (Original work published 1789).

Berlin, J. A. (1993). Poststructuralism, semiotics, and social-epistemic rhetoric: Converging agendas. In T. Enos & S. C. Brown (Eds.), *Defining the new rhetorics* (pp. 137–153). Newbury Park, CA: Sage.

Bertens, H. (1995). *The idea of the postmodern: A history.* London: Routledge.

Bizzell, P. (1990). Beyond anti-foundationalism to rhetorical authority: Problems defining "cultural literacy." *College English, 52,* 661–675.

Boatright, J. R. (1995). Aristotle meets Wall Street: The case for virtue ethics in business. *Business Ethics Quarterly 5,* 353–359.

Boatright, J. R. (2000). *Ethics and the conduct of business* (3rd ed.). Upper Saddle River, NJ: Prentice Hall.

Bok, S. (1978). *Lying: Moral choice in public and private life.* New York: Pantheon.

Bowden, P. (1997). *Caring: Gender-sensitive ethics.* London: Routledge.

Bowie, N. (1993). The moral obligations of multinational corporations. In T. L. Beauchamp & N. E. Bowie (Eds.), *Ethical theory and business* (4th ed, pp. 519–531). Englewood Cliffs, NJ: Prentice Hall.

Bowie, N. (1996). Relativism, cultural and moral. In T. Donaldson & P. H. Werhane (Eds.), *Ethical issues in business* (5th ed, pp. 91–95). Upper Saddle River, NJ: Prentice Hall.

Brabeck, M. (1993). Moral judgment: Theory and research on differences between males and females. In M. J. Larrabee (Ed.), *An ethic of care: Feminist and interdisciplinary perspectives* (pp. 33–48). New York: Routledge.

Branscomb, A. W. (1994). *Who owns information? From privacy to public access.* New York: Basic Books.

Branscomb, E. S. (1993). Trademarks: Caveat scriptor. *Technical Communication, 40,* 97–99.

Brenkert, G. G. (1993). Strict products liability and compensatory justice. In T. L. Beauchamp & N. E. Bowie (Eds.), *Ethical theory and business* (4th ed., pp. 198–203). Englewood Cliffs, NJ: Prentice Hall.

Brinson, J. D., & Radcliffe, M. F. (1996). *An intellectual property law primer for multimedia and web developers* [Online]. Available: <http://www.eff.org/pub/

Intellectual_Property/multimedia_ip_primer.paper> [1998, November 13].

Brockmann, R. J., & Rook, F. (Eds.). (1989). *Technical communication and ethics.* Washington, DC: Society for Technical Communication.

Broughton, J. M. (1993). Women's rationality and men's virtues: A critique of gender dualism in Gilligan's theory of moral development. In M. J. Larrabee (Ed.), *An ethic of care: Feminist and interdisciplinary perspectives* (112–139). New York: Routledge..

Bryan, J. (1992). Down the slippery slope: Ethics and the technical writer as marketer. *Technical Communication Quarterly, 1*, 73–88.

Bryan, J. (1995). Seven types of distortion: A taxonomy of manipulative techniques used in charts and graphs. *Journal of Technical Writing and Communication, 25*, 127–179.

Bunch, C. (1992). A global perspective on feminist ethics and diversity. In E. B. Cole & S. Coultrap-McQuin (Eds.), *Explorations in feminist ethics: Theory and practice* (176–185). Bloomington, IN: Indiana University Press.

Callinicos, A. (1990). *Against postmodernism: A Marxist critique.* New York: St. Martin's Press.

Camm, B. L., Ross, K., & Scott, G. (1993). Product liability: How it affects the writing and design of instruction manuals for the United States and the European Community. In *Proceedings of the 40th International Technical Communication Conference* (pp. 56–59). Arlington, VA: Society for Technical Communication.

Campbell, J. (1995). *Understanding John Dewey.* Chicago: Open Court.

Carr, A. Z. (1993). Is business bluffing ethical? In T. L. Beauchamp & N. E. Bowie (Eds.), *Ethical theory and business* (4th ed., pp. 449–454). Englewood Cliffs, NJ: Prentice Hall. This is an abridged version of the 1968 *Harvard Business Review* version, published in the January-February issue, 143–159.

Carson, R. (1962). *Silent spring.* Boston: Houghton Mifflin.

Cavanaugh, G. F., Moberg, D. J., & Velasquez, M. (1995). Making business ethics practical. *Business Ethics Quarterly, 5*, 399–418.

Chodorow, N. J. (1978). *The reproduction of mothering: Psychoanalysis and the sociology of gender.* Berkeley, CA: University of California Press.

Ciulla, J. (1992) Breathing new life into a corporate code of ethics. In J. Mahoney & E. Vallance (Eds.), *Business ethics in a new Europe* (pp. 177–189). Norwell, MA: Kluwer.

Clapes, A. L. (1993). *Softwars: The legal battles for control of the global software industry.* Westport, CT: Quorum.

Clark, G. (1987). Ethics in technical communication: A rhetorical approach. *IEEE Transactions on Professional Communication, 30*, 190–195.

Cleek, M. A., & Leonard, S. L. (1998). Can corporate codes of ethics influence behavior? *Journal of Business Ethics, 17*, 619–630.

Cohen, M. R. (1954). *American thought: A critical sketch.* Glencoe, IL: Free Press.

Cole, E. B., & Coultrap-McQuin, S. (1992). Toward a feminist conception of moral life. In E. B. Cole & S. Coultrap-McQuin (Eds.), *Explorations in feminist ethics: Theory and practice* (pp. 1–11). Bloomington, IN: Indiana University Press.

Cole, E. B., & Coultrap-McQuin, S. (Eds.). (1992). *Explorations in feminist ethics: Theory and practice.* Bloomington, IN: Indiana University Press.

Committee for Economic Development. (1989). *Who should be liable? A guide to policy for dealing with risk.* New York: Committee for Economic Development.

Copyright Clearance Center. (1997). *Guidelines for creating a policy for copyright compliance* [online]. Available: <http://www.copyright.com/News/Guidelines.html> [1998, November 12].

Craig, R. J. (1994). *The no-nonsense guide to achieving ISO 9000 certification.* New York: ASME Press.

Cramton, P. C., & Dees, J. G. (1996). Promoting honesty in negotiation: An exercise in practical ethics. In T. Donaldson & P. H. Werhane (Eds.), *Ethical issues in business* (5th ed., pp. 143–177). Upper Saddle River, NJ: Prentice Hall.

Cressey, D. H., & Moore, C. A. (1983). Managerial values and corporate codes of ethics. *California Management Review, 25,* 53–77.

Darwall, S. (1980). Is there a Kantian foundation for Rawlsian justice? In H. G. Blocker & E. H. Smith (Eds.), *John Rawls' theory of social justice: An introduction* (pp. 311–345). Athens, OH: Ohio University Press.

De George, R. T. (1986). Ethical dilemmas for multinational enterprise: A philosophical overview. In W. M. Hoffman, A. E. Lange, & D. A. Fedo (Eds.), *Ethics and the multinational enterprise* (pp. 39–46). Lanham, MD: University Press of America.

De George, R. T. (1995). *Business ethics* (4th ed.). Englewood Cliffs, NJ: Prentice-Hall.

Dewey, J. (1922). *Human nature and conduct.* In J. A. Boydston (Ed.), *The works of John Dewey: The middle works,* 1899–1924 (Vol. 14). Carbondale, IL: Southern Illinois Press, 1976–1983.

Dewey, J. (1929). *The quest for certainty: A study of the relation of knowledge and action.* New York: Minton, Balch.

Doheny-Farina, S. (1989). Ethics and technical communication. In C. H. Sides (Ed.), *Technical and business communication: Bibliographic essays for teachers and corporate trainers* (pp. 53–73). Urbana, IL: National Council of Teachers of English.

Dombrowski, P. M. (1994). Ethics. In P. M. Dombrowski (Ed.), *Humanistic aspects of technical communication* (pp. 181–198). Amityville, NY: Baywood.

Donaldson, T. (1989). *The ethics of international business.* New York: Oxford University Press.

Dragga, S. (1996). "Is this ethical?" A survey of opinion on principles and practices of document design. *Technical Communication, 43,* 255–265.

Dragga, S. (1997). A question of ethics: Lessons from technical communicators on the job. *Technical Communication Quarterly, 6,* 161–178.

Drivon, L. E. (1990). *The civil war on consumer rights.* Berkeley, CA: Conari.

Dunfee, T. W. (1993). The role of ethics in international business. In T. W. Dunfee & Y. Nagayasu (Eds.), *Business ethics: Japan and the global economy* (pp. 63–80). Dordrecht, Netherlands: Kluwer.

Ebejer, J. M., & Morden, M. J. (1993). Paternalism in the marketplace: Should a salesman be his buyer's keeper? In T. L. Beauchamp & N. E. Bowie (Eds.),

Ethical theory and business (4th ed., pp. 472–474). Englewood Cliffs, NJ: Prentice Hall.

Evan, W. M., & Freeman, R. E. (1993). A stakeholder theory of the modern corporation: Kantian capitalism. In T. Beauchamp & N. Bowie (Eds.), *Ethical theory and business* (3rd ed., pp. 101–105). Englewood Cliffs, NJ: Prentice Hall.

Ewin, R. E. (1995). The virtues appropriate to business. *Business Ethics Quarterly, 5,* 833–842.

Faigley, L. (1992). *Fragments of rationality: Postmodernity and the subject of composition.* Pittsburgh, PA: University of Pittsburgh Press.

Farrell, H., & Farrell, B. J. (1998). The language of business codes of ethics: Implications of knowledge and power. *Journal of Business Ethics, 17,* 587–601.

Feldman, F. (1978). *Introductory ethics.* Englewood Cliffs, NJ: Prentice Hall.

Field, T. G. (1996). *Copyright for computer authors. Basic IP information* [Online]. Available: <http://www.fplc.edu/tfield/copysof.htm> [1998, November 11].

Field, T. G. (1998). *Copyright on the Internet. Basic IP information* [Online]. Available: <http://www.fplc.edu/tfield/copyNet.htm [1998, November 11].

Fisher, B. (1995). Documenting an ISO 9000 quality system. *Technical Communication, 42,* 482–491.

Flanagan, O., & Jackson, K. (1993). Justice, care, and gender: The Kohlberg-Gilligan debate revisited. In M. J. Larrabee (Ed.), *An ethic of care: Feminist and interdisciplinary perspectives* (pp. 69–84). New York: Routledge.

Flood, R. L. (1993). *Beyond TQM.* Chichester, UK: Wiley.

Flower, L. (1993). Cognitive rhetoric: Inquiry into the art of inquiry. In T. Enos & S. C. Brown (Eds.), *Defining the new rhetorics* (pp. 171–190). Newbury Park, CA: Sage.

Ford, R. C., & Richardson, W. D. (1994). Ethical decision making: A review of the empirical literature. *Journal of Business Ethics, 13,* 205–221.

Foster, P., & Loew, J. (1997, July 17). *Intellectual property survey* [Online]. Available: TECHWR-L@listserv.okstate.edu [1998, November 15].

Foucault, M. (1970). *The order of things: An archaeology of the human sciences.* London: Tavistock.

Foucault, M. (1972). *The archaeology of knowledge* (A. M. S. Smith, Trans.). London Tavistock.

Freadman, R., & Miller, S. (1992). *Re-thinking theory: A critique of contemporary literary theory and an alternative account.* Cambridge, England: Cambridge University Press.

Friedman, M. (1996). The social responsibility of business is to increase its profits. In T. Donaldson & P. H. Werhane (Eds.), *Ethical issues in business: A philosophical approach* (5th ed., pp. 222–227). Upper Saddle River, NJ: Prentice Hall. This is an abridged version of the essay originally published in the *New York Times Magazine,* September 13, 1970.

Galbraith, J. K. (1958). *The affluent society.* New York: Houghton Mifflin.

Garfinkel, S. L., Stallman, R. M., & Kapor, M. (1996). Why patents are bad for software. In P. Ludlow (Ed.), *High noon on the electronic frontier: Conceptual issues in cyberspace* (pp. 35–45). Cambridge, MA: MIT Press.

Gilligan, C. (1982). *In a different voice: Psychological theory and women's development.* Cambridge, MA: Harvard University Press.

Gilligan, C. (1993). Reply to critics. In M. J. Larrabee (Ed.), *An ethic of care: Feminist and interdisciplinary perspectives* (pp. 207–214). New York: Routledge.

Grassian, V. (1981). *Moral reasoning: Ethical theory and some contemporary moral problems.* Englewood Cliffs, NJ: Prentice Hall.

Griffin, J. (1989). When do rhetorical choices become ethical choices? In R. J. Brockmann & F. Rook (Eds.), *Technical communication and ethics* (pp. 63–70). Washington, DC: Society for Technical Communication.

Guillot, G. H. (1998) *All about trademarks* [Online]. Available: <http://www.ggmark.com/welcome.html> [1998, December 15].

Habermas, J. (1973). A postscript to "Knowledge and human interests." *Philosophy and the Social Sciences, 3,* 157–185.

Habermas, J. (1990). *Moral consciousness and communicative action* (C. Lenhardt & S. W. Nicolsen, Trans). Cambridge, MA: MIT Press.

Haezrahi, P. (1969). The concept of man as end-in-himself. In R. P. Wolff (Ed.), *Foundations of the metaphysics of morals, with critical essays* (pp. 292–318). Indianapolis, IN: Bobbs-Merrill

Hall, D. G., & Nelson, B. A. (1989). Integrating professional ethics into the technical writing course. In R. J. Brockmann & F. Rook (Eds.), *Technical communication and ethics* (pp. 73–81). Washington, DC: Society for Technical Communication.

Hare, R. M. (1984, Spring/Summer). Commentary. *Business and Professional Ethics Journal, 3 & 4,* 23–28.

Heckel, P. (1996). Debunking the software patent myths. In P. Ludlow (Ed.), *High noon on the electronic frontier: Conceptual issues in cyberspace* (pp. 63–107). Cambridge, MA: MIT Press.

Helyar, P. S. (1992). Products liability: Meeting legal standards for adequate instructions. *Journal of Technical Writing and Communication, 22,* 125–147.

Herrington, T. K. (1995). Report of the Department of the Treasury on the Bureau of Alcohol, Tobacco, and Firearms investigation of Vernon Wayne Howell also known as David Koresh. IEEE *Transactions on Professional Communication, 38,* 151–157.

Hewlett-Packard. (1998). *The H-P way* [Online]. Available: <http://www.hp.com/abouthp/hpway.html> [1998, December 20].

Hoft, N. L. (1995). *International technical communication: How to export information about high technology.* New York: Wiley.

Holley, D. M. (1993). A moral evaluation of sales practices. In T. L. Beauchamp & N. E. Bowie (Eds.), *Ethical theory and business* (4th ed., 462–472). Englewood Cliffs, NJ: Prentice Hall.

Horton, W. (1993). The almost universal language: Graphics for international documents. *Technical Communication, 40,* 682–693.

Huber, P. W. (1988). *Liability: The legal revolution and its consequences.* New York: Basic Books.

Huber, P. W., & Litan, R. E. (1991). Overview. In P. W. Huber & R. E. Litan (Eds.), *The liability maze: The impact of liability law on safety and innovation* (pp. 1–27). Washington, DC: The Brookings Institution.

Hudson, W. D. (1980). *A century of moral philosophy*. New York: St. Martin's Press.

Hume, D. (1888). *A treatise of human nature* (L. A. Selby-Bigge, Ed.). Oxford: Clarendon Press.

International Organization for Standardization. (1999). *Welcome to ISO Online!* [Online]. Available: <http://www.iso.ch/> [1999, January 4].

Jackall, R. (1988). *Moral mazes*. New York: Oxford University Press.

Jamal, K., & Bowie, N. E. (1995). Theoretical considerations for a meaningful code of professional ethics. *Journal of Business Ethics, 14*, 703–714.

Johnson, N. (1984). Ethos and the aims of rhetoric. In R. J. Connors, L. S. Ede, & A. A. Lunsford (Eds.), *Essays on classical rhetoric and modern discourse* (pp. 98–114). Carbondale, IL: Southern Illinois University Press.

Johnson & Johnson. (1998). Credo [Online]. Available: http:<www.johnsonand johnson.com/ who_is_jnj/cr_usa.html> [1998, December 20].

Jones, D. (1998). *Technical writing style*. Boston: Allyn and Bacon.

Kaner, C., & Pels, D. (1998). *Bad software: What to do when software fails*. New York: Wiley.

Kant, I. (1969). *Foundations of the metaphysics of morals*. In R. P. Wolff (Ed.) & L. W. Beck (Trans.), *Foundations of the metaphysics of morals, with critical essays*. Indianapolis, IN: Bobbs-Merrill. All quotations from Kant use the standard pagination from the Konigliche Preussische Akademie der Wissenschaft edition (Berlin, 1902–1938).

Kaptein, M., & Wempe, J. (1998). Twelve Gordian knots when developing an organizational code of ethics. *Journal of Business Ethics, 17*, 853–869.

Katz, S. B. (1992). The ethic of expediency: Classical rhetoric, technology, and the Holocaust. *College English, 54*, 255–275.

Kerber, L. K. (1993). Some cautionary words for historians. In M. J. Larrabee (Ed.), *An ethic of care: Feminist and interdisciplinary perspectives* (pp. 102–107). New York: Routledge.

Kettner, M. (1993). Scientific knowledge, discourse ethics, and consensus formation in the public domain. In E. R. Winkler & J. R. Coombs (Eds.), *Applied ethics: A reader* (pp. 28–45). Oxford: Blackwell.

Kinneavy, J. L. (1986). *Kairos*: A neglected concept in classical rhetoric. In J. D. Moss (Ed.), *Rhetoric and praxis: The contribution of classical rhetoric to practical reasoning* (pp. 79–105). Washington, DC: Catholic University of America Press.

Kittay, E. F., & Meyers, D. T. (1987). Introduction. In E. F. Kittay & D. T. Meyers (Eds.), *Women and moral theory* (pp. 3–16). Totowa, NJ: Rowman & Littlefield.

Kohlberg, L. (1981). *Essays on moral development. Vol. 1.: The philosophy of moral development*. San Francisco: Harper & Row.

Kohlberg, L. (1984). *Essays on moral development. Vol. 2.: The psychology of moral development*. New York: Harper & Row.

Kremers, M. (1989). Teaching ethical thinking in a technical writing course. *IEEE Transactions on Professional Communication, 32*, 58–61.

Kuester, J. R., & Nieves, P. A. (1998). *Hyperlinks, frames and meta-tags: An intellectual property analysis* [Online]. Available: <http://www.patentperfect.com/ idea.htm> [1998, December 16].

Kuhn, T. S. (1970). *The structure of scientific revolutions* (2nd ed.). Chicago: University of Chicago.

Lanham, R. A. (1988). The 'Q' Question. *South Atlantic Quarterly, 87,* 653–700.

Lawrence, F. B. (1975, October 27). Whose ethics guide business? *Industry Week,* 25.

Lickona, T. (Ed.). (1976). *Moral development and behavior: Theory, research, and social issues.* New York: Holt, Rinehart and Winston.

Limaye, M. R., & Victor, D. A. (1991). Cross-cultural business communication research: State of the art and hypotheses for the 1990s. *Journal of Business Communication, 28,* 277–299.

Luria, Z. (1993). A methodological critique. In M. J. Larrabee (Ed.), *An ethic of care: Feminist and interdisciplinary perspectives* (pp. 199–203). New York: Routledge.

Lustig, M. W., & Koester, J. (1999). *Intercultural competence: Interpersonal communication across cultures* (3rd ed.). New York: Longman.

Lyons, D. (1965). *Forms and limits of utilitarianism.* Oxford Clarendon Press.

Lyotard, J. F. (1991a). *Just gaming* (W. Godzich, Trans.). Minneapolis, MN: University of Minnesota Press.

Lyotard, J. F. (1991b). *The postmodern condition: A report on knowledge.* (G. Bennington & B. Massumi, Trans.). Minneapolis, MN: University of Minnesota Press.

Machrone, B. (1990). The look-and-feel issue: The evolution of innovation. In M. D. Ermann, M. B. Williams, & C. Gutierrez (Eds.), *Computers, ethics, and society* (pp. 295–298). New York: Oxford.

MacIntyre, A. (1982). *After virtue: A study in moral theory* (2nd ed.). Notre Dame, IN: University of Notre Dame Press.

MacPherson v. Buick Motor Company, 217 N.Y. 382 (1916).

Maggio, R. (1997). *Talking about people: A guide to fair and accurate language.* Phoenix, AZ: Oryx.

Manley, W. W. (1991). *Executive's handbook of model business conduct codes.* Englewood Cliffs, NJ: Prentice Hall.

Manning, R. (1992). Just caring. In E. B. Cole & S. Coultrap-McQuin (Eds.), *Explorations in feminist ethics: Theory and practice* (pp. 45–54). Bloomington, IN: Indiana University Press.

Martin, W., & Sanders, S. P. (1994). Ethics, audience, and the writing process: Bringing public policy issues into the classroom. *Technical Communication Quarterly, 3,* 147–163.

Matthews, M. C. (1987). Codes of ethics: Organizational behavior and misbehavior. In *Research in corporate social performance* (Vol. 9, pp. 107–130). Greenwich, CT: JAI Press.

McCabe, D. L., Trevino, L. K., & Butterfield, K. D. (1996). The influence of collegiate and corporate codes of conduct on ethics-related behavior in the workplace. *Business Ethics Quarterly, 6,* 461–476.

McGuire, E. P. (1988). *The impact of product liability* (Research Report No. 908). New York: The Conference Report.

Michaelson, H. (1990). How an author can avoid the pitfalls of practical ethics. *IEEE Transactions on Professional Communication, 33,* 58–61.

Microsoft Corporation. (1997). *Getting started with Microsoft® FrontPage® 98.* Redmond, WA: Author.

Mill, J. S. (1971). *Utilitarianism: With critical essays.* (S. Gorovitz, Ed.). Indianapolis, IN: Bobbs-Merrill. (Orginal work published 1863).

Miller, C. R. (1979). A humanistic rationale for technical writing. *College English,* 40, 610–617.

Miller, C. R. (1989). What's practical about technical writing? In B. E. Fearing & W. K. Sparrow (Eds.), *Technical writing: Theory and practice* (pp. 14–24). New York: Modern Language Association.

Miller, C. R. (1993). Rhetoric and community: The problem of the one and the many. In T. Enos & S. C. Brown (Eds.), *Defining the new rhetorics* (pp 79–94). Newbury Park, CA: Sage.

Miller, T. P. (1991). Teaching professional writing as social *praxis. Journal of Advanced Composition,* 11, 57–72.

Molander, E. A. (1987). A paradigm for design, promulgation and enforcement of ethical codes. *Journal of Business Ethics,* 6, 619–631.

Moon, J. D. (1995). Practical discourse and communicative ethics. In S. K. White (Ed.), *The Cambridge companion to Habermas* (pp. 143–169). Cambridge, England: Cambridge University Press.

Moore, G. E. (1903). *Principia ethica.* Cambridge, England: Cambridge University Press.

Murphy, P. (1995). Corporate ethics statements: Current status and future prospects. *Journal of Business Ethics,* 14, 727–740.

Nader, R. (1965). *Unsafe at any speed.* New York: Brossman.

Nash, L. L. (1992). American and European corporate ethics practices: A 1991 survey. In J. Mahoney & E. Vallance (Eds.), *Business ethics in a new Europe* (pp. 155–176). Norwell, MA: Kluwer.

National Safety Council. (1999). *Unintentional injuries are among leading causes of death in the U.S., National Safety Council Web site* [Online]. Available: http://www.nsc.org/news/nrrptinj.htm [1999, December 6].

Norris, C. (1993). *The truth about postmodernism.* Oxford, England: Blackwell.

Novak, M. (1996). *The fire of invention, the fuel of interest: On intellectual property.* Washington, DC: AEI Press.

Nunner-Winkler, G. (1993). Two moralities? A critical discussion of an ethic of care and responsibility versus an ethic of rights and justice. In M. J. Larrabee (Ed.), *An ethic of care: Feminist and interdisciplinary perspectives* (pp. 143–156). New York: Routledge.

O'Mahoney, B. (1998a). *Basic. The copyright website* [Online]. Available: <http://www.benedict.com/edge/basic.htm> [1998, November 14]

O'Mahoney, B. (1998b). *Web issues. The copyright website.* [Online]. Available: <http://www.benedict.com/edge/webiss.htm> [1998, November 14].

Ornatowski, C. M. (1992). Between efficiency and politics: Rhetoric and ethics in technical writing. *Technical Communication Quarterly,* 1, 91–103.

Paine, L. S. (1996). Managing for organizational integrity. In T. Donaldson & P. H. Werhane (Eds.), *Ethical issues in business* (5th ed., pp. 494–507). Upper Saddle River, NJ: Prentice Hall.

Parfit, D. (1986). *Reasons and persons.* New York: Oxford University Press.

Perica, L. (1972). Honesty in technical communication. *Technical Communication, 15,* 2–6.

Pierce, M. A., & Henry, J. W. (1996). Computer ethics: The role of personal, informal, and formal codes. *Journal of Business Ethics, 15,* 425–437.

Pincoffs, E. L. (1986). *Quandaries and virtues: Against reductivism in ethics.* Lawrence, KS: University Press of Kansas.

Porter, J. E. (1993). Developing a postmodern ethics of rhetoric and composition. In T. Enos & S. C. Brown (Eds.), *Defining the new rhetorics* (pp. 207–226). Newbury Park, CA: Sage.

Possin, K. (1991). Ethical argumentation. *Journal of Technical Writing and Communication, 21,* 65–72.

Powledge, T. M. (1980). Morals and medical writing, *Medical Communications, 8,* 1–10.

Preston, I. L. (1975). *The great American blow-up: Puffery in advertising and selling.* Madison, WI: University of Wisconsin Press.

Priest, G. L. (1988). Products liability law and the accident rate. In R.E. Litan & C. Winston (Eds.), *Liability: Perspectives and policy* (pp. 184–222). Washington, DC: The Brookings Institution.

Publishers win important fair use victory. (1996). *CCC Online* [Online]. Available: <http://www.copyright.com/News/MDSDecision.html> [1998, November 1].

Quinton, A. (1973). *Utilitarian ethics.* New York: St. Martin's Press.

Rachels, J. (1985). Can ethics provide answers? In M. Velasquez & C. Rostankowski (Eds.), *Ethics: Theory and practice* (pp. 22–30). Englewood Cliffs, NJ: Prentice Hall.

Rachels, J. (1986). *The elements of moral philosophy.* New York: McGraw-Hill.

Rachels, J. (1993). Moral philosophy as a subversive activity. In E. R. Winkler & J. R. Coombs (Eds.), *Applied ethics: A reader* (pp. 110–130). Oxford: Blackwell.

Raiborn, C. A., & Payne, D. (1990). Corporate codes of conduct: A collaborative conscience and continuum. *Journal of Business Ethics, 9,* 879–889.

Raiborn, C. A., & Payne, D. (1996). TQM: Just what the ethicist ordered. *Journal of Business Ethics, 15,* 963–972.

Randall, D. M., & Gibson, A. M. (1990). Methodology in business ethics research: A review and critical assessment. *Journal of Business Ethics, 9,* 457–471.

Raugust, M. C. (1992). Feminist ethics and workplace values. In E. B. Cole & S. Coultrap-McQuin (Eds.), *Explorations in feminist ethics: Theory and practice* (pp. 125–130). Bloomington, IN: Indiana University Press.

Rawls, J. (1971). *A theory of justice.* Cambridge, MA: Harvard University Press.

Riley, K. (1993). Telling more than the truth: Implicature, speech acts, and ethics in professional communication. *Journal of Business Ethics, 12,* 179–196.

Romain, D. (1992). Care and confusion. In E. B. Cole & S. Coultrap-McQuin (Eds.), *Explorations in feminist ethics: Theory and practice* (pp. 27–37). Bloomington, IN: Indiana University Press.

Rosch, W. L. (1990). The look-and-feel issue: The copyright law on trial. In M. D. Ermann, M. B. Williams, & C. Gutierrez, (Eds.), *Computers, ethics, and society* (pp. 288–295). New York: Oxford University Press.

Rose, L. (1995). *Netlaw: Your rights in the online world.* Berkeley, CA: Osborne McGraw Hill.

Ross, W. D. (1930). *The right and the good.* New York: Oxford University Press.

Roth, B. (1993). Is it quality improves ethics or ethics improves quality? *Journal for Quality and Participation, 16,* 6–9.

Rubens, P. (1981). Reinventing the wheel? Ethics for technical communicators. *Journal of Technical Writing and Communication, 11,* 329–339.

Rutter, R. (1991). History, rhetoric, and humanism: Toward a more comprehensive definition of technical communication. *Journal of Technical Writing and Communication, 21,* 133–153.

Ryan, M. P. (1998). *Knowledge diplomacy: Global competition and the politics of intellectual property.* Washington, DC: Brookings Institution Press.

Sanders, S. P. (1997). Technical communication and ethics. In K. Staples & C. Ornatowski (Eds.), *Foundations for teaching technical communication: Theory, practice, and program design* (pp. 99–117). Greenwich, CT: Ablex.

Scaltsas, P. W. (1992). Do feminist ethics counter feminist aims? In E. B. Cole & S. Coultrap-McQuin (Eds.), *Explorations in feminist ethics: Theory and practice* (pp. 15–26). Bloomington, IN: Indiana University Press.

Schlegelmilch, B. (1998). *Marketing ethics: An international perspective.* London: International Thomson Business Press.

Scruton, R. (1982). *Kant.* Oxford: Oxford University Press.

Secor, M. J. (1987). Recent research in argumentation theory. *The Technical Writing Teacher, 14,* 337–354.

Settle, S. M., & Spigelmyer, S. (1984). *Product liability: A multibillion-dollar dilemma.* New York: American Management Association.

Shaw, W. H. (1993). *Business ethics* (2nd ed.). Belmont, CA: Wadsworth.

Shaw, W. H. (1995). *Moore on right and wrong: The normative ethics of G. E. Moore.* Dordrecht, Netherlands: Kluwer.

Sher, G. (1987). Other voices, other rooms? Women's psychology and moral theory. In E. F. Kittay & D. T. Meyers (Eds.), *Women and moral theory* (pp. 178–189). Totowa, NJ: Rowman & Littlefield.

Shimburg, H. L. (1977). President's plans—1977–78. *Technical Communication, 24,* 30–31.

Shimburg, H. L. (1978). Ethics and rhetoric in technical writing. *Technical Communication, 25,* 16–18.

Sigma Xi. The Scientific Research Society. (1986). *Honor in science.* New Haven, CT: Author.

Silber, J. R. (1968). The Copernican revolution in ethics: The good reexamined. In R. P. Wolff (Ed.), *Kant: A collection of critical essays* (pp. 266–290). Notre Dame, IN: University of Notre Dame Press.

Smart, J. J. C., & Williams, B. (1973). *Utilitarianism: For and against.* Cambridge: Cambridge University Press.

Smith, A. (n.d, 1776). An inquiry into the nature and causes of the wealth of nations. New York: Modern Library.

Smith, H. J. (1989). From caveat emptor to caveat venditor: Some legal concerns for technical communicators. In *Proceedings of the 36th International Technical*

Communication Conference (pp. MG 49–51). Washington, DC: Society for Technical Communication.

Smith, H. T., & Shirk, H. N. (1996). The perils of defective documentation: Preparing business and technical communicators to avoid product liability. *Journal of Business and Technical Communication, 10,* 187–202.

Society for Technical Communication. (1998). Ethical guidelines for technical communicators [Online]. Available: <http://www.stc-va.org/publications frame.html> [1998, December 15].

Solomon, R. (1992). *Ethics and excellence: Cooperation and integrity in business.* New York: Oxford University Press.

Sorell, T., & Hendry, J. (1994). *Business ethics.* Oxford: Butterworth-Heinemann.

Steeples, M. M. (1994). The quality-ethics connection. *Quality Progress, 27,* 73–75.

Stevens, B. (1994). An analysis of corporate ethical code studies: "Where do we go from here?" *Journal of Business Ethics, 13,* 63–69.

Stone, C. (1975). *Where the law ends.* New York: Harper & Row.

Strate, L., & Swerdlow, S. (1987). The maze of the law: How technical writers can research and understand legal matters. *IEEE Transactions on Professional Communication, 30,* 136–148.

Strobel, L. P. (1980). *Reckless homicide? Ford's Pinto trial.* South Bend, IN: And Books.

Sullivan, D. L. (1990). Political-ethical implications of defining technical communication as a practice. *Journal of Advanced Composition, 10,* 375–386.

Thrush, E. A. (1997). Multicultural issues in technical communication. In K. Staples & C. Ornatowski (Eds.), *Foundations for teaching technical communication: Theory, practice, and program design* (pp. 161–177). Greenwich, CT: Ablex.

Toulmin, S. (1985). The tyranny of principles. In N. E. Bowie (Ed.), *Making ethical decisions* (pp. 138–151). New York: McGraw-Hill.

Tronto, J. C. (1989). Women and caring: What can feminists learn about morality from caring? In A. M. Jaggar & S. R. Bordo (Eds.), *Gender/body/knowledge: Feminist reconstructions of being and knowing* (pp. 172–187). New Brunswick, NJ: Rutgers University Press.

Tronto, J. C. (1993). Beyond gender theory to a theory of care. In M. J. Larrabee (Ed.), *An ethic of care: Feminist and interdisciplinary perspectives* (pp. 240–258). New York: Routledge.

Tufte, E. R. (1997). *Visual explanations: Images and quantities, evidence and narrative.* Cheshire, CT: Graphics Press.

Tyler, L. (1992). Ecological disaster and rhetorical response: Exxon's communications in the wake of the Valdez spill. *Journal of Business and Technical Communication, 6,* 149–171.

United States Code [Online]. (1998). Available: <http://uscode.house.gov/usc. htm> [1998, December 10].

U.S. Bureau of the Census. (1998). *Statistical abstract of the United States: 1998.* Washington, DC: U.S. Government Printing Office.

U.S. Copyright Office. (1998). *Copyright law of the United States* [Online]. Available: <http://lcweb.loc.gov/copyright/title17> [1998, November 12].

U.S. Patent and Trademark Office. (1998a). *What is a patent?* [Online]. Available: <http://www.uspto.gov/web/offices/pac/doc/general/whatispa.htm> [1998, November 17].

U.S. Patent and Trademark Office. (1998b). *Basic facts about registering a trademark* [Online]. Available: <http://www.uspto.gov/web/offices/pac/doc/basic/basic_facts.htm> [1998, November 19].

Velasquez, M. G. (1998). *Business ethics: Concepts and cases* (4th ed.). Upper Saddle River, NJ: Prentice Hall.

Verschoor, C. C. (1997, October). Principles build profits. *Management Accounting*, 42–46.

Walker, L. J. (1993). Sex differences in the development of moral reasoning: A critical review. In M. J. Larrabee (Ed.), *An ethic of care: Feminist and interdisciplinary perspectives* (pp. 157–176). New York: Routledge.

Walzer, A. E., & Gross, A. (1994). Positivists, postmodernists, Aristotelians, and the *Challenger* disaster. *College English, 56*, 420–433.

Warnock, M., *Ethics since 1990* (3rd ed.). Oxford, England: Oxford University Press.

Wartzman, R. (1987, October 9). Nature or nurture? Study blames ethical lapses on corporate goals. *Wall Street Journal*, p. 21.

Weber, N. (1989). *Product liability: The corporate response* (Research Report No. 893). New York: The Conference Board.

Weiner, R. S. (1998). Copyright in a digital age: Practical guidance for information professionals in the midst of legal uncertainty. *CCC Online* [Online]. Available: <http://www.copyright.com/News/DigitalAge.html> [1998, November 16].

Weiss, E. H. (1993). The technical communicator and ISO 9000. *Technical Communication, 40*, 234–238.

Wellbank, J. H., Snook, D., & Mason, D. T. (1982). *John Rawls and his critics: An annotated bibliography*. New York: Garland.

Wells, S. (1986). Jürgen Habermas, communicative competence, and the teaching of technical discourse. In C. Nielson (Ed.), *Theory in the classroom* (pp. 245–269). Urbana, IL: University of Illinois Press.

Wicclair, M. R., & Farkas, D. K. (1989). Ethical reasoning in technical communication: A practical framework. In R. J. Brockmann & F. Rook (Eds.), *Technical communication and ethics* (pp. 21–25). Washington, DC: Society for Technical Communication.

Williams, C. (1997). Intel's Pentium chip crisis: An ethical analysis. *IEEE Transactions on Professional Communication, 40*, 13–19.

Winkler, E. E. (1993). From Kantianism to contextualism: The rise and fall of the paradigm theory in bioethics. In E. R. Winkler & J. R. Coombs (Eds.), *Applied ethics: A reader* (pp. 343–365). Oxford: Blackwell.

Winkler, E. E., & Coombs, J. R. (1993). Introduction. In E. R. Winkler & J. R. Coombs (Eds.), *Applied ethics: A reader* (pp. 1–8). Oxford, England: Blackwell.

Winsor, D. A. (1988). Communication failures contributing to the Challenger accident: An example for technical communicators. *IEEE Transactions on Professional Communication, 31*, 101–107.

Wood, J. T. (1994). *Who cares?: Women, care, and culture*. Carbondale, IL: Southern Illinois University Press.

Yoos, G. (1979). A revision of the concept of ethical appeal. *Philosophy and Rhetoric*, 12, 41–58.

Young, J. C. (1961). Responsibilities of writers and editors to readers. *STWP Review*, 14–16.

Index

About the Author

MIKE MARKEL is Director of Technical Communication at Boise State University. The former editor of IEEE *Transactions on Professional Communication*, Markel is the author of numerous articles and five other books on technical communication, including the textbook *Technical Communication*, now in its sixth edition.